"*Wrestling in Britain* provides a thorough rereading of this important form but, more than this, it contributes to and reimagines narratives of British sports history, performance and popular culture. The scholarship in this volume also provides readers with new insights into celebrity, the development of television, and media production. The first full-length study of British professional wrestling history, it is a welcome, dynamic addition to many diverse fields."

– *Claire Warden, De Montfort University, UK*

"As British professional wrestling finds itself in a period of resurgence, *Wrestling in Britain* serves as a timely interrogation of the history of this unique leisure pursuit. Litherland's work reflects on wrestling's complex relationship with 'reality' across a number of fields, and illustrates a historical context which can help make sense of contemporary practices of sport, celebrity, and fandom."

– *Tom Phillips, University of East Anglia, UK*

Wrestling in Britain

At the intersection of sport, entertainment and performance, wrestling occupies a unique position in British popular culture. This is the first book to offer a detailed historical and cultural analysis of British professional wrestling, exploring the shifting popularity of the sport as well as its wider social significance.

Arguing that the history of professional wrestling can help us understand key themes in sport, culture and performance that span the nineteenth and twentieth centuries, it addresses topics such as: attitudes towards violence, representations of masculinity, the media and celebrity culture, consumerism and globalisation. By drawing on a variety of intellectual traditions and disciplines, the book explores the role of power in the development of popular cultural forms, the ways in which history structures the present, and the manner in which audiences construct identity and meaning through sport.

Wrestling in Britain: Sporting Entertainments, Celebrity and Audiences is fascinating reading for all students and researchers with an interest in media and cultural studies, histories and sociologies of sport, or performance studies.

Benjamin Litherland is a member of the Centre for Participatory Culture at the University of Huddersfield, UK. He is a media and cultural studies scholar, and his existing research portfolio demonstrates a diverse and interdisciplinary approach to the study of media, film, and sports and games.

Routledge Research in Sports History

The *Routledge Research in Sports History* series presents leading research in the development and historical significance of modern sport through a collection of historiographical, regional and thematic studies which span a variety of periods, sports and geographical areas. Showcasing ground-breaking, cross-disciplinary work from established and emerging sport historians, the series provides a crucial contribution to the wider study of sport and society.

For a full list of titles in this series, please visit www.routledge.com/sport/series/RRSH

Available in this series:

5 A Social History of Tennis in Britain
Robert Lake

6 Association Football
A Study in Figurational Sociology
Graham Curry and Eric Dunning

7 Taekwondo
From a Martial Art to a Martial Sport
Udo Moenig

8 The Black Press and Black Baseball, 1915–1955
A Devil's Bargain
Brian Carroll

9 Football and Literature in South America
David Wood

10 Cricket: A Political History of the Global Game, 1945–2017
Stephen Wagg

11 Wrestling in Britain
Sporting Entertainments, Celebrity and Audiences
Benjamin Litherland

Wrestling in Britain

Sporting Entertainments, Celebrity and Audiences

Benjamin Litherland

LONDON AND NEW YORK

First published 2018
by Routledge
2 Park Square, Milton Park, Abingdon, Oxon OX14 4RN

and by Routledge
711 Third Avenue, New York, NY 10017

Routledge is an imprint of the Taylor & Francis Group, an informa business

© 2018 Benjamin Litherland

The right of Benjamin Litherland to be identified as authors of this work has been asserted by him in accordance with sections 77 and 78 of the Copyright, Designs and Patents Act 1988.

All rights reserved. No part of this book may be reprinted or reproduced or utilised in any form or by any electronic, mechanical, or other means, now known or hereafter invented, including photocopying and recording, or in any information storage or retrieval system, without permission in writing from the publishers.

Trademark notice: Product or corporate names may be trademarks or registered trademarks, and are used only for identification and explanation without intent to infringe.

British Library Cataloguing in Publication Data
A catalogue record for this book is available from the British Library

Library of Congress Cataloging in Publication Data
A catalog record for this book has been requested

ISBN: 978-0-8153-8571-4 (hbk)
ISBN: 978-1-351-18044-3 (ebk)

Typeset in Sabon
by Taylor & Francis Books

Contents

Acknowledgements viii

Introduction: 'We don't look on wrestling as a sport': introducing sporting entertainment 1

1 The field vs the stage 22

2 'Are the bouts rigged?': The enduring possibility of sporting entertainment 53

3 'Equally vociferous both for and against': Compromise, conflict and pleasure 83

4 Villains, blue-eyes and the melodrama of celebrity 114

5 'Everything is eventually going to find its way on the goggle-box': Television and spectacle 147

Epilogue 177

Index 182

Acknowledgements

This book is the product of two institutions: the University of Sussex and the University of Huddersfield. The work is based on research from my PhD, and I want to thank my supervisors, Andy Medhurst and Lucy Robinson. I will forever be grateful for their time, dedication, belief and energy in this project, and their work, ideas, and approaches are at the heart of this study. The book is also informed by the staff and my fellow postgraduates at Sussex, who supported and inspired me in all ways great and small.

Similarly, staff and postgraduates at the University of Huddersfield have been supportive in turning my PhD thesis into the book presented here. In particular, The Centre for Participatory Culture, and its directors, Cornel Sandvoss and Matt Hills, have been good mentors and friends, helping to develop ideas and approaches while fostering an exciting space where research can flourish.

My partner, Rachel, is crucial to this work in untold ways, and it truly would have not been possible without her. Since embarking on my academic career, my family – Gill, Mick, Hannah, William – have provided sustained financial and emotional support. I have spent hours and hours talking about and watching wrestling with my friends, and I am grateful to have such knowledgeable people in my life.

Archives staff have been helpful and patient. Thanks to the University of Sussex library, Mass Observation Archive, the National Fairground Archive, the London Metropolitan Archive, the ITA/IBA/Cable Authority Archive, Carlisle Archive Centre, the National Football Museum, the National Library, and the National Archives.

Finally, my MA and PhD were funded by the Arts and Humanities Research Council, and elements from my MA dissertation and PhD thesis are represented in this work. Without that support, I would not have been able to pursue this work, and I hope that they long continue to support scholars who would otherwise not have been able to study at postgraduate level and beyond.

Introduction

'We don't look on wrestling as a sport': introducing sporting entertainment

On Saturday, 20 June 1981, Big Daddy wrestled Giant Haystacks at London's Wembley Arena. It was billed as the ultimate grudge match between the ultimate foes, a 'no rounds, no submissions, no time limit' contest between two colossal men apparently settling a feud that had been bubbling since the mid-1970s. Though both large, in height and weight, their characters were even larger. As Nancy Banks-Smith, *The Guardian*'s television critic, explained:

> Giant Haystacks is bad. He is not only bad, he is big 'n' mean 'n' hairy 'n' ornery 'n' nearly seven feet 'n' 40 stone ... Big Daddy, 23 peculiarly pallid stones is good. He has a heart as big as all outdoors and size 12 boots. His topper glistens with gold sequins; his at-the-shoulder cape waves like wings.[1]

After two minutes and 50 seconds of the big men bumping and knocking against one another, Big Daddy knocked Giant Haystacks to the floor for the count-out win. The match was not the most watched match in British wrestling history, Big Daddy's match with Mighty John Quinn two years earlier had attracted a larger, and indeed more excited crowd, to the same arena, and the 1963 F.A. Cup Final day's match between Jackie Pallo and Mick McManus had captured a larger television audience. The match between the two, however, holds a special place in how British professional wrestling is remembered. When *World of Sport Wrestling* was brought back for a one-off special on New Year's Eve, 2016, photos of Big Daddy and Giant Haystacks were regularly used in the press to illustrate that story.[2] Their centrality in media memories about professional wrestling in Britain emerges from a combination of things. The sight of them, exceptionally big and undeniably charismatic, shone through, and their feud had been a regular fixture of British wrestling throughout the 1970s. Their 1981 match, furthermore, was the last great match that fully captured the public's attention before *World of Sport*'s cancellation in 1985, and then British wrestling's cancellation on ITV in 1988.

The wrestler's stature, and Big Daddy and Giant Haystacks' prominence, illustrate something else about the sport. In simple terms, Daddy and Haystacks offer a good illustration of something that seems apparent to most commentators: professional wrestlers were showpeople, not 'athletes'. 'They are no less in show business', one *Daily Mail* article claimed, 'than Danny la Rue or the Muppets. Wrestlers are the last stand-up comics.'[3] Wrestlers, then, are concerned with entertainment, not winning or competition. The BBC put it simply, explaining to the national press, 'We don't look on wrestling as a sport. Wrestlers are entertainers.'[4] At best, professional wrestling is what the Independent Television Authority described as a 'sporting entertainment'.[5] Big Daddy and Giant Haystacks could only exist in a world that stressed performance over sporting competition, and they are partly fondly recalled because they encapsulated something that everyone implicitly understood about wrestling.

That professional wrestling is not a 'real' sport in any commonly understood sense will not be a surprise to readers. It has been the cornerstone of journalistic analysis alongside one of the central arguments in most academic studies. Sharon Mazer, for example, has argued that

> to watch wrestling and then to write about performance is to attempt to confront and come to terms with the significance of a highly popular performance practice as it intersects, exploits, and finally parodies the conventions of both sport and theatre.[6]

Similarly, Heather Levi explains that wrestling 'occupies a space between sport, ritual and theatre and is thus capable of drawing its power from all of those genres'.[7] Despite those intersections, however, the most sustained academic arguments about professional wrestling have been developed by those working broadly in Theatre Studies or Media Studies,[8] as represented by the most recent edited collection, entitled *Performance and Professional Wrestling*.[9] These studies have often focused on the performed nature, following Roland Barthes' suggestion that, 'wrestling is not a sport, it is a spectacle'.[10] Influenced by Barthes, and often taking a semiotic approach, at their core, most of these studies are attracted to professional wrestling's 'fakery', its illusions, spectacle and dramatic tendencies and the meanings, representations and ideologies therein. This can be seen in the ways in which theorists have attempted to claim professional wrestling as a form of melodrama,[11] identity drama,[12] ritual drama,[13] passion play,[14] contact improvisational dance,[15] commedia dell'arte,[16] and televised carnivalesque.[17] Critics have often been drawn to the forms of dramatic representation – specifically between good and evil – and the operation of stereotypes within the text.[18]

I do not want to dismiss these readings and analyses out of hand. All offer, with varying degrees of understanding and insight, appropriate comparisons to other cultural forms. It is hard not to watch a televised professional wrestling match from either side of the Atlantic from the past fifty years without encountering or recognising the high degree of theatrics and dramatics alluded to by these writers, especially in the case of Big Daddy and Giant Haystacks.

These insights have undoubtedly been a useful starting point, both for the study of professional wrestling at large and the work presented here. Professional wrestling has not been a sport by any modern definition since the 1920s: there is no legitimate competition, gambling is a rare feature or attraction, and the ideologies of sport are disregarded or even inverted. On a textual level, then, professional wrestling certainly exists on the cusp of the sporting and the theatrical. The problem with such a reading is that it risks taking sport, and for that matter theatre, to be an unchanging, natural phenomenon. Sport, like any text or practice, is a highly structured, socially reproduced cultural form that is the product and result of specific economic, cultural and social conditions and historical processes.

As with most cultural forms that exist in our day-to-day lives, we take sport for granted, and these processes remain hidden from view. Few people will have dedicated much time to considering what features or forms, codes or conventions, are needed for something to be classified as 'sport'. This is probably fair. Aside from a few games that might occasionally throw up an intriguing pub table debate between friends ('is darts *really* a sport?'), for those playing or watching it, sport simply exists. Studying professional wrestling confronts some of the key tensions and questions about what sport is. Is sport for participating or spectating? If the latter, are the benefits of sporting competition based on gambling, entertainment and laughter, or the former, healthiness, morality and leadership? Should sportsmen and sportswomen receive a wage for their time and troubles or does payment represent professionalism and a threat to the amateur ideal? Should sport be played by everyone in local fields and parks or be watched on stages and televisions? 'Is there even,' to borrow a rhetorical question from Martin Johnes, 'such a thing, a singular concept, called sport?'[19]

While not quite as casual in their approaches, sports studies have generally not gravitated towards sports that challenge the perceived internal logic *of* sport. Cultural anthropologists and historians might have engaged in their own version of the pub table dispute, asking questions about the differences between play and sport and how this establishes itself in non-capitalist and capitalist societies.[20] Work by Allen Guttmann, furthermore, has done a good job of establishing shifts from festival sports to 'modern' sporting cultures, that embrace 'secularism, equality, specialization, rationalization, bureaucratization, quantification, records'.[21] Generally speaking, for modern, Western audiences the meaning of sport is apparently common sense: a competition between individuals or groups testing physical skill, speed, accuracy or strength, and this has been reflected in many scholarly discussions. Robert Reinehart, describing the emergence of 'alternative' sports, reflects on how athletes might answer this question, settling on 'What is sport is a moot question.'[22] Similarly, in Wray Vamplew's excellent book on the economics of sport, he refuses to even engage in the debate, claiming that 'except on the fringes, sport is generally recognisable and that any attempt … to further classify or delineate … runs the risk … of confusing the goalposts with the bedposts'.[23]

Such an approach is perfectly valid for Vamplew's purposes, but given the nature of professional wrestling, this book is precisely interested in the fringes (and for that matter how the fringes interact with 'centres' of power). When we begin to problematize 'sport', seeking types of physical display that may sit on the fringes, numerous examples can be considered. Activities such as figure skating, high diving and ballroom dancing can all be considered competitive, but to be so rely on independent adjudicators making aesthetic judgements. Hippodramatic horse riding, rope dancing, tumbling, trapeze artistry, tightrope walking, juggling, sword throwing, and many other physical activities that can be witnessed on the circus and variety stage use similar or even identical skills and bodily actions to those found in sport, but are very clearly defined as 'theatre'. One can quite conceivably imagine such displays, with a tweak here and there regarding showmanship and performance conditions, as Olympic events. And what about entertainments such as ITV's 1990s show *Gladiators*, or bodybuilding, all of which can sit uncomfortably on the boundaries of sporting contest and theatrical display? The boundaries between sport and other recreational forms are arbitrary, often permeable, sometimes barely visible, and regularly contested.

Conversely, a significant question remains why other sports did not develop in a manner alongside professional wrestling. In many regards, professional wrestling is a perfect sport, offering narratives of competition combined with exceptional physical prowess, bodily control, speed and strength. Given the success of professional wrestling on television, whether in Britain, America, Mexico, Japan, or many countries besides, it seems remarkable that other sports have not followed professional wrestling's lead in pre-arranging contests. Asking audiences to part with their money to watch an event in which quality and entertainment are left to chance seems an improbable business model in a century which saw ever-increasing Fordism and standardisation across cultural and economic commodities.[24] Moreover, it is not difficult to imagine other sports in a model not dissimilar to the sporting entertainments of wrestling. It does not take large amounts of imagination to whisk away the whites of Wimbledon, or the hushed silence of the 100 m Olympic final, or the polite handshakes before a rugby match and replace them with brightly coloured costumes, 'good' and 'bad' characters, and matches where sport is prearranged, performed solely for entertainment. Some critics of contemporary sporting cultures might suggest that sport in fact already does this (see Chapter 5), but, as fun as imagining sports in this way might be, such a fantasy does not necessarily sit comfortably. Indeed, if upon reading this paragraph you have had an instinctive reaction, thinking that such changes would mean that sport was no longer sport, that very well might illustrate the point that we have fundamental beliefs about what sport *should* look like.

Professional wrestling, and other sports imagined in this manner, are simply not sport as we understand it. Fair play, competition and handshakes just seem *natural*. Natural they are not, though. These elements are the result of a hard-fought competition between actors, agents and institutions looking to control sport's meanings, rules and values. This book does not offer a formalist or essentialist description of sport, dance or theatre while testing professional wrestling as a text against such definitions. Moreover, it does not take sport for granted, assuming the way in which sport looks today is how sport was always going to look. As we will see in Chapter 1 and Chapter 2, numerous sports in the eighteenth and nineteenth centuries continued relationships with the stage, and performed sporting entertainments were a very real possibility for how sport might otherwise have developed. Boundaries between sport and the theatre exist, but they are socially, politically and culturally reproduced and policed, by those involved with theatre and sport and by wider society.

While histories of American and Mexican wrestling have been written, this is the first monograph-length study of (professional) wrestling in Britain. In addition to developing analysis about professional wrestling, it seeks to challenge pre-existing histories of sport, and considers alternative models for sport's development. It also poses new theoretical contributions to how audiences can be studied in history, and the role of celebrities in contemporary cultures. The book explores how sport has been constructed historically, recognising that what we take for granted today had to first be established in the past. It also develops and combines a set of critical theories to understand how 'sport' and 'theatre' are reproduced, shaping audience expectations and forms of representation. Professional wrestling, the book proposes, can be understood as an enduring possibility for sport, serving as a marker for what sport could have been, a point of comparison which proves sports legitimacy and naturalness.

Fields, terrains and coordinates

If the above shows anything, it is that professional wrestling fundamentally challenges academic disciplines (or perhaps it demonstrates the limitations of academic disciplines). To critically assess professional wrestling, this book necessarily moves between disciplines and sub-disciplines, placing circus history alongside contemporary celebrity studies, forcing sports history into conversations with feminist literature studies. Simply put, it is a work of cultural studies, drawing on the 'anti-disciplinary' instincts of that approach,[25] embracing the fact that 'cultural studies is not one arm of the humanities so much as an attempt to use all of those arms at once'.[26] This theoretical bricolage is not a mere intellectual exercise, but stems from the conviction that a full understanding of professional wrestling demands such an approach. While the scholarship on wrestling described above has made a number of rich contributions to understanding its cultural position, a creative movement across theoretical and disciplinary boundaries is essential to develop a full picture of British professional wrestling's role in history. In working in this model, the book adds to a debate larger than wrestling itself, about the role of power in the construction of popular cultural forms, the ways in which history structures the present, and the manner in which different audiences construct meaning and identity in their uses of media and sporting texts.

While the book draws on a variety of intellectual traditions, then, it houses those arguments in a combination and dialogue between three overarching metatheories, explored in turn below. These theories inform, structure and anchor the arguments, and allow for the exploration that is needed. The first, given my self-declared embrace of cultural studies, should be unsurprising: Gramscian hegemony and Stuart Hall's conception of politics as 'terrain'. The second, Pierre Bourdieu's analysis of fields. The third, Georg Simmel's notion of modernity as produced by intersecting social circles. Taken together, the book argues that fields have terrains, are produced via conflict and compromise, and that individuals find their space in those terrains through a set of social coordinates. From sporting organisations and governmental bodies, to audiences, both those who love or hate a text, to the types of codes and conventions in journalistic representation, the book proposes that all forms of response are produced by and produce a field's terrain.

The first metatheory the book draws upon, Antonio Gramsci's conception of hegemony, and its adoption and adaptation by theorists attached or sympathetic to the Birmingham Centre for Contemporary Cultural Studies, will be familiar to most scholars of media, popular culture and sport. In brief, hegemony is the theory of how dominant groups negotiate and govern by consent. Moving beyond Marxist analyses of history and culture that described social control and class conflict in literal terms, for a generation of writers interested in media, sports and popular culture, the utilisation of Gramsci's work allowed for aspects of social control and power while simultaneously allowing room for working-class agency, operating as a middle ground between structuralism and culturalism.[27] The attraction of hegemony is clear: it moves notions of power away from something that is wielded to something that is coercive and manifested in a number of subtle ways. Using this model, 'the bourgeoisie can become a hegemonic, leading class only to the degree that bourgeois ideology is able to accommodate, to find some space for, opposing class cultures and values'.[28] In this reading, ruling groups control the ideological meanings of sport and leisure without necessarily producing class conflict or coercion in the sense of physical violence or threat thereof. Through a mixture of different forms of control, the model of sport and leisure being 'controlled' by the bourgeoisie was retained, but at the same time the working classes had a role in the ways in which sport and leisure were remade.

At its most polemical, however, the hegemony model tends to see power structures as part of the social control thesis, albeit with the might of the police force, magistrates and industrialists being swapped for a more nuanced description of cultural control.[29] While hegemony still sits in the background of many contemporary analyses, it has fallen out of favour in some disciplines, partly because its explanatory power has dwindled. As noted by Richard Holt, 'If crudely handled, the idea of hegemony simply degenerates into a bland proposition about the manipulation of the masses by controlling cliques.'[30] Studies in many sports have shown that to think simply in terms of bourgeoisie and proletariat is to misunderstand how sport and popular culture were experienced by such groups, and class has been broken up and divided into more nuanced competing class fractions and sub-hegemonies, demonstrating that clear middle-/working-class divides need further consideration and context.[31]

Combining the insights gleaned from Gramsci, however, with Pierre Bourdieu's description of fields offers a solution that allows this book to reinvigorate the relevance and vibrancy of both models. Field theory's great strength is the way in which it asks key questions about the role of organisations and institutions. As Bourdieu and Wacquant (1992) claim:

> The notion of field does not provide ready-made answers to all possible queries in the manner of the grand concepts of 'theoreticist theory' which claims to explain everything and in the right order. Rather its major virtue ... is that it promotes a mode of construction that has to be rethought anew every time. It forces us to raise questions: about the limits of the universe under investigation, how it is 'articulated,' to what and to what degree, etc.

In keeping with Bourdieu's work more generally, fields are surprisingly simple concepts grounded in dense empirical work.[32] At its most basic, a field is an autonomous and unique social space, 'having its own laws of functioning independent of those of politics and the economy ... endowed with particular institutions and obeying specific laws'.[33] Bourdieu is rightly adamant that a field cannot be understood by one-dimensional, economic readings of the base and superstructure. Instead, fields exist in the wider social field, creating mutually dependent, sometimes antagonistic, relationships between other fields. Changes in one field, then, may cause changes in another, functioning 'somewhat like a prism which refracts every external determination: demographic, economic or political events are always retranslated according to the specific logic of the field'.[34] Finally, contained within each field are subfields which, like fields, contain a unique set of 'logic, rules and regularities' while still observing the forms of capital inherent in the broader field.[35]

Bourdieu conceptualises fields as being 'simultaneously a *space of conflict and competition*, the analogy here being with a battlefield'.[36] It is also a battlefield which is shaped by previous encounters. Those who have control over a field can scar and mark the field and provide advantages in future skirmishes. Writing about changes to the artistic field, Bourdieu argues that:

> The direction of change depends on the state of the system of possibilities ... inherited from history. It is these possibilities which define what it is possible or not possible to think or do at a given moment in any determined field.[37]

Continuity is actively reproduced by those it already favours, and advantages in the struggles are bequeathed to those who support its structures. While change can be produced by new entrances into the field, or existing agents and institutions combining their capitals to mount challenges, transformation still exists within a limited set of historical possibilities. Ultimately, control over the field is a set of conflicts mounted by different individuals or agents bringing with them all their available forms of capital, both in the field itself and elsewhere, played out in the structure and rules of the field as it exists. These battles are tactical and predominantly, though crucially not always, won by those with the most forms of capital (economic, cultural, social, symbolic and derivatives thereof).

Bourdieu turned his attention to sport on several occasions,[38] and his emphasis on the uniqueness of the sporting field is important. One of sports history's greatest achievements in the last 30 years has been to establish the distinctiveness of sport while placing it in a larger frame of social and historical development, allowing for 'its own tempo, its own evolutionary laws, its own crises, in short, its specific chronology'.[39] The book is broadly concerned with how the sporting and exercise field came into being, and how its key tensions were negotiated. As Bourdieu claims:

> [T]he social definition of sport is an object of struggles, that the field of sporting practices is the site of struggles in which what is at stake, *inter alia*, is the monopolistic capacity to impose the legitimate definition of sporting practice and of the legitimate function of sporting activity – amateurism vs. professionalism, participant sport vs. spectator sport, distinctive (elite) sport vs. popular (mass) sport.[40]

Thinking about professional wrestling in relation to the sporting field is critical to understanding its development. Rather than offering an essentialist description of sport, building a typology that inherently excludes professional wrestling, studying the historical genesis and then maintenance of the sporting field offers a more complex history. Thinking in terms of fields offers an opportunity to observe historical participants and their own policing and maintaining of boundaries and those who pass through them. Using these measurements, professional wrestling in the twentieth century belonged to the sporting field. Professional wrestling looked, felt and was experienced like a sport. It was used as an example in debates about the role, purpose and meaning of sport. Professional wrestling was displayed in grounds and stadiums created and maintained by other sports. Many ex-amateur wrestlers became pro-wrestlers, agents, or promoters. Until the 1930s, professional wrestling was covered in sporting magazines and in the sporting pages of the mainstream press. From the 1930s onwards, professional wrestling appeared as part of televised sports broadcasting. The fact that so much energy has been spent claiming that professional wrestling is not a sport, whether in academia or beyond, is testament to the huge amount of investment and dedication we all have in delineating and sustaining a field's boundaries.

Seeing fields as a place of battle is useful, and sometimes they evidently are, but this approach is limited. If we combine the notion of fields as autonomous and unique spaces, complete with their own values and ideologies, with Gramsci and British cultural studies, however, then we get closer to the complex ways in which fields operate. In simple terms, compromise is often just as likely a tactic as conflict. Stuart Hall offers a summary of the ways in which individuals experience power: 'incorporation, distortion, resistance, negotiation, recuperation', and these are very much successful tactics on the field.[41] At any given time, subfields and fields may compromise to mutually profit; negotiations may delay or disrupt the war; and incorporation may be a key tool for survival. A field may well be a battlefield, but it simultaneously contains both guerrilla tactics and advanced methods of negotiation and peacekeeping. In the history of sports, these conflicts and compromises have played out differently in different sports, shaped by the wider social field and the types of capital and groupings involved at those moments. Choosing when to go to battle and when to negotiate, when to attack and when to defend, helps us to understand the histories of any given field. As a metaphor, Stuart Hall's description of politics as a terrain is powerful for thinking about fields. In simple terms, the terrain is the ground upon which the boundaries and contours of the field are laid out, and the nature of the terrain shape the conflicts and compromises that take place. Individuals, associations and groups place themselves on the terrain of the battlefield, and use the environment, the topology of the map, as needed. Terrains are produced by how groups form, the alliances and allegiances they have for one another, and the types of capital or power each have access to.

Finally, building on Georg Simmel, the book proposes that a field's terrain is partially structured by a field's intersection with other fields. In so doing, the book is able to overcome a potential limitation of field theory by modelling more comprehensively the nature of interactions and movements between and across fields as they are experienced by individual actors, and how those interactions shape the terrain itself. For Simmel, individuality in a modern society is produced by the number of social circles one exists in. Starting with the family, and building up to career, friendship groups, clubs and other distinct social groups, then:

> The groups to which individuals belong form, as it were, a system of coordinates in such a way that each additional one defines the individual more exactly and unambiguously. The attachment to any given one of them still leaves individuality wide latitude; however, the more there are, the more unlikely it is that yet other persons will manifest the same combination of groups, that this many circles would yet again intersect at any *one* point.[42]

Social circles, of course, are much less formal than Bourdieu's fields, lacking the bureaucratic institutions, formal structures or defining values and ideologies. Even so, the notion of intersecting fields is vital to understanding how the terrain of a field is produced. If instead of studying a field itself, we studied an egocentric experience of them, then we'd see that the individual in modern society is defined by membership of many fields. Memberships of these fields may involve personal and localised negotiation of competing habitus and capital, as individuals make sense of the push and pull that fields enact upon them. Furthermore, in their movement across different fields, individuals build a type of meta-habitus, a bank of habits and understandings that can be drawn upon, depending on the social space they find themselves. As discussed in Chapter 3, watching sport, consuming television, and one's own response to those texts, demonstrate the conflicts and compromises of a given field, albeit battles that are much more impressionistic and phantasmagorical. Because of this, all of us have stakes in a variety of fields at any given time.

A field's terrain can partly be mapped by analysing an individual's key intersections with other fields. Though impossible to share the same set of coordinates as another person, it is very possible to share a very similar set of coordinates (or what Bourdieu would call 'proximity in social space'[43]), and one is likely to find a similar set of values and ideologies, and therefore a similar set of shared 'enemies', the closer someone is to your coordinates. This is especially important for the historical development of professional wrestling (and other sports' refusal to develop as a theatrical entertainment). During the formation of the field, entrepreneurial showpeople operated in both the theatrical and sporting fields. Those groupings battled (or attempted to battle) sporting organisations and groupings whose intersections were in the medical or religious or educational fields. The important point is that the terrain of the field was produced by intersections, however. Chapter 5 looks at the expansion of the media field, particularly television, after the Second World War, involving a flux of media workers into the sporting field, radically altering the terrain. Taken together, social groups formed at a micro level, fields formed at a macro level, fields experienced changes in the political, industrial and economic fields, and individuals existed across multiple formations. To put it simply, this was a multifaceted and constantly moving social map that was difficult to negotiate, and where small structural changes in one part of the culture might have unintended consequences in another.

What is sport? Who it is for? What is its purpose? Such seemingly simple questions have involved a complex set of groups, cliques and factions seeking to carve out their own meanings, values and pleasures. Sometimes changes in the field of sport have refracted much bigger social changes or pressures from outside of the field, and sometimes they have involved more specific debates contained to the field itself, albeit with social actors retaining social roles beyond the field. Understanding a field is fundamentally a historical question, because power dynamics and terrains are always rooted in history. As Stuart Hall has argued about the final decades of the nineteenth century:

> The more we look at it, the more convinced we become that somewhere in this period lies matrix of factors and problems from which *our* history – and our peculiar dilemmas – arise. Everything changes – not just a shift in the relations of forces but a reconstitution of the terrain of political struggle itself. It isn't just by chance that so many of the characteristic forms of what we think of as 'traditional' popular culture either emerge from or emerge in their distinctive modern form.[44]

Ultimately, a field's terrain is immensely influential. In terms of sport and the media, the terrain helps to explain how texts are produced, how they are consumed, and the available meanings to those who consume them. Chapter 3 demonstrates that the conflicts between audiences and fans about meaning or pleasures of a text are always shaped by positions in the field and broader structures. Chapter 4 demonstrates how key a field's terrain is in structuring the codes and conventions of a celebrity, and how we understand them. Anyone who has ever claimed that professional wrestling is not a real sport, for instance, has been expressing the values and ideologies of the sporting field. These values and ideologies are the result of conflicts and compromises made during the genesis of the sporting field in the nineteenth century which still shape the terrain as it exists today. The terrain of the field shapes the common sense or hegemony (or what Bourdieu calls doxa) of a cultural form, and thinking beyond those common-sense notions requires critical historical consideration, working across multiple methods, and drawing on a variety of sources.

Methodology

Studying the history of professional wrestling poses difficulties. Characterised by the ephemeral nature of historical documentation, archives are notoriously trying at the best of times. In addition to the complications faced by all historical researchers, wrestling presents its own unique dilemmas. Wrestling is an umbrella term for hundreds of various competitive combat sports that existed across counties, countries and historical contexts. Rooted in festival cultures, each has their own distinct styles, meanings and has been pugnacious in their resistance to succumbing to nationalising and internationalising tendencies of other sporting cultures.[45] The professional and amateur versions share little in common, but their histories are intertwined and one cannot explain the former without reflecting on the latter (and vice versa). To understand the development of professional wrestling, one first needs to understand the multiple local styles that are found across England, both historically and contemporarily. As a series of regional sports, wrestling left scattered and incomplete accounts, rooted in folk traditions and inconsistent record-keeping from village to village, region to region.

As a national and international entertainment, however, professional wrestling has never had anything resembling a national organisation with a set of central governing bodies, clubs, or formal structures. Professional wrestling developed in the late nineteenth and early twentieth centuries as a transnational entertainment, taking influence from American carnival promoters, British music hall showpeople, and French vaudeville, establishing distinct touring patterns in Australasia, America and Europe. Further research will no doubt reveal influences and relationships across the globe. During the twentieth century, professional wrestling had established highly distinct promotions and styles in North America, Europe, Japan and Mexico. The closest the sport came to such a group in Britain, Joint Promotions in the second half of the twentieth century, still consisted of regional wrestling organisations and did not have a monopoly over the sport in the same way that other sporting bodies retained.

Without a clear local/national/international organisation consolidating power, obvious archives where one can study the history of 'wrestling' are not especially forthcoming. For wrestling, unlike, say, association football, there are no institutionalised archives comprehensively detailing company records or finances. This reveals something about how the terrains of a field are created. In adding to the theoretical approaches above, we might posit that those in prominent positions upon the terrain of a field leave written legacies, and usually attract financial support to sustain, document and digitise those records. If paperwork and written archives are often sought to establish historical record and legacies, serving as documents that shape the possibilities and terrains of a field, wrestling promoters have usually been reluctant to engage in these legacies.

Aggravating the lack of formal or institutional records is something quite specific to professional wrestling. *Kayfabe*, a term reflecting wrestling's carnival roots (see Chapter 3 and Chapter 4), refers to wrestling's insistence on its own legitimacy, with narratives from the fictional world apparently expanding into 'real' life, and this extends into written and archival sources. British wrestler biographies maintained the illusion that professional wrestling is a competitive sport, for example, and in letters to Independent Television wrestling promoters spoke about wrestling as a legitimate sport. Analysing these sources requires care, though arguably this type of source analysis merely adds a specificity to the types of investigation that all historians are involved with. Kayfabe has also complicated the types of records that have been kept. Promoters have never been the most diligent with regards to company finances or paperwork,[46] partly because leaving detailed reports of the fakery and trickery involved in the performance would have caused problems for promoters, given the fact that newspapers were often eager to provide evidence for such accusations.

To bypass these issues, the research for this book has involved the consultation of a range of primary sources spanning a variety of fields and institutions. The records have sometimes been kept by those who opposed wrestling, they sometimes appear in spaces or institutional archives where wrestling was tangential, and often they reveal professional wrestling's relationship intersections with other subfields and fields. That is one of the strengths of the book, helping to frame the theoretical analysis above, placing wrestling into a variety of spaces and seeing the competing and conflicting notions of what wrestling is for, both historically and across institutions and organisations. Wrestling's performativity is often continued into these spaces, and in seeking to untangle ballyhoo from promoters from misunderstandings of concerned outsiders, the work analyses the role of promotional cultures in sustaining histories, narratives and ideologies of any given field.

For example, the book examines local archives (particularly the Cumbrian record archives), where diligent local historians have done a good job of preserving some of the area's rich sporting history. In the absence of an official professional wrestling archives understanding the working structure of Joint Promotions, the cartel of affiliated promoters who described themselves as something akin to a national sporting organisation, is difficult to ascertain with any accuracy, but IBA/ITA's detailed written archives provide records of ITV and professional wrestling's relationship. The archive documents audience internal correspondence, external correspondence with Joint Promotions, and minutes of meetings. In examining these sources, the book analyses the relationship between sporting organisations and both the sporting field and other fields, in addition to their role in reproducing particular values and capitals

The book also explores the role of sporting organisations in policing differences between the theatrical and sporting fields, and the influence of showpeople and promoters on the production, promotion and dissemination of professional wrestling. It draws on showmen's autobiographies, particularly Charles Cochran, who were heavily involved in professional wrestling's development. The pitfalls of these sources are apparent, doubly so knowing the showmen involved and their renown for hyperbole, and these are complicated further by kayfabe. Where possible, then, their claims are tested against records and photographs from the National Fairground Archive (Sheffield) and Belle Vue archives (Manchester) alongside press reports, taking advantage of digitised and searchable newspaper and magazine archives. Elsewhere, in seeking to understand why professional wrestling developed in the manner that it did, the chapter explores minutes and memos from the National Football Museum regarding the Football Association's resistance to theatrical football contests. In so doing, it offers an intriguing example of how sport's relationship to theatrical and sporting spaces was negotiated and performed.

Given the book's emphasis on conflict and compromise, it also draws on local and national government archives, particularly at moments when professional wrestling has been especially concerning to these institutions. In the 1930s and 1940s, London County Council (LCC) placed the sport under a large degree of scrutiny, and the Home Office (HO) conducted their own research on the sport. In these two sets of records, there were letters of complaint from concerned correspondents, letters and internal memos between branches of government and sporting organisations, and detailed police and governmental reports from the wrestling matches themselves. Such analysis reflects the ways in which governmental power produces a field's terrain, and how cultural forms that are seen to resist broader ideological meanings or values face conflict within the field by those beyond the field. It also gives detailed responses of people not involved with professional wrestling.

Studying audiences remains a difficult enterprise, and this is complicated by studying audiences in history. Where social science and media studies researchers can design methodologies that locate the audience, and often ask them specifically designed questions, historical audiences have long since disappeared. Despite this, the book offers a detailed study of professional wrestling audiences, their pleasures and their displeasures. This is made possible by drawing upon a range of archival materials. First of these is the records in the Mass Observation (MO) project. The Mass Observation project grew out of a desire to understand the pleasures and cultures of the urban working classes, one of the results was a detailed study of Bolton's various everyday practices in the 1930s. In keeping with other MO methods,[47] Bolton's all-in wrestling fans were invited to write to the project via the local newspaper, answering the question:

> What do you like about all-in wrestling? Make it short and snappy or long and argumentative. Anything you like. The Prizes will go to those whose replies are judged to be the most straightforward and sincere.[48]

Clearly, this was a self-selecting sample, and considering the judges were the all-in wrestling promoters, those writing to the competition may have been inclined to write positive reviews, although some attendees used the opportunity to complain about the conduct of wrestlers and audiences. The MO provides a reasonably detailed overview of the multifarious, at times contradictory, ways audiences could read and enjoy all-in wrestling. Throughout the book, quotes are presented as given in the archives, including spelling and grammatical errors. Correcting and disciplining the century-old language of young working-class people would rob them of their voices, and repeated use of *sic* can fracture sentences and appear patronising.

A second source of audience data is from the accounts of both the LCC and HO, which include lengthy descriptions of how audiences responded and reacted to events. Though these are through the eyes of police officers, they give some sense of how audiences were seen by those in power. Finally, Independent Television's regulator, Independent Broadcasting Authority (IBA)/Independent Television Authority (ITA), have archives including detailed letters from audiences, both for and against wrestling, and crucially quantitative audience research by Ian Dobie and Mallory Wober.[49] In bringing these archives together, the book explores the different ways audiences have understood professional wrestling, and the manner in which audiences exist upon and reproduce a field's terrain.

Finally, newsreel, film and television recordings, have allowed me to see historical examples of a sport that has always been very visual and visceral. These have helped complicate or support some of the above accounts. This has clearly been helped by digitization projects (like those of the British Film Institute and British Pathé) combined with other forms of digital archives and fan preservations. Between YouTube, online collectors and DVDs, some of wrestling's appearances on television have been viewed. For the media historian, however, television recordings are a double-edged sword: they are excellent records but much early footage has been lost, and this is true with regards to professional wrestling. The vast majority of early broadcasts, particularly from the 1950s and 1960s, were not retained. Recordings from the late 1960s and 1970s, however, are more readily available. Being an audio-visual medium, where television wrestling matches have survived, they leave a vivid record of the performance as it was seen, if not experienced, by audiences at home. Overall, the breadth and depth of these sources have allowed the book to build up a complex history of British wrestling, from its appearances in early modern festivals through to its broadcasts on global, multi-channel broadcasting. It analyses professional wrestling from the view of broadcasters, audiences, promoters, showpeople, and government organisations.

Structure of the book

Chapter 1 is concerned with the development of the sporting field, and how the key tensions and debates created and sustained the terrain of the field. To examine a fielded society is to trace the moment in which a society becomes differentiated enough to sustain them.[50] The sporting field emerges at 'the moment from which there began to be constituted a field of competition within which sport was defined as a specific practice, irreducible to a mere ritual game or festive amusement'.[51] The chapter explores wrestling's relationship to festival cultures before the establishment of the economic and industrial fields, and how prize-fighting and wrestling became ensconced in the world of theatre and popular entertainment. Facing pressure from fields elsewhere in society, many sports sought support and relief, or developed elsewhere, in other fields, whether medicine, military, educational or entertainment. In the latter, sport became a key attraction on the stage. As these different forms of sport came together in the middle of the nineteenth century, key debates about the role of sport took place, ultimately creating the terrain of the sporting field.

Chapter 2 assesses the critical role of sporting organisations in policing and negotiating the sporting field, and attributes professional wrestling's embrace of entertainment to the sport's lack of coherent national or international institution. It explores the influence and impact of theatrical showpeople on sport in the early twentieth century, particularly in professional wrestling's emergence as an entertainment on the music hall stage. It then proposes that professional wrestling serves as an enduring possibility of what sport might have looked like, and as an enduring possibility as a warning for the rest of the field. By the 1920s and 1930s, promoters had foregone legitimate competition entirely, swapping sport for spectacle. In flaunting so many of the sporting field's established values, the sport was met with widespread resistance, from government, other sporting organisations and the press.

Despite this resistance, promoters and wrestlers compromised, setting up the Mountevans Committee to remove some more of the violent and performance aspects while retaining wrestling's pre-arranged and entertainment-orientated nature. From this, Joint Promotions, a cartel-like organisation that protected members in Britain, was established, and this group were in a prime position to gain monopoly broadcasting rights with ITV. The chapter is a study in the way intersections, and agents' coordinates from these overlaps, shape social groupings and thus the terrain of a field, and the way that terrain influences the ideologies and battles in that social space. Developing Bourdieu's notion of 'discarded possibles', the chapter is adamant that sport is not 'natural' and that professional wrestling's development was a very real possibility for other sports. Wrestling served as a type of spectre for the rest of the field, a reminder of sport's relationship with the stage before the formation of the field.

Whereas Chapter 1 and Chapter 2 are concerned with clearly defined conflicts between named organisations and agents, Chapter 3 moves to the imagined and phantasmagorical spaces of audiences. Audiences, the chapter proposes, exist on the terrain of the field, taking part in the wider battles about sport's meanings, and its pleasures. The sporting field was produced and reproduced by a wide variety of individuals who had some sort of stake in what sport is, and this chapter outlines that theoretical contribution to both field theory and audience studies. The chapter explores key sites of contention about what professional wrestling is, including performances of violence, the display of bodies, comedy, and subversions of masculinity. These pleasures, furthermore, were laced with questions about wrestling's authenticity, and audience's understanding of that performativity. Many of the pleasures and displeasures outlined in this chapter can be explained by professional wrestling's intersection with the theatrical fields, and these are explored in further detail.

If a field's terrain shapes audience's expectations, reading positions, and identities, Chapter 4 assesses how fields structure texts. In particular, it is concerned with how fame operates in professional wrestling, and what that tells us about the nature of celebrity culture in a fielded society. The chapter analyses the moral structure of professional wrestling, detailing narratives that are structures around good guys (blue-eyes or babyfaces in wrestling sub-cultural language) and bad guys (heels/villains). As part of this analysis, it assesses and then critiques existing scholarship that explores professional wrestling through morality plays and melodrama. Though professional wrestling can be considered melodramatic, it suggests, that is because all celebrity culture is imbued with what Peter Brooks described as the melodramatic mode.[52] Celebrities-as-melodrama can be explained by the fielding of society in the eighteenth century, specifically the growth of commercial culture alongside the journalistic field. During this time, newspapers stripped out the complexities and nuances of public figures, and turned them into quasi-fictionalised characters. For professional wrestlers, music hall entrepreneurs fictionalised and embellished these characters, ultimately leading to the form of quasi-fictionalised, highly performative professional wrestling personas of the twentieth century. Caught between competing fields, performers in professional wrestling feel melodramatic and fictionalised because they lack supporting representational logics of the field.

Finally, Chapter 5 is interested in the ways in which intersecting fields shape each other, and how changes in one field subsequently change the terrain in another. To do this, it explores television's influence on the media field, and then how those influences radically altered the sporting field and professional wrestling. It explores the growth and development of Independent Television, and how wrestling became a signature of that channel. It then assesses how television changed professional wrestling as a text. It also examines the discarded possibility of Pay-TV, and how experimentations with that technology changed ownership structures, before examining the World Wrestling Federation's expansion into the UK via Sky television. It concludes by suggesting that the sporting field now more broadly occupies a position historically occupied by professional wrestling,

Notes

1 Nancy Banks-Smith, 'Clash of the Titans: Nancy Banks-Smith Witnesses the Triumph of Good Over Evil in the Wrestling Ring', *The Guardian*, 22 June 1981, p. 9.
2 See, for example, Mark Jefferies, 'World of Sport wrestling to return to TV on Saturdays after massive success of special', *The Mirror*, 23 March 2017. Available at: www.mirror.co.uk/tv/tv-news/world-sport-wrestling-return-tv-10087890
3 Herbert Kretzmer, 'Charge of the Heavy Brigade . .', *Daily Mail*, 16 July 1979, pp. 18–19.
4 Clifford Davies, 'Ring Stars Join Variety Union: Wrestlers Fight for Bigger TV Purse', *Daily Mirror*, 23 April 1962, p. 11.
5 Letter from H.W. Abby, Dale Martin Promotions, to Lew Grade and Howard Thomas, 21 Jan. 1966, Sporting Events 'Wrestling' vol. 1, IBA, Box 01097.
6 Sharon Mazer, *Professional Wrestling: Sport and Spectacle* (Jackson, MS, 1999), p. 3.
7 Heather Levi, *The World of Lucha Libre: Secrets, Revelations, and Mexican National Identity* (Durham, NC, 2008). p. 6.
8 See Nicholas Sammond (ed.), *Steel Chair to the Head: The Pleasure and Pain of Professional, Wrestling* (Durham, NC, 2005).
9 Broderick Chow, Claire Warden, and Eero Laine (eds), *Performance and Professional Wrestling*, (London, 2017).
10 Roland Barthes, *Mythologies*, trans. Annette Lavers (Reading, 1993), pp. 15–25.
11 Henry Jenkins, '"Never Trust a Snake": WWF Wrestling as Masculine Melodrama', in Aaron Baker and Todd Boyd (eds), *Out of Bounds: Sports, Media and the Politics of Identity* (Bloomington, IN, 1997), pp. 48–81; Gerald Craven and Richard Moseley,

'Actors on the Canvas Stage: The Dramatic Conventions of Professional Wrestling', *The Journal of Popular Culture*, 6(2), (1972), pp. 326–336.
12 Thomas Henricks, 'Professional Wrestling as Moral Order', *Sociological Inquiry*, 44(3), (1974), pp. 177–188.
13 Michael R. Ball, *Professional Wrestling as Ritual Drama in American Popular Culture* (Lewiston, NY, 1990).
14 Gregory P. Stone, 'Wrestling – The Great American Passion Play', in Eric Dunning (ed.), *Sport: Readings from a Sociological Perspective* (Toronto, 1971), pp. 301–335.
15 Cynthia J. Novack, 'Looking at Movement as Culture: Contact Improvisation to Disco', *The Drama Review*, 32(4), (1988), pp. 102–119.
16 Barthes, *Mythologies*, p. 17.
17 John Fiske, *Understanding Popular Culture* (London, 1989), pp. 83–102.
18 John W. Campbell, 'Professional Wrestling: Why the Bad Guys Win', *Journal of American Culture*, 19(2), (1996), pp. 127–132; Jeffery J. Mondak, 'The Politics of Professional Wrestling', *The Journal of Popular Culture*, 23/2, (1989), pp. 139–149.
19 Martin Johnes, 'British Sports History: The Present and the Future', *Journal of Sport History*, 35(1), (2008), p. 68.
20 Allen Guttmann, *From Ritual to Record: The Nature of Modern Sports* (New York, 2004).
21 Ibid., p. 16.
22 Robert E. Reinehart, 'Emerging Arriving Sport: Alternatives to Formal Sport', in Jay Coakley and Eric Dunning (eds), *Handbook of Sports Studies* (London, 2002), p. 516.
23 Wray Vamplew, *Pay Up and Play the Game: Professional Sport in Britain, 1875–1914* (Cambridge, 1988), p. xv.
24 Garry Whannel, *Fields in Vision: Television Sport and Cultural Transformation* (London, 1992), p. 84.
25 Nicholas Daly, 'Interdisciplinarity and Cultural Studies', *Victorian Review*, 33(1), (2007), pp. 18–21.
26 Hua Hsu, 'Stuart Hall and the Rise of Cultural Studies', *The New Yorker*. Available at: www.newyorker.com/books/page-turner/stuart-hall-and-the-rise-of-cultural-studies
27 Tony Bennett, 'Popular Culture and the "Turn to Gramsci"', in Tony Bennett, Colin Mercer and Janet Woollacott (eds), *Popular Culture and Social Relations* (Milton Keynes, 1986), pp. xi–xix.
28 Ibid., p. xv.
29 John Hargreaves, *Sport, Power and Culture* (Oxford, 1986).
30 Richard Holt, *Sport and the British: A Modern History* (Oxford, 1989), p. 363.
31 Norman Baker, 'Whose Hegemony? The Origins of the Amateur Ethos in Nineteenth Century English Society', *Sport in History*, 24(1), (2004), pp. 1–16.
32 See Pierre Bourdieu, *The Field of Cultural Production: Essays on Art and Literature*, trans. Randal Johnson (Cambridge, 2012); Pierre Bourdieu, *The Rules of Art: Genesis and Structure of the Literary Field*, trans. Susan Emanuel (Cambridge, 1996).
33 Bourdieu, *The Field of Cultural Production*, pp. 162–163.
34 Ibid., p. 164.
35 Pierre Bourdieu and Loïc J. D. Wacquant, *An Invitation to Reflexive Sociology* (Chicago, 1992), p. 104.
36 Ibid., p. 17.
37 Bourdieu, *The Rules of Art*, p. 206.
38 Pierre Bourdieu, 'Sport and Social Class', *Social Science Information*, 17, (1978), pp. 819–840; Pierre Bourdieu, 'The State, Economics and Sport', *Culture, Sport, Society*, 1(2), (1998), pp. 15–21; Bourdieu writes about the Olympics as a field of production in *On Television* (New York, 1996), pp. 79–81.

39 Bourdieu, 'Sport and Social Class', p. 821.
40 Ibid., p. 826.
41 Stuart Hall, 'Notes on Deconstructing the Popular', in Raphael Samuel (ed.), *People's History and Socialist Theory* (London, 1981), p. 236.
42 Georg Simmel, 'The Intersection of Social Circles', in Georg Simmel, *Sociology: Inquiries into the Construction of Social Forms*, vol. 1 (Leiden, 2009), pp. 371–372.
43 Pierre Bourdieu, *Practical Reason: On the Theory of Action* (Cambridge, 2001), pp. 10–11.
44 Italics in original, Hall, 'Notes on Deconstructing the Popular', p. 229.
45 Katrin Bromber, Birgit Krawietz and Petar Petrov, 'Wrestling in Multifarious Modernity', *The International Journal of the History of Sport*, 31(4), (2014), pp. 91–404.
46 Fiona A.E. McQuarrie, 'Breaking Kayfabe: "The History of a History" of World Wrestling Entertainment', *Management & Organizational History*, 1(3), (2006), p. 242.
47 Ian Gazeley and Claire Langhamer, 'The Meanings of Happiness in Mass Observation's Bolton', *History Workshop Journal*, 75(1), (2013), p. 166.
48 Ibid.
49 Ian Dobie and Mallory Wober, *The Role of Wrestling as a Public Spectacle: Audience Attitudes to Wrestling as Portrayed on Television* (London, 1978).
50 George Steinmetz, 'Bourdieu, Historicity, and Historical Sociology', *Cultural Sociology*, 5(1), (2011), p. 54.
51 Bourdieu, 'Sport and Social Class', p. 821.
52 Peter Brooks, *The Melodramatic Imagination: Balzac, Henry James, Melodrama and the Mode of Excess* (New Haven, CT, 1976).

Bibliography

Baker, Norman, 'Whose Hegemony? The Origins of the Amateur Ethos in Nineteenth Century English Society', *Sport in History*, 24(1), (2004), pp. 1–16.
Ball, Michael R., *Professional Wrestling as Ritual Drama in American Popular Culture*, Lewiston, NY, Edwin Mellen Press, 1990.
Barthes, Roland, *Mythologies*, trans., Annette Lavers, Reading, Vintage Press, 1993.
Bennett, Tony, *'Popular Culture and the "Turn to Gramsci"'*, in Tony Bennett, Colin Mercer and Janet Woollacott (eds), *Popular Culture and Social Relations*, Milton Keynes, Open University Press, 1986, pp. xi–xix.
Bourdieu, Pierre, 'Sport and Social Class', *Social Science Information*, 17, (1978), pp. 819–840. Bourdieu, Pierre, 'Genesis and Structure of the Religious Field', *Comparative Social Research*, 13, (1991), pp. 1–44.
Bourdieu, Pierre, *On Television*, New York, The New Press, 1996a.
Bourdieu, Pierre, *The Rules of Art: Genesis and Structure of the Literary Field*, trans. Susan Emanuel, Cambridge, Polity, 1996b.
Bourdieu, Pierre, *The State Nobility: Elite Schools in the Field of Power*, trans. Lauretta C. Clough, Cambridge, Polity, 1996c, pp. 261–336.
Bourdieu, Pierre, 'The State, Economics and Sport', *Culture, Sport, Society*, 1(2), (1998), pp. 15–21.
Bourdieu, Pierre, 'Rethinking the State: Genesis and Structure of the Bureaucratic Field', in George Steinmetz (ed.), *State/Culture: State-Formation After the Cultural Turn*, Ithaca, NY, Cornell University Press, 1999.
Bourdieu, Pierre, *Practical Reason: On the Theory of Action*, Cambridge, Polity, 2001.
Bourdieu, Pierre, *The Field of Cultural Production: Essays on Art and Literature*,

trans. Randal Johnson, Cambridge, Polity, 2012. Bourdieu, Pierre, and Wacquant, Loïc J. D., *An Invitation to Reflexive Sociology*, Chicago, University of Chicago Press, 1992.

Bromber, Katrin, Krawietz, Birgit and Petrov, Petar, 'Wrestling in Multifarious Modernity', *The International Journal of the History of Sport*, 31(4), (2014), pp. 391–404.

Brooks, Peter, *The Melodramatic Imagination: Balzac, Henry James, Melodrama and the Mode of Excess*, New Haven, CT, Yale University Press, 1976.

Campbell, John W., 'Professional Wrestling: Why the Bad Guys Win', *Journal of American Culture*, 19(2), (1996), pp. 127–132.

Chow, Broderick, Warden, Claire, and Laine, Eero (eds), *Performance and Professional Wrestling*, London, Routledge, 2017.

Craven, Gerald and Moseley, Richard, 'Actors on the Canvas Stage: The Dramatic Conventions of Professional Wrestling', *The Journal of Popular Culture*, 6(2), (1972), pp. 326–336.

Daly, Nicholas, 'Interdisciplinarity and Cultural Studies', *Victorian Review*, 33(1), (2007), pp. 18–21.

Dobie, Ian, and Wober, Mallory, *The Role of Wrestling as a Public Spectacle: Audience Attitudes to Wrestling as Portrayed on Television*, London, Independent Broadcasting Authority, 1978.

Fiske, John, *Understanding Popular Culture*, London, Routledge, 1989.

Gazeley, Ian and Langhamer, Claire, 'The Meanings of Happiness in Mass Observation's Bolton', *History Workshop Journal*, 75(1), (2013), pp. 159–189.

Guttmann, Allen, *From Ritual to Record: The Nature of Modern Sports*, New York, Columbia University Press, 2004.

Hall, Stuart, 'Notes on Deconstructing the Popular', in Raphael Samuel (ed.), *People's History and Socialist Theory*, London, Routledge, 1981, pp. 227–240.

Hargreaves, John, *Sport, Power and Culture*, Oxford, Polity, 1986.

Henricks, Thomas, 'Professional Wrestling as Moral Order', *Sociological Inquiry*, 44(3), 1974, pp. 177–188.

Jenkins, Henry, '"Never Trust a Snake": WWF Wrestling as Masculine Melodrama', in Aaron Baker and Todd Boyd (eds), *Out of Bounds: Sports, Media and the Politics of Identity*, Bloomington, IN, Indiana University Press, 1997, pp. 48–80.

Johnes, Martin, 'British Sports History: The Present and the Future', *Journal of Sport History*, 35(1), (2008), pp. 65–71.

Levi, Heather, *The World of Lucha Libre: Secrets, Revelations, and Mexican National Identity*, Durham, NC: Duke University Press, 2008.

Mazer, Sharon, *Professional Wrestling: Sport and Spectacle*, Jackson, MS, University Press of Mississippi, 1999.

McQuarrie, Fiona A.E., 'Breaking Kayfabe: "The History of a History" of World Wrestling Entertainment', *Management & Organizational History*, 1(3), (2006), pp. 227–250.

Mondak, Jeffery J., 'The Politics of Professional Wrestling', *The Journal of Popular Culture*, 23(2), (1989), pp. 139–149.

Novack, Cynthia J., 'Looking at Movement as Culture: Contact Improvisation to Disco', *The Drama Review*, 32(4), (1988), pp. 102–119.

Reinehart, Robert E., 'Emerging Arriving Sport: Alternatives to Formal Sport', in Jay Coakley and Eric Dunning (eds), *Handbook of Sports Studies*, London, Sage, 2002, pp. 504–520.

Sammond, Nicholas (ed.), *Steel Chair to the Head: The Pleasure and Pain of Professional Wrestling*, Durham, NC, Duke University Press, 2005.

Simmel, Georg, 'The Intersection of Social Circles', in Georg Simmel, *Sociology: Inquiries into the Construction of Social Forms*, vol. 1, Leiden, Brill, 2009, pp. 363–408.

Steinmetz, George, 'Bourdieu, Historicity, and Historical Sociology', *Cultural Sociology*, 5(1), (2011), pp. 45–66.

Stone, Gregory P., 'Wrestling – The Great American Passion Play', in Eric Dunning (ed.), *Sport: Readings from a Sociological Perspective*, Toronto, University of Toronto Press, 1971, pp. 301–335.

Vamplew, Wray, *Pay Up and Play the Game: Professional Sport in Britain, 1875–1914*, Cambridge, Cambridge University Press, 1988.

Whannel, Garry, *Fields in Vision: Television Sport and Cultural Transformation*, London, Routledge, 1992.

Chapter 1

The field vs the stage

Speaking to a local radio station in the 1960s, with the glitz, glitter and glamour of televised professional wrestling at its height, one old, retired Cumbrian wrestler declared that 'wrestling ... was a game for the field not the stage'.[1] Though his frustration is perhaps understandable, it also revealing. Since the nineteenth century, sport has been characterised by intensely and intrinsically held beliefs about what sport *is*, what it is *for*, and *who* it is for. It was for competition, health, and helped to instil values beneficial to the individual and nation. These values, the chapter suggests, can be traced to the establishment of the sporting field, some time in the mid-nineteenth century. While such values are never set in stone, and there have been slow changes to these underlying conceptions, it is with remarkable consistency that the values derived from the genesis of the sporting field structure our sense of what sport is. The core notion of sport for the field rather than the stage is to some degree foundational.

Sport did not have to be this way, though. Before the genesis of the field, sport had a range of meanings and values depending on the context in which it took place. This chapter begins by charting the history of wrestling's relationship to the festival and agricultural cultures before a period that can be loosely described as 'industrialism'. It also assesses discussions about the new economic order's impact on festival and sporting cultures, and posits that many sports that survived the onslaught of industrialism found support, if only in passing, in developing cultural fields. One of those fields was the theatrical field, and combat sports like prize-fighting and wrestling began to be performed on the stage, emphasising entertainment. This was, the chapter posits, a different sporting culture to the one that emerged in the nineteenth century, and it is this history that professional wrestling can be understood as a continuation of.

The chapter then examines the emergence of the sporting and exercise field, a space which sought to establish key values around amateurism, rational recreation, and sport for health. Sport was deeply intertwined with ideologies about British men in industry and empire. The culture that produced the philosophy of rational recreation, the notion that leisure should be culturally and morally uplifting, was also a culture that valued capitalist enterprise. The greatest challenge to rational recreation, aside from the fact that the working classes were not an acquiescent group eager to be told how to spend their free time, was the on-going commercialisation of culture. Some members of the middle class, with enough social and symbolic capital to have influence, argued for rational recreation, but there were equal numbers who saw leisure as an economic and commercial possibility. Where Bourdieu often categorises fields as spaces of conflict, the chapter explores the ways that compromises are made, dependent on the terrain of the field. By the twentieth century, the key contours and terrains had been established: with limited and controlled forms of professionalism operating in some sports and elsewhere purer notions of amateurism being pursued. Due to wrestling's regional nature, it resisted the growth of a national sporting field, and did not comfortably operate on the forming terrain. Because of these complexities, wrestling occupied an uncomfortable position in the sporting field, a position that cultural entrepreneurs would take advantage of in the twentieth century.

Scenes from a low life

Types of wrestling and pugilism, like many sports in the early modern period, were a regular feature in quotidian lives and the festival calendar. Records of wrestling can be found scattered across Britain, but certain areas were famed for their styles. Robert W. Malcolmson lists 'Cornwall, Devon, Bedfordshire, Northamptonshire, Norfolk, Cumberland, and Westmoreland',[2] to which can be added Lancashire, an important region for the development of the catch-as-catch-can style at the end of the nineteenth century. When Joseph Strutt, a folklorist writing at the turn of the nineteenth century, described wrestling, he was keen to point out, 'the entirely different systems of wrestling developed in different parts of the kingdom is a slight but genuine proof of the great variety of nationalities and tribes that were involved in the making of England'.[3] Though they shared the most basic of rules (attempting to throw or keep an opponent on the ground), the differences were often more noticeable than their similarities. In the Lake District, Cumberland and Westmoreland, wrestling matches started with a unique hold where '[e]ach man places his chin on his opponent's right shoulder and grasps him round the back. The left arm is over the opponent's right and the right arm under the opponent's left arm.'[4] In Cornwall and Devon participants wore a jacket which provided a focus for holds, and wrestling on the ground was forbidden. The former allowed kicking where the latter did not.[5] Lancashire wrestling had a reputation for being particularly violent, with kicking and choking and a tendency to be fought on the ground.[6] Wrestling, like most sports in the medieval and early modern period, was hyper-locally organised and informal, with variations in rules even from one village to the next.

In its everyday form, wrestling was practised outside alehouses and on village greens, or it might simply have taken the form of children playing in a manner not dissimilar to today of children kicking around a football in the park. It is important to stress that sport was a regular feature throughout the year.[7] In the historiography of sports pre-dating the eighteenth century, there is sometimes a danger in celebrating and focusing on festivals and ignoring their more banal relatives. While this can be an easy trap to fall into, it is a one that is perhaps easy to understand: festivals were big, boisterous and colourful affairs that captured the attention of visitors, surveyors, diarists and antiquarians. For these reasons, festival culture is the best-documented and most vivid form of archival evidence of popular culture. Sport was a regular feature of the carnival calendar. Football and rugby historians, for example, have long stressed inter-village matches played on Shrove Tuesday as being the pre-industrial antecedents of their modern counterpart,[8] and cock throwing was closely linked to Shrove Tuesday.[9] Pugilism and wrestling tournaments were similarly regularly conducted as part of the larger festival event. In 1758, William Borlase described the relationship in Cornwall between festivals, feasts and wrestling traditions:

> Every parish has its annual feast, and at such time (however poor at other times of the year) everyone will make a shift to entertain his friends and relations on the Sunday, and on the Monday and Tuesday all business is suspended, and the young men assemble and hurl or wrestle, or both, in some part of their parish of the most public resort.[10]

Carnival was a disruption from the hard-working lives of the rural poor and an event that brought most, if not all, the local community together to laugh and play, and the rituals, symbols and imagery of festivals celebrated the visceral, carnal pleasures divorced from the harsh lived experiences of agricultural labour. Festivals punctuated the calendar providing an abundance of food, sex, laughter and a subversion of power that was not permissible at other times of the year.[11] In this context, sport provided an important arena for expressions of anger and violence while maintaining the boundaries of licensed disorder as opposed to outright illegality. Wrestling had the potential to be a highly ferocious affair with blood, broken bones and even death. Richard Holt offers one description of a fight in Lancashire which records:

> [P]arties mutually agreeing to fight 'up and down', which includes the right of kicking on every part of the body and in all possible situations, and of squeezing the throat or 'throttling' to the verge of death. At races, fairs and on other public occasions contests of this nature are watched by crowds of persons who take part on each side ... that death often occurs in such battles will not be extraordinary.[12]

Yet for all the excited rhetoric of this account, excessive violence was likely to be the exception rather than the rule. In practice, wrestling was closer to Adrian Harvey's conclusions about folk football: 'most games appear to have been comparatively good natured ... [and] good humoured rather than violent'.[13] It was physical, and blood might be spilled, but the matches themselves were rarely about settling scores or attempting to do permanent damage to one's opponent. Frustration and anger were likely contained to the match itself and remained spontaneous and easily passed.

Despite this, forms of pugilism caught the attention of social reformers. Questions about social control have permeated historical accounts of sports, leisure and popular culture in the industrial revolutions.[14] Influenced by Marxist traditions, much of the earliest sport and leisure history work focused on attacks, suppression and conflict aimed at the customs and cultures of the poor and working classes. Paying attention to the eighteenth century and early nineteenth century,[15] this view articulated the destruction of older, pre-industrial forms of leisure by a toxic mixture of industrialism, urbanisation, and the growth of a capitalist middle class. In the city and under the eyes of capitalists and factory bosses, such accounts claim, sharper conceptions of time and work brought an end to more casual forms of leisure and play.[16] The key denunciation about traditional forms of popular culture was that they tempted workers away from employment and destroyed the discipline that was needed for modern industrial production.[17] Government laws and reforms were made to have material consequences with the 1839 Metropolitan Police Act, whose 'major objective', according to Robert Storch, 'was the closer and more efficient regulation and organisation of quotidian life' which had 'profound' implications for popular culture.[18] The establishment of a police force proper and changes in local and national government created a more intense focus on the sport.

In some ways, pugilism, wrestling and prize-fighting appear to be ideal case studies for this model. The sports existed as regional 'from-below' entertainment linked to festival cultures, before facing numerous objections and other forms of pressure from industrialists, the police, magistrates, the church, and other moral reformers. Given that forms of pugilism and wrestling encouraged many of the qualities deemed unworthy of a civilized mind – booze, betting and bloodlust – the sports were frequently attacked. When arguments against prize-fighting were aired in public they often stressed the 'disrupting' nature of the sport for workers. Prize-fighting remained a popular and regular distraction, even as festival cultures began to be replaced by more organised weekly doses of leisure, and the sport's relationship with Saint Monday remained strong throughout the first decades of the nineteenth century. It was for good reason that George Davis dedicated his poem *Saint Monday: Scenes from a Low Life* to the prize-fighters Tom Johnson, Richard Humphreys (*sic*) and Daniel Mendoza.[19]

Edward Hyde East, MP and judge, warned that prize fights appealed to, and in some ways produced, the 'idle' and 'disorderly'.[20] Such criticisms were sung in harmony with claims that the sport was violent and degrading. The emergence and spread of Methodism and Anglicanism petitioned against bodily pleasures such as drink and sport. The Rev. Edward Barry argued in 1789 that it was a 'direct violation of every law, of humanity, and common decency'.[21] Wrestling also suffered censures: in Cornwall, with its strong Methodist leanings, ministers frequently denounced wrestling competitions. An 1829 letter explained why local miners should not be tempted by the sport:

> Why do you not go to the wrestling? ... Because I can employ my time better. Because it is throwing my money away. Because I wish not to be seen in bad company. Because I would not encourage idleness, folly and vice. Because I should set a bad example. Because God has forbidden it.[22]

Be that as it may, how popular or successful were such denouncements? Such narratives tend to overlook the large amount of continuity expressed.[23] Elsewhere, the idea that a singular industrial revolution could be written about was overtaken by studies that stressed regionality.[24] Further, there has been some revision about the unevenness of such pressure, the regional dimensions of such debates, and the speed with such sports responded to these controls.[25] Simply put, many sports and leisure activities flourished throughout the industrial revolution, albeit while adapting to the new social field in which they belonged.

As lofty as some of the reforming rhetoric undoubtedly was, prize-fighting and wrestling did not seem to particularly suffer a decline. Prize-fighting's apparent illegality, for example, did not stop it flourishing in the 1790s, 1800s, and 1810s, and again in the 1860s. During one of pugilism's especially prominent periods in the 1790s, a trilogy of fights between Daniel Mendoza and John Humphreys attracted and excited thousands of spectators and dozens of newspaper reports, discussed further in Chapter 4. Legitimate contests were a common occurrence in the south and other fights took place, albeit with less frequency, all over England. To legally by-pass its dubious status, legitimate fights would be held in the countryside with large crowds dutifully following the event.[26] Often, fights would pass without incident. Likewise, those who wished to suppress wrestling met with limited triumphs.

Similarly, wrestling continued across the country throughout the late eighteenth and early nineteenth centuries. In both Cumbria and Cornwall, there is some reference to a decline in wrestling in the final decades of the eighteenth century, but it is hard to accurately assess what this means. In 1807, one reverend claimed wrestling in Cornwall was a 'very rare occurrence'.[27] A similar decline was recorded in Cumbria in the 1770s.[28] As Michael Tripp asks, though, were contemporaries referring to 'overall numbers ... those entering tournaments, or simply the absence of informal wrestling so prevalent in Carew's day?' He then adds, 'another possible interpretation is that these writers were referring to a decline amongst their own class'.[29] Just as anti-sports reformers were often eager to embellish their perceived successes, pro-sport arguments, from folklorists and other antiquarians, often imagined and romanticised the past to pass comment on the passing from the age of 'innocence' to 'experience'.

For all the arguments about the policing of the proletariat's entertainments and moral force of rational recreation, debates about popular culture in industrialising Britain did not fit comfortably into simple class binaries, and the control of leisure was never simply 'a contest between proletarians in the red corner and bosses in the blue'.[30] A complicated picture of sport and leisure history has emerged in which a broad section of individuals, institutions and agents, all with competing values and ideas, have shaped sport, and where class and hegemony are divided into class fractions and sub-hegemonies.[31] Certainly, many of the sports that did survive the nineteenth century were those who had participants or supporters who had the economic, social or cultural capital to withstand outside challenges. Blood sports such as bear baiting and cock throwing often lacked the capital to sustain such threats. There was no unified resistance from the working classes and few culturally, socially or economically rich backers provided sufficient support. Conversely, entire sports could come together to protect themselves from outside attacks, as Mike Huggins' work on horse racing found that 'vertical ties of common interest often bound competing groups'.[32]

Another way of analysing this history, then, is to think about the role of fields. Festival sports belonged to a society that was reasonably unstructured, rural, and intensely local. Big structures, like economic trade and politics were presided over by an obvious power structure incorporating royalty, its immediate court, the landed elites they sponsored, and the church. Political and economic power congregated in the hands of a limited few, and the possibility of separate, functioning fields did not exist because, according to George Steinmetz, 'undifferentiated societies ... do not have fields that are relatively autonomous from the dominant powers'.[33] Between 1700 and 1775, economic, religious, cultural and political fields emerged, indicating that 'the creation of ... modern society [is seen] by the differentiation of state and market power and more generally the making of fields'.[34] Dramatic changes to the private market, and incentives to trade and loan, were accompanied by industrial innovations and the eventual restructuring of the workforce and subdivision of labour. During this time, politics, business, education, literature, theatre, medicine and many other fields and subfields were defined in relation to one another in the field of power. Fields emerged as autonomous, and institutions, groups and agents were actively attempting to shape the boundaries while policing the capital, and exchange rates, available within.

The establishment of one field changed the terrain of the wider social field, and those changes were refracted and reflected elsewhere. For the purpose of this study, an autonomous economic field saw a shift from a participatory festival and agricultural culture to a commercial culture which demonstrated sharper divisions between work and leisure, and popular commercial entertainments emerged to entertain workers in the growing industrial centres. By the end of the century, leisure was moving away from localised, semi-rural and communal pleasures to an increasingly urbanised,[35] national, professionalised, institutionalised, and profitable commodity sold in a competitive, commercial marketplace. Without the relative safety and protection afforded by fields, and with the removal of patronage and lack of interest from cultural entrepreneurs or sometimes even audiences, many traditional pastimes did not survive the century. Sports that flourished, however, were often sports that could find bureaucratic or institutional support in some of these establishing and emerging fields, with agents who had some significant degree of economic or cultural capital. To do so, they often had to adapt to the wider societal battles that existed in a fielding society, including conflicts and compromises with the economic and industrial fields. For sports like wrestling and prize-fighting, and indeed other commercially orientated sports like pedestrianism, this support came from the popular cultural fields, with backing from showpeople, publicans and other commercial entertainers.

Sparring in the most fashionable and scientifical style

Evidence abounds for the genesis and establishment of the theatrical fields in the eighteenth century. Cultural entrepreneurs, free from older forms of sponsorship and patronage, provided these audiences with their cultural wares.[36] By the 1820s, over one hundred theatres had been built in urban centres across England.[37] Circus, arguably the defining Georgian and early-Victorian entertainment, was born in London in 1773. In the early 1800s, nine cities across England could boast of a permanent or semi-permanent wooden structure where circus was performed, and by the 1820s, London alone had nine circuses.[38] Fairs and wakes that survived into the nineteenth century, and these were plentiful, became more entertainment-focused and continued to offer professional theatre booths and gaffs.[39] Commercial entertainments borrowed and adapted existing and older cultural forms. A diverse range of amusements that had previously been offered by itinerant performers were presented at the circus or fairgrounds.[40] Now, however, they were presented with a sleeker and professionalised mode and display, each establishing their own specific terrains.

Facing pressure from the economic and industrial fields, sporting events sought ideological or economic protection in other fields, borrowing the language of training, medicine or entertainment. While sport was not of central importance in the growing fields, having support from those with economic, cultural or bureaucratic capital to resist challenges usually helped. Continuing from commercial boxing venues and amphitheatres in the early part of the eighteenth century (see Chapter 4), many sports found space and support in the commercial popular cultures. Circuses, singing saloons, theatres, gaffs, public houses, and fairgrounds were regularly used as a space to demonstrate and exhibit sporting competitions. The histories of theatre and sport have usually been written separately, with academic disciplines usually clustering around the boundaries policed by fields themselves. As Hugh Cunningham suggested in the 1980s:

There are histories of sport, of drama, of the pantomime, and of the circus. Yet what is most striking is the connections between these different forms of entertainment, connections so strong that one can speak of this world of entertainment as part of one close-knit popular culture. All these forms of entertainment were frankly commercial in nature, all aimed to attract spectators, all employed professionals ... It was no accident that wrestling could be seen at the Eagle Tavern, soon to become the Grecian Saloon, and not simply coincidence that Pierce Egan was at home in both the theatre and the prize-ring, nor that so many of these forms of entertainment could be witnessed at the horse race or fair.[41]

When one begins looking for connections between sport and the stage, one finds an intense network of related agents and institutions with a seemingly shared set of values, ideologies, languages, capitals and beliefs. Archers, for example, dressed and exhibited in American Indian costumes.[42] A cricket match, specifically designed to elicit laughter, was held between physically disabled men.[43] In pedestrianism, a sport which publicans and showpeople had firm control of, Samantha Oldfield has noted the arrival of the America star, Louis 'Deerfoot' Bennett, in 1849.[44] On arrival, he toured as part of his own circus-athletic troupe which featured a display of sporting acts and exhibitions. The show drew on popular troupes associated with circuses and fairgrounds, including characterisation and costume. Accounts of the tour indicate that the show was about entertainment first and foremost.

> [Wearing] native clothing with 'wolfskin cloak' and 'buckskin moccasins', his racing apparel being 'tights, and wearing a girdle richly ornamented with floss silk and feathers, and also a slight belt, to which several small bells were attached'. Deerfoot would present his war-cry, a 'yell so shrill, ear-splitting, and protracted' when he defeated his opponents and the performance element of the races added to their entertainment value.[45]

Perhaps the greatest example of a sport thriving in the fairgrounds, theatres, and singing saloons was pugilism, and prize-fighters and wrestlers became an important feature of this urban, commercial popular culture. Their performances were not sporting contests, but displays that were referred to by contemporaries as *sparring*. The primary purpose of sparring was to entertain while providing a simulacrum of the sport. Pierce Egan, the most famous and prolific journalist of the Fancy, the influential subculture attached to commercial sporting cultures, offered a pithy summary of what he considered sparring to be. It was, he wrote, a 'mock encounter; but, at the same time, a representation, and, in most cases, an exact one, of real fighting'.[46] His description hints at the tensions between the sport proper, that is legitimate competitions that took place in the fields, and its theatrical equivalent. Advertisements for sparring often stressed their verisimilitude. One advert, for example, claimed: 'the exhibition is a novelty in the catalogue of such displays, inasmuch as the men set-to on a stage fifteen feet square, attired in their flannel drawers and colours as near as possible to represent the real conflict'.[47]

Yet sparring was both safer and more profitable than legitimate competition. Legitimate competitions posed the very real possibility of injury or even death. Even the most successful fighter faced a professional career that, by default, would never stretch into old-age. Prize-fighting was a sport that privileged speed and endurance. No matter what a fighter did to cover the blows, there were only so many times that they could suffer repeated impacts to the head. At best, there were opportunities for a few boxers to remain in the sport after retirement, as trainers, seconds, and referees. The real potential to earn enough to retire comfortably was greatly enhanced by the prospect of theatrical exhibitions. Exhibition fights were gloved affairs, serious damage was restricted, and the brutality of the long legitimate contests was almost completely removed.[48] Though we should maintain a certain amount of scepticism with regards to crowd sizes at prize-fighting fights in the country,[49] estimates of thousands or tens of thousands hoping to see the fight do not seem wildly misplaced. Contemporary and historical sources had difficulty in recording accurate attendances – the lack of tickets, turnstiles and stewards – it also made charging for the events problematic. While there were occasional attempts to collect money from spectators at the big open-air events,[50] the probability is that for the majority of the crowd the biggest financial outlays were travel, alcohol and betting. None of these costs, though, were likely to find their way to the participants involved (unless, of course, one fighter had a particularly nefarious relationship with a bookie). Prize-fighting sometimes offered big purses, but these were one-off payments.

Theatrical exhibitions offered the solution for prize-fighters to gain money from their skills. One newspaper report suggested that an exhibition in 1806 was attended by 700 patrons, each paying 2s6d,[51] about a day's wage for an unskilled labourer. This seems to be a good indicator of audience sizes and admission costs.[52] Harvey estimates that it was not uncommon for a successful and well-known prize-fighter to earn £50–£100 a week,[53] an estimate that is not far away from Mendoza's claim of earning 25 guineas a night for a three-night-run in Manchester.[54] Compared to skilled labourers, a pugilist's week-long engagement with a theatre might be equivalent to a year's wages.[55] Admission charges and tickets, then, or at the very least extended contracts with big theatres and circuses, were a much more direct way for the pugilists to profit from their labour. It also offered a lucrative and regular form of employment that might also extend their short careers.[56]

Proliferating entertainment venues, in London and the provinces, meant there were plenty of places for prize-fighters to spar and plenty of demand for their skills, from both theatrical managers and audiences. In his autobiography, Daniel Mendoza recorded where he performed throughout the 1790s, and the range of venues is indicative of the sorts of venues where the most popular prize-fighters were hired. At the height of his fame, Mendoza received, 'from the proprietors of various country theatres very liberal offers of engagement'.[57] He was, 'engaged ... on very liberal terms for three nights, to exhibit the art of self-defence at Covent Garden Theatre, and had the satisfaction of experiencing, each night, the most flattering reception from the audience'.[58] In 1790, he toured Lancashire and Scotland's theatres. Soon after, Mendoza was employed by Astley to perform in Dublin and Liverpool, two of the many circuses he had established across the country.

Mendoza, though certainly one of the most recognisable prize-fighters of the period, was not unique in this regard. Without the space to offer an exhaustive list, a brief description of the pubs, theatres and circuses which displayed sparring during the late-eighteenth and early-nineteenth century offers a glimpse of the coverage given to the entertainment: the Peahen Tavern[59], Sadler's Wells,[60] Garrick Head,[61] Royal Circus,[62] the Lyceum,[63] Sans Souci Theatre,[64] Howes and Cushing,[65] Ginnett's,[66] and Pablo Fanque's.[67] Prize-fighters appeared in large cities and smaller provincial towns. Tenting circuses, after the introduction of American circuses in the 1830s, took these entertainments even further afield. By the late 1820s, pugilists were appearing in so many different locations in so many cities around the country that *Bell's Life in London* could produce a half-joking, half-serious poem entitled 'Movements of the Pugilistic Stars', listing where particular boxers might be on any given day.[68] Wrestling, although to a lesser extent, could also be found on the stage and in the circus ring. These included the Grecian Saloon (an early precursor to the music hall),[69] Pantheon Theatre,[70] and later in the century, P.T. Barnum's Greatest Show on Earth.

Circuses and theatres were the domain of the well-known star performers. For lesser-known pugilists there were the prize-fighting exhibitions which toured the fairgrounds and horse racing meets. In these booths, sparring exhibitions were supplemented by open challenges for locals to last a predetermined time in the ring for a prize (a gimmick that professional wrestling continued on the music hall stage). In his memoirs, David Prince Miller, performing in a boxing booth for the first and last time, recorded touring the fairgrounds of Yorkshire. He had, he complained, 'all the rough customers to contend with ... during the first day's exhibition ... a great strong butcher came into the place to show off his pugilistic talents'.[71] At Bartholomew fair, one newspaper clipping recorded 'a man who had hired a room for the purpose, bellowed aloud to the mob as follows: "Walk up, Gentlemen and Ladies, to see the wonderful boxing. Here's sparring in the most fashionable and scientifical style."'[72] Boxing booths and wrestling booths, performing sparring exhibitions or invited challenges, were a regular feature of many fairs, and remained so throughout the nineteenth century and much of the twentieth century.[73]

Yet for all functions of these events, in sparring performances, Harvey succinctly notes, 'providing entertainment was a presiding concern'.[74] Importantly for how professional wrestling was performed later around the turn of the twentieth century (see Chapter 3), prize-fighting exhibitions interacted with, and were influenced by, the performance traditions they appeared alongside. Sparring exhibitions were ensconced in the world of theatricality, and, along with much Georgian popular culture, exhibited the variety elements that would characterise the music hall later in the century. At the circus, sparring was part of the wider bill and was performed next to the acts that were fashionable at the time. On the fairground, boxing booths were competing with other gaffs and stalls for the audience's attention, evidenced by the Bartholomew fair caller's bellowing to audiences. On the stage, at both public houses and theatres, sparring was presented alongside other performances. Examples include sparring being presented at the Lyceum next to a 'variety of entertainments; with music and singing'.[75] At an 1822 show sparring featured next to a romantic melodrama, a performance of a scene from *Tom and Jerry*, the playing of a fiddle, a performance of tricks with ladders, and a comic pantomime.[76] Harvey records that, 'sport was presented as a number of attractions at pubs, such as the mixture of songs, comedy and boxing held at the Garrick Head'.[77]

Appearing next to other forms of performance influenced the way sparring exhibitions were presented. In keeping with the clowning and physical comedy that could be seen at the circus, one review of an exhibition in 1819 described how two boxers 'performed a "burlesque set-to", which excited much laughter'.[78] In one of the first national tours in the 1790s, Mendoza travelled and performed with a famed comedian who offered comic routines and impersonations of famous boxers.[79] At the Royal Circus, sparring was presented as the centrepiece of the pantomime, *The Spirit of the Fancy*. Little information about the performance has survived except for a short review which described it as 'undoubtedly the best of its kind that has been produced on that stage'. This, if nothing else, hints that boxing melodramas were not uncommon.[80] In one of Mendoza's tours, he 'paired up with a Mr Stretton in a show mixing instruction in self-defence with popular songs and sketches by composer and entertainer Charles Dibdin'.[81]

Adapting to the entertainment environment in which they found themselves, prize-fighters and wrestlers possessed and displayed other skills. Acting talent was required for pantomimes like *The Spirit of the Fancy*. At one sparring performance, Tom Hickman danced a 'Lancashire Clog Hornpipe in Real Clogs'.[82] David Prince Miller is not a typical example of a boxing showman, but his adaptability suggests something of the culture that produced him: at various points in his career he was, '[an] impersonator of a black giantess, prize-fighting sparer, conjurer, equestrian, fortune teller, employee of Wombwell, magician, [and] manager of the Royal Adelphi Theatre, Glasgow'.[83] Miller's own description of his engagement in a fairground boxing booth indicates the ease in which a sparring exhibition might borrow other showmen and women from other performances.

> I next proceeded to Halifax, in Yorkshire, where there were several shows, and, among other entertainments, an exhibition of sparring. The

arrangements for this affair were not completed, and, being at the time a strapping fellow, I had the offer of an engagement, which I accepted, and figured as the Warwickshire Champion.[84]

The evidence for these theatrical sparring tours is rich, but this is not to say that sparring exhibitions had completely overtaken legitimate competitions. Prize-fighters were still expected to compete in fights to prove their worth. Success in the fields, though, likely corresponded to success on the stage. One big fight or victory that caught the public's attention was often enough to sustain several years of performances. Often, a fight that managed to garner press and public attention would be a catalyst for a theatrical tour. It was not unheard of for the two participants of a fight to undertake a tour to capitalise on the recognition the two brought together. *Bell's Life*, for instance, reported that 'Barney, in company with Arthur Matthewson, his late successful antagonist, are exhibiting their *accomplishments* at Cheltenham, in their progress on a *sparring* tour.'[85]

The shared world of popular culture, in which prize-fighters were as comfortable on the stage as they were fighting in the field, is important. In the late eighteenth and early nineteenth centuries, 'there was a substantial commercial sporting culture that was almost as sophisticated as its successors of forty or so years later'.[86] This model of sporting exhibition, though, was very different to what followed in the second half of the nineteenth century. There was no natural split between sport and theatre, if anything sport and theatre were comfortable bedfellows. These relationships may seem incongruous to modern observers. Indeed, the unease that many people have in describing professional wrestling as sport today is testament to that analysis. This is due to the emergence and convergence of a very different sporting culture in the nineteenth century, one that mostly eschewed theatricality. Harvey argues that 'It was the onset of the "amateur" ideal that was to impede this progress. The upper and middle classes, far from promoting and fostering commercial sport, came to oppose it bitterly.'[87] Professional prize-fighters shared values and capitals with the circus performers, legitimate and illegitimate actors, and fairground entertainers. Putting on a good show, providing value for money, and creating and sustaining forms of celebrity were central tenets of the prize-fighting and sparring profession. Crucially, the 'common sense' notion of what sport is, and what sport is separate *from*, did not always exist as such. If not for the ideology and discourse of amateurism later in the century, and its high degree of influence at the genesis of the sporting field, this form of spectator sport – married to the popular and commercial stage – might have quite feasibly been the dominant sport today. The notion of 'sporting entertainments' can be traced to these early commercial sporting cultures; professional wrestling's development can be considered as a logical continuation of values and ideologies in a number of sporting displays.

Can the ancient sport be saved?

The sporting culture described above was one entwined with the world of commercial popular culture, but that was not the only space in which a version of something we might describe as sport existed. A particularly important space where sport found support and structure was in the educational field. Some time around the beginning of Victoria's reign, the now well-established narrative posits, public schools were looking to reform and modernise schooling. Sport was a key component in these plans. Always popular with some students, sport became something to be retooled and embraced rather than outlawed and policed. In giving games rules, sport was considered something that kept the boys out of trouble. From the riots and uprisings that had periodically undermined power structures through to keeping the boys thoughts 'pure' and hands from exploring their own or each other's bodies (or at least only on the field and not in the dorm rooms),[88] competitive team sports were seen by heads as antidotes to some of the 'disciplinary' problems encountered in the school.[89] Sport, in line with rational recreationist arguments, was celebrated for the moral and ideological traits it could instil in their pupils: community, competition, healthiness in mind and body, robustness, stoicism, and good grace in victory or defeat. Sport, therefore, was designed to train the future leaders of England, empire and industry.[90]

The sporting ethos taught at some of the public schools was, by the 1850s, adopted by advocates of Evangelicalism and Anglican moralists. Like public school masters – and a great number of people who signed up to this ideology were ex-public school boys – muscular Christians saw in sport the potential for character building and nation building. In addition to the qualities that the public schools believed sport could imbue, muscular Christianity railed against the damaging effects that were supposedly infecting modern, urban living. Sport, so the argument went, produced healthy, clean, masculine men rather than the dirty, sickly and effeminate men that city living and industrialism were believed to be creating. Muscular Christianity encouraged a very particular type of masculinity that was firmly placed within Victorian, industrialist culture: it encouraged self-discipline[91] and 'moral' standing and was the missionary wing of public school sports.

Though looking very similar on the surface, sport, depending on the social space where it took place, had different, often competing, meanings. The commercial sporting culture described above was a very different sporting culture to that promulgated in the Victorian public school, which was a very different sporting culture to the one that existed in the army, which in turn was a very different sporting culture to the forms of exercise recommended by those in the medical profession. At the beginning of the nineteenth century, therefore, 'sport' involved a variety of meanings, values and pleasures depending on the field in which it existed: sport for entertainment; sport for school discipline and pride; sport for training; sport for health. There were unmistakably distinct similarities, though, and as the nineteenth century continued, these different forms of practising sport began to coalesce, emerging as a distinctive and autonomous field. In so doing, it brought together the disparate sporting activities that had previously belonged to other fields and searched for commonalities and shared values. Writing about France in 1900, but recognising the earlier genesis in England, Jaques deFrance has suggested that:

> As all these activities lost their original way of being performed, they tended to get closer to each other, to aggregate, to be incorporated into a common space, and to acquire some common features ... gymnastics, sports and other forms of bodily exercises confronted one each other and began to search for common principles and common forms of organization. We can speak, in that case, of a field of sports and physical activities.[92]

During the merging of these groups into a shared space, debates, challenges and confrontations about how the field was to be structured were a common occurrence. As Mike Huggins has explained about the period, 'ownership of particular sports, their core values and the place of competition and winning were all debated'.[93] The establishment of the field involved a divergent group of agents looking to control, dominate and legitimate the various ideological, political and social meanings of sport. Arguments about whether sport was for health or entertainment, training or gambling, persisted, often in highly emotional and personal terms. To put it simply, the period between 1830 and 1860 was a period of great upheaval: some sports were created, others ceased to exist. Radical changes were enacted to sports that survived, and a whole swathe of sporting bodies and organisations were born. By the end of the nineteenth century, the specific topography of the field had been established.

Part of the pattern during the formation of the field was sports becoming nationally and then internationally organised. After completing their studies and embarking on their professional careers, and with sport now a well-respected pastime that stood as pillar of English masculinity and morality, former public school boys sought to continue playing the sports that had been a formative part of their childhood and adolescent years.[94] The public schools created a set of rules which were then distributed through 'the middle-class administrators who could secure them almost immediate national recognition through that intimate community of interest which the English know as the old-boy network'.[95] As a term, the old-boy network is indicative of a particular class, gender and power inflection that sought to control sport, and also sought to close it off from people not part of that network. That power was exerted and institutionalised in the ruling and governing bodies that were formed over the course of the 1860s. Encouraged by improvements in communications and transport, sporting organisations provided national rules so teams from across the country could play one another. Indeed, the genesis of the sporting field can be traced to the establishment of such bodies, and it is unsurprising that

Bourdieu claims a field becomes autonomous with the establishment of 'set of specific institutions'.[96] Sporting bodies' roles were to establish, enforce and sustain the negotiated values, capitals and ideologies of the field. Organisations and administrators were designed to sustain, protect and distribute these new versions of sport. They served to encourage and organise competition between members; helped to police disputes; publicly promoted the ethos and ethics of sport and their rational recreation; and attempted to control, with differing degrees of success, commercialisation. With a set of rules that could be observed across the whole of the country, sports became nationalised and regional teams competed against one another without the inconveniences of squabbles about regional and/or school variations.

As well as codifying rules, these groups established a potent and powerful discourse about how sport should be played. Tony Mason offers a strong summary of what was considered the amateur ideal:

> [P]laying for the side and not for the self. Being modest and generous in victory and staunch and cheerful in defeat. Playing the game for the game's sake: there might be physical and moral benefits but there should be no other rewards and certainly not prizes and money. No player should ever intentionally break the rules or stoop to underhand tactics. Hard but fair knocks should be taken and given courageously and with good temper.[97]

Who decided how a sport was played, and what it meant to the people playing and watching, were the central debate while the sporting field established its autonomy. Those who encouraged muscular Christianity and the discourse of amateurism often argued that it was 'grounded in a belief that it served to promote social stability by diverting men from drink, crime and political agitation or increasing the extent of social class intercourse'.[98] Increasing social intercourse may have been named by some of the participants involved, but for others the amateur ideology was just as much about keeping the classes separate rather than bringing them closer together. At times, amateurism was merely a concerted effort to gain control of sport and exclude and limit those taking part in the field. The Amateur Athletic Club famously excluded:

> Any gentlemen who has ever competed in an open competition or for public money, or for admission money, or with professionals for a prize, public money, or admission money, and who has ever, at any period of his life taught, pursued, or assisted in the pursuit of athletic exercised as a means of livelihood, or is a mechanic, artisan or labourer.[99]

In Bourdieusian terms, class can be described as a combination of social, cultural and symbolic capital, and those with similar amounts of cultural and economic capital, or 'proximity in social space', will likely, but not always, share similar interests, desires and motives.[100] As he stresses, however, 'This does not mean that they constitute a class in Marx's sense, that is, a group which is mobilized for common purposes, and especially against another class.'[101] Often, for example, the conflicts in the sporting field were not based on class in a simple sense, but between the same classes with slight differentiations and interpretations on what constituted amateurism, or debates about which school's rules should be adopted. During the formation of the field, individuals sought to form bonds with those who shared similar interests, values or tastes, and those with shared values often had similar social coordinates operating across intersecting fields. Active members in the sporting field retained roles in other fields, whether in industry, religion, education or theatre, and in the sporting fields individuals sought alliances with those sharing similar intersecting coordinates. The sporting organisation's powers partly derived from the capitals that were translated and refracted from the other fields they were part of. The public schools, universities, military and educational fields retained a higher status in the broader social field, and its members often had more economic, social and cultural capital. The intersectional power of their positions meant that the foundational values of the field reflected their view of what sport should look like, and this was closer to games they played in school than the theatrical, entertainment-orientated sports on the stage. Battles in the field, then, were tactical and predominantly won by those with the most forms of capital, economic, cultural, social, symbolic and derivatives thereof, and how these translated into the emerging field itself. These intersecting coordinates, and the terrain they produced, helped to generate the micro tensions between groups and individuals (disputes about which universities' rules should be adopted and adapted at a national level) but also the fundamental disagreements about what sport was for.

Showpeople's interpretation of sport, while often coming from those we might consider middle class, operated on a terrain without the capitals to fully resist this intersectional power. The amateur gentleman, a figure representing the coordinates of the sporting field, the public school, the church and industry, was positioned in contrast to 'professional' sportspeople. Professionalism, with its links to entertainment, profit, and the working classes, was seen to be a threat to the spirit in which sport should be played. Moreover, so it was argued, how was the amateur who practised after work supposed to compete with someone who practised daily and made their living from the sport?[102] Other critics felt that professionalism would lead to players being open to bribery: 'Men who were paid to win,' Vamplew summarises a prevalent view of the time, 'could also be paid to lose.'[103] The outright opposition to professionalism was in part a response to the type of theatrical performances that commercial sporting cultures had adapted to in the first half of the century. These tensions and conflicts, however, played out in different sports in different ways, subject to the types of organisations, support and broader historical context. Where the Amateur Athletic Association was substantially successful, boxing and wrestling posed deeper problems for the new sporting field.

Frustrated by boxing's continued relationship with the stage and fairgrounds, The Fancy, the influential subculture, who had sponsored the sport, drifted away in the early decades of the nineteenth century. There were continued, and failed, attempts to create appropriate and effectual ruling groups: The Fair Play Club in 1828 and the Pugilistic Benevolent Association in 1852.[104] Without a body, prize-fighters were still attracted to the stage, and after Jem Ward's retirement in 1832 followed 30 years of confusion about champions and championships.[105] Further successful attempts were made to bring boxing into the sporting field. Between 1867 and 1885 when the Marquess of Queensberry lent his title and social prestige to a challenge cup and set of rules that had been designed by John Graham Chambers. The new rules stipulated that boxing gloves should be worn always, introduced timed rounds, and finally banned wrestling holds; they privileged the 'scientific' style of boxing rather than brute strength and endurance; gloves allowed respectable men to compete without the worry of bloodied and bruised faces. The new sport belonged to the amateur athletic landscape, and Queensberry cups were competed for as part of the Amateur Athletic Club's yearly championships.[106]

In 1891, the National Sporting Club (NSC) became home to the organisation of boxing in England. The club awarded titles and, from 1908, Lonsdale belts. Like other sporting bodies of the period, the NSC attempted to control professionalism in the sport by attempting to limit competitors to fighting at their venues. While the Lonsdale belts could add prestige to a fighter, however, 'not surprisingly the Lonsdale belts failed to keep boxers within the NSC's stable ... Though British champions could only be crowned at the NSC, they refused to grant its directors monopolistic control of their careers and were enriched elsewhere.'[107] Andrew Horrall also highlights the ways in which boxers looked to earn money for their professionalism, in ways remarkably similar to what prize-fighters had been doing in the Georgian period. John L. Sullivan, the first world champion of Queensberry rules, followed a tradition of rarely defending his title. Instead, he starred in stage melodramas and music hall sparring exhibitions across America before visiting England briefly in 1888. When he was finally defeated by Gentleman Jim Corbett in 1892, Corbett followed a very similar pattern to Sullivan, touring theatres and music halls.[108]

One of the most enduring legacies of the Queensberry rules was the attempt to 'rescue' boxing from the performance tradition that it had become firmly associated with. The character of the professional boxer who won his championship at all costs and then retreated into the world of the fairground, carnival and circus was the very antithesis of what amateurism was supposed to stand for. A divorce between boxing and entertainment industries was never straightforward, though, and there was never any instantaneous rupture. Yet for all these continuing relationships with the stage, and the continuing influences on boxing, there existed an element of control by a sporting body. Importantly, boxing had something that resembled a national organisation. There was an agreed-upon set of rules and an expectation that boxers should act a certain way, even if they often fell short of those expectations. The NSC might not have had complete control over the sport or its sportsmen, but it had *some* control, and could regulate contests, especially for English championship matches. This was a delicate and precarious agreement, but it did seem to curb some of the more grandiose relationships with the stage that had been present in boxing 50 years earlier. In 1929, as will be argued in Chapter 2, facing the possibility of operating outside of a recognised governing body, the sport instituted the British Boxing Board of Control.

Wrestling occupied an even more precarious position during the formation of the field. Where sports like football, rugby and cricket all embraced national and international bodies, codified rules and organised national competitions, local wrestling styles resisted such developments, remaining highly local in both organisation and competition. In the face of highly bureaucratised and nationalised sporting bodies, local wrestling groups retained hyper-local organisation into the second half of the nineteenth century. Wrestling in Cumbria consisted of several local groups (often by town or village), who organised the annual competition but exerted little control over the sport as a whole.[109] Wrestling had also had some successes in London and other cities throughout the nineteenth centuries, particularly for immigrants to the industrial centres.[110] Competitions were held in the Cumberland style in Manchester, Liverpool and at the Islington Agricultural Hall in London; and in the Cornwall style in London throughout much of the nineteenth century. Organisers, however, kept the sport regional. The Cumberland and Westmorland Wrestling Society, based in London, restricted competition to 'natives of Cumberland and Westmoreland, and at the discretion of the committee to other North-country men, to whom suitable prizes shall be given to be wrestled for'.[111] The exclusion of non-northern counties competitors was a rule that expanded to all wrestling events competing in the Cumberland and Westmoreland style, be it in London or at the local fairs. There was clearly a reluctance by local groups to establish a national competition or series of leagues. There were other attempts in 1898[112] and 1904[113] (with links to the AAA) to establish obvious national amateur wrestling organisations, but these struggled to gain national control. While there was some resistance in terms of establishing a clear and nationally recognised wrestling organisation, there were greater challenges facing the purist supporters of amateurism.

The establishment of the sporting field resisted older models of commercial sporting culture, and produced a range of sporting organisations bodies, supported by intersections of other fields, who policed the concept of what sport was for. This was a very specific attempt to control sport, both financially and culturally, with the conscious goal of limiting the influence of dominating professional sportsmen, spectator sports audiences, and the theatrical and circus managers. They did not succeed totally in this regard, but their attempt was successful insofar as establishing the field's capital and doxa, both *on* the sport's field and *in* the sporting field. While they were successful in establishing key values around the amateur ideal, and sport for health, the application of the amateur ideal in its purest form was short-lived.

Compromise and contradiction

In his account of commercialised sport, Wray Vamplew states that the working classes were not overly keen on playing sport, but 'they did not mind watching others play and, as entrepreneurs were quick to realise, they were even willing to pay for the privilege'.[114] There were several ways in which entrepreneurs and investors might have hoped to have drawn a profit from investing in organised sport in the late Victorian era, from the more traditional organisers of sport publicans and bookmakers to the caterers, property developers, and commercial sponsors of big contests. Holt and Vamplew have expressed some doubt about profit being the sole reason for investment, and their contributions have served to muddy earlier assumptions about economic factors being the primary motive of sporting entrepreneurs.[115] Such individuals were clearly interested in acquiring cultural, social and symbolic capital as well. Tranter, summarising these views, however, declares that 'a desire to make money out of sport was clearly an important, perhaps even the most important, motive for participation'.[116] It is hard to disagree: growing numbers of spectators at football matches, cricket games and athletic meets were matched by the construction of purpose-built stadiums designed to hold thousands of people, an expansion that could be witnessed in the parallel growth of variety theatres and music halls discussed later in this chapter. Fifty-eight football clubs moved into purpose-built stadia between 1889 and 1910. This, however, was a very different type of commercial sporting culture to the ones connected to the stage earlier in the century.

The level of investment, and potential profit, changed the number of professionals involved in sport. Audiences and crowds, it was believed by entrepreneurs and club directors, came to see a talented team win a tight-run match.[117] Talented players needed to be paid to train and avoid the distraction of work. Professionalism and commercialism went hand in hand. Holt summarises that, 'Professionalism was the limited form through which amateurs permitted market forces to enter the world of sport.'[118] Spectator sports drew angered responses from some commentators and reformers versed in the public school and amateur ideology of what sport should be. Instead of helping to promote the healthy bodies and healthy minds for industry and empire that the muscular Christians had hoped to promote in the previous decades, spectator sport supposedly encouraged idleness and passiveness. Despite some disgruntled voices, commercialism was nurtured and encouraged. Simply put, there was too much money to be made from professional sports, and those with the economic capital with the ability to enter the field (in building stadiums and setting up clubs) would likely have other forms of capital (social, economic and cultural) to challenge the dominant amateur ethos.

Sporting bodies, reluctantly perhaps, allowed limited forms of spectatorship and professionalism on one condition: sporting authorities managed, restricted and maintained bureaucratic control over the sport, competitors and associated competitions. The forms that professionalism could be manifested were highly restricted, with limitations like wage caps, restrictions on players' transfers, and a strict enforcement of sporting rules and some acknowledgement of amateur sporting ideology, including stresses on competition and fair play. A 'respectable' sporting body was central to maintaining the 'respectability' of sport, upholding its virtues as outlined by the emergence of amateurism, while adapting to the commercial reality that sport was a popular amusement for spectators. In analysing the negotiations, it is clear that fields were not always a system of conflict as Bourdieu describes. Rather, and closer to Antonio Gramsci's conception of hegemony, alliances were made, negotiations were frequent, and compromises were found. As was outlined in the Introduction, if fields are battlefields, then they encompass a vast range of warfare techniques. The field's topography was shaped by how social groupings and organisations found space, the conflicts and compromises enacted by those groupings.

Virtually all agents and institutions in the sporting field felt the consequences of amateurism and the growth of commercialism, but the compromises and changes bore out differently in different sports. Sports, moreover, responded to the establishment of this terrain in different ways, shaped by the capitals involved and the historical moment in which they took place. Association football, a popular spectator sport that had deep roots in working-class communities, allowed professionalism from the mid-1880s onwards,[119] albeit with professionalism restricted by wage caps until the 1960s.[120] Tensions and compromises in rugby, as Tony Collins has persuasively identified, resulted in the sport splitting in two, with Rugby League in north being professionalised and Rugby Union in the South continuing to support amateurism.[121] For those who demanded a strict form of amateurism, any form of professionalism threatened the very existence of the amateur ideal. Pierre de Coubertin, the founder of the Olympic Games, once claimed:

> We must uphold the noble and chivalrous character of athleticism, which has distinguished it in the past, so that it may continue effectively to play the admirable role in the education of modern peoples that was attributed to it by Greek masters. Human imperfection always tends to transform the Olympic athlete into a circus gladiator. A choice must be made between these two incompatible approaches to athletics. To defend against the spirit of gain and professionalism that threatens to invade them, amateurs in most countries have established complex legislation that replete with compromise and contradiction.[122]

Just as wrestling had resisted a coherent national body, wrestlers also seemed reluctant to embrace the negotiated values of amateurism. In opposition to the values of amateurism, wrestlers in Lancashire, Cumbria and Devonshire had always competed for prizes. But debates about professionalism, different to that in amateur sport more widely, materialised in local wrestling tournaments. In 1864, the two most successful wrestlers in Cumbria's history, Jameson and Wright, were banned from competing at an event.[123] Arguments and explanations were familiar. Claims abounded that athletes who trained all year would always be likely to win in competition against those who practised sport as a hobby:[124] Jameson and Wright had started to travel around the country entering all competitions in the Cumberland and Westmorland style. It was nearly always one of the two of them who won the large purses. The most damaging rumour, though, was that the pair had been 'barneying', throwing falls for bets backed on oneself. This was widely disregarded by those who wrote letters of support to the local press (not necessarily a resounding declaration of innocence, but important nevertheless).[125] The fact remained that it was distinct possibility. Similar arguments about 'faggoting', Cornish wrestling's equivalence of barneying, plagued the sport in the south-west.[126] In the southern counties, this distrust was said to be one of the main causes of wrestling's decline in popularity.[127] In the north, a newspaper report similarly blamed barneying for the disinterest in the local sport:

> Wrestling is a game of the past. One by one tournaments of the north ... have been allowed to drop out of existence. The professors of the sport have themselves mostly to blame. What is known as 'barneying,' or 'liging doon,' became much too prevalent; real rivalry languished, and the sport dropped and died.[128]

The Cumberland and Westmorland Wrestling Society, based in London, was disbanded in 1887 due to these problems.[129] It was the closest the sport had to a national organisation. Cornish, Lancastrian and Cumbrian wrestling events and tournaments were demonstrating a fall in entrants and attendance in the final decades of the century. In 1886, Ben Cooper, a respected and much decorated but retired champion, remarked,

> [T]hat the taste or the inclination for wrestling is dying out cannot be denied; I have been watching this for years and when I compare the numbers of first-class wrestlers of my time of wrestling with the few and scanty numbers of the present day, I can come to no other conclusion.[130]

Barneying and faggoting aside, writers, both contemporary and historical, have offered other possibilities for the decline in local wrestling events. The Cumbrian local press blamed national sports, particularly boxing and football, for appealing to the younger generation at the cost of older, traditional sports.[131] Lyn Murfin places such assimilation over a longer period but comes to a similar conclusion: 'Increasing integration of Cumbria into a national sporting culture, in which boxing figured, but Cumberland and Westmoreland style wrestling did not, must have been an important factor in wrestling's decline.'[132] Tripp similarly attributes the appearance of cricket and rugby to Cornwall's decreasing interest in its local wrestling tradition.[133] He also cites the crystallisation of mass leisure industries and the success of the time/work discipline as further factors.[134]

In a context in which many sports were formed and then flourished, local wrestling traditions were struggling in the face of a national and international sporting culture supported by large capital investments and secure sporting government bodies. Within the sporting field, there were few agents or institutions supporting local wrestling traditions. Those that did often lacked the economic, social or symbolic capital needed to establish the sports as national events. For the few observers sympathetic to the sport, the decline in wrestling presented a problem to be fixed. A *Daily Mail* editorial in 1898 cheerfully declared 'an idea prevails, however, that a revival of the sport can be brought about by means of amateur competitions'.[135] Local wrestling competitions resisted the strictest definitions of professionalism and amateurism, having a strong local tradition of prizes for winners. This resistance to acquiescing to a national sporting culture, and the inability to establish a middle-class sporting body at a national or international level, meant that wrestling developed in a slightly different direction to that of other sports.[136] Instead, as we will see in Chapter 2, wrestling continued to be displayed in theatrical and entertainment fields, and this would ultimately alter the manner in which professional wrestling developed.

Conclusion

Given the ease with which it could be performed, combat sports and variations of wrestling existed across Britain in the pre-industrial era. Highly local, such sports were deeply embedded in the agricultural and festival cultures. With the fielding of society in the eighteenth century, the earliest commercial sporting cultures were displayed in circuses, theatres and the fairgrounds, and emphasised entertainment and profit. The genesis of a sporting and exercise field in the second half of the nineteenth century, however, involved the convergence of primarily the education, military, medical and cultural fields. Various agents and institutions competed and compromised to control the meaning and structures.

The greatest debates and power struggles about the role of sport circled around professionalism and amateurism and spectator and participatory sports. These two positions, roughly represented by public schools, muscular Christians, and adherents of the Olympic Games ethos, in one corner, and professional players and capitalists, in the other, had given birth to the sporting field in the late nineteenth century. The resulting compromises between the agents and institutions produced the spectator sports that dominated England and beyond for the twentieth century. Nearly every sport broadly subscribed to the amateur ideals, privileged the ideologies of fair play, but allowed room for some profit to be made via entrance fees, spectatorship, all the while restricting and policing professional players. Critical to this transformation were the sporting bodies that had bureaucratised, centralised and codified the rules. Groups policed sportsmen and women and provided national competitions and a national sporting culture. Glimpses of what sports might have been earlier in the century – sprinting as part of circus troupes complete with costumes and characters, cricket games involving the people with disabilities for amusement – had, for the most part, been greatly restricted. By the end of the nineteenth century, the purpose and meaning of sport had often existed at a precariously balanced compromise: sport was to be considered a moral good, but professional matches, enclosed and providing entertainments to paying customers, were tolerated by the old amateur purists.

Lacking a coherent sporting body, professional wrestling, as we will see in Chapter 2, continued to be influenced by those whose chief concern was providing entertaining spectacles and profits. Such relationships were not 'unnatural', though. The earliest commercial sporting cultures had emerged in these social milieus, but the arrival of the amateur sporting ethos had changed the nature and fundamental values of the sporting field. In this regard, we might view professional wrestling's development in the late nineteenth and early twentieth centuries as a snapshot of how sport might otherwise have developed had the commercial sporting cultures of the early nineteenth century been allowed to continue unhindered. The debates about the role of entertainment in sport, however, were only just beginning, and wrestling would serve as the model and/or warning for the rest of the sporting field for the remainder of the twentieth century.

Notes

1 Clicker wrestling notes, 16 Feb. 1973, Cumbria Archive Centre, DSO 48/25.
2 Robert W. Malcolmson, *Popular Recreations in English Society, 1700–1850* (Cambridge, 2007), p. 43.
3 Joseph Strutt, *The Sports and Pastimes of the People of England* (London, 1801), p. 69.
4 W.R. Mitchell, cited in Ian Ward, 'Lakeland Sport in the Nineteenth Century', unpublished doctoral thesis (Liverpool, 1985), p. 47.
5 Michael Tripp, 'Persistence of Difference: A History of Cornish Wrestling', unpublished doctoral thesis (Exeter, 2009), pp. 86–87.
6 Richard Holt, *Sport and the British: A Modern History* (Oxford, 1989), p. 18.
7 Tony Collins and Wray Vamplew, *Mud, Sweat and Beers: A Cultural History of Sport and Alcohol* (Oxford, 2002), p. 5.
8 Adrian Harvey, *Football: The First Hundred Years: The Untold Story* (London, 2013); Eric Dunning and Kenneth Sheard, *Barbarians, Gentlemen and Players: A Sociological Development of Rugby Football* (New York, 1979).
9 Kathleen Kete, 'Animals and Ideology: The Politics of Animal Protection in Europe', in Nigel Rothfels (ed.) *Representing Animals* (Bloomington, IN, 2002), pp. 19–34.

10 William Borlase, *The Natural History of Cornwall* (Oxford, 1758), p. 301.
11 Mikhail Bakhtin, *Rabelais and His World*, trans. Helene Iswolsky (Bloomington, IN, 1984).
12 Holt, *Sport and the British*, p. 18.
13 Harvey, *Football*, p. 9.
14 This emphasis is reflected in the titles and subtitles of work, Peter Bailey's *Leisure and Class in Victorian England: Rational Recreation and the Contest for Control, 1830–1885*; A.P. Donajgrodzki's edited collection, *Social Control in Nineteenth Century Britain*; Eileen Yeo and Stephen Yeo, 'Ways of Seeing: Control and Leisure versus Class and Struggle', in Eileen Yeo and Stephen Yeo (eds), *Popular Culture and Class Conflict, 1590–1914: Explorations in the History of Labour and Leisure* (Sussex, 1981), pp. 128–154.
15 For a detailed overview of the industrial revolution and popular culture historiography, see Emma Griffin, 'Popular Culture in Industrializing England', *The Historical Journal*, 45(3), (2002), pp. 619–635.
16 Peter Burke, 'The Invention of Leisure in Early Modern Europe', *Past & Present*, 14(1), (1995): Joan-Lluis Marfany, 'Debate: The Invention of Leisure in Early Modern Europe', *Past & Present*, 156(1), (1997), pp. 174–191.
17 Susan Easton, Alun Howkins, Stuart Laing, Linda Merricks; and Helen Walker, *Disorder and Discipline: Popular Culture from 1550 to the Present* (Aldershot, 1988), p. 56; Douglas A. Reid, 'The Decline of Saint Monday 1766–1876', *Past & Present*, 71(1), (1976), p. 84; Mark Judd, '"The Oddest Combination of Town and Country", Popular Culture and the London Fairs, 1800–1860', in John K. Walton and James Walvin (eds), *Leisure in Britain 1780–1939* (Manchester, 1983), p. 13.
18 Robert D. Storch, 'Persistence and Change in Nineteenth-Century Popular Culture', in Robert D. Storch (ed.) *Popular Culture and Custom in Nineteenth-Century England* (London, 1982), p. 14.
19 Reid, 'Saint Monday', p. 79.
20 Edward Hyde East, *A Treatise of the Pleas of the Crown*, vol. 1 (London, 1803), p. 270.
21 Edward Barry, *A Letter on the Practice of Boxing* (London, 1789), p. 7.
22 John Graham Rule, 'The Labouring Miner in Cornwall c. 1740–1870' (Warwick, 1971), p. 326.
23 Hugh Cunningham, *Leisure in the Industrial Revolution c. 1780–c.1880* (New York, 1980); J. M. Golby and A.W. Purdue, *The Civilisation of the Crowd: Popular Culture in England, 1750–1900* (London, 1984).
24 John K. Walton and James Walvin (eds), *Leisure in Britain, 1780–1939* (Manchester, 1983).
25 Griffin, 'Popular Culture in Industrializing England', p. 623.
26 William Hazlitt, *William Hazlitt: Selected Writings* (Oxford, 2009), pp. 117–128.
27 Tripp, *Persistence of Difference*, p. 109.
28 Mike Huggins, 'The Regular Re-invention of Sporting Tradition and Identity: Cumberland and Westmorland Wrestling c.1800–2001', *The Sports Historian*, 21(1), (2001), pp. 38–39.
29 Tripp, *Persistence of Difference*, p. 109.
30 Eileen Yeo and Stephen Yeo, 'Ways of Seeing: Control and Leisure versus Class and Struggle', p.143.
31 Norman Baker, 'Whose Hegemony? The Origins of the Amateur Ethos in Nineteenth Century English Society', *Sport in History*, 24(1), (2004), pp. 1–16.
32 Mike Huggins, *Flat Racing and British Society, 1790–1914* (London, 1999), p. 11.
33 George Steinmetz, 'Bourdieu, Historicity, and Historical Sociology', *Cultural Sociology*, 5(1), (2011), p. 54.

34 Craig Calhoun, 'For the Social History of the Present: Bourdieu as Historical Sociologist', in Philip S. Gorski (ed.), *Bourdieu and Historical Analysis* (Durham, NC, 2013), p. 37.
35 Michael Harris, 'Sport in the Newspapers Before 1750: Representations of Cricket, Class and Commerce in the London Press', *Media History*, 4(1), (1998), p. 24.
36 Jane Moody, *Illegitimate Theatre in London, 1770–1840* (Cambridge, 2007), p. 148.
37 Hugh Cunningham, 'Leisure and Culture', in *The Cambridge Social History of Britain 1750–1950* vol. 2, *People and their Environment* (Cambridge, 1993), p. 294.
38 Helen Stoddart, *Rings of Desire: Circus History and Representation* (Manchester, 2000), p. 16.
39 John K. Walton and Robert Poole, 'The Lancashire Wakes in the Nineteenth Century' in Robert D. Storch (ed.) *Popular Culture and Custom in Nineteenth-Century England* (London, 1982), pp. 112–113; Robert Poole, 'Oldham Wakes', in John K. Walton and James Walvin (eds), *Leisure in Britain, 1780–1939* (Manchester, 1983), p. 79.
40 Brenda Assael, *The Circus and Victorian Society* (Charlottesville, VA, 2005), p. 2; Stoddart, *Rings of Desire*, p. 13.
41 Cunningham, *Leisure in the Industrial Revolution*, p. 36.
42 Adrian Harvey, *The Beginnings of a Commercial Sporting Culture in Britain, 1793–1850* (Aldershot, 2004), p. 174.
43 Ibid.
44 Samantha Oldfield, 'Running Pedestrianism in Victorian Manchester', *Sport in History*, 34(2), (2014), p. 233.
45 Ibid.
46 Pierce Egan, *Boxiana; or Sketches of Modern Pugilism...*vol. 2 (London, 1824), pp. 16–17.
47 Classified advertisement, *Bell's Life in London and Sporting Chronicle*, 13 Mar. 1842, p. 1.
48 Brailsford, *Bareknuckles*, p. 132.
49 Allen Guttmann 'English Sports Spectators: The Restoration to the Early Nineteenth Century', *Journal of Sport History*, 12(2), (1985), p. 114.
50 John Ford *Prizefighting: The Age of Regency Boximania* (Devon, 1971), p. 98.
51 Anon., 'Sparring Contest', *The Morning Post*, 30 Apr. 1806, p. 3.
52 Ford, *Prizefighting*, p. 141.
53 Harvey, *Commercial Sporting Culture*, p. 200.
54 Daniel Mendoza, *Memoirs of the Life of Daniel Mendoza Containing a Faithful Narrative of the Various Vicissitudes of his Life and an Account of the Numerous Contests in Which he has Been Engaged, With Observations on Each* (London, 1816), p. 167.
55 Harvey, *Commercial Sporting Culture*, p. 200.
56 Brailsford, *Bareknuckles*, p. 146; Kenneth Gordon Sheard, *Boxing in the Civilising Process* (Cambridge, 1992), pp. 140–141.
57 Mendoza, *Memoirs*, p. 175.
58 Ibid., p. 135.
59 Brailsford, *Bareknuckles*, p. 46.
60 Ibid.
61 Harvey, *Commercial Sporting Culture*, p. 170.
62 Anon., 'News', *World*, 22 May 1789, p. 2.
63 Classified advertisement, *World*, 19 Jan. 1790, p. 1.
64 Anon., 'Liverpool Fancy', *Bell's Life in London and Sporting Chronicle*, 20 May 1832, p. 3.
65 Classified advertisement, *Liverpool Mercury*, 3 Jul. 1861, p. 1.

66 Anon., 'The Ring', *Bell's Life in London and Sporting Chronicle*, 30 Mar. 1862, p. 6.
67 Anon., 'The Ring', *Bell's Life in London and Sporting Chronicle*, 15 Sept. 1861, p. 6.
68 Anon., 'Movements of the Pugilistic Stars', *Bell's Life in London and Sporting Chronicle*, 23 Aug. 1829, p. 3.
69 Cunningham, *Leisure in the Industrial Revolution*, p. 36.
70 Anon., 'Wrestling and Other Athletic Amusements', *Bell's Life in London and Sporting Chronicle*, 3 Jan. 1836, p. 3.
71 David Prince Miller, *The Life of a Showman and the Managerial Struggles…With Anecdotes and Letters of Some of the Most Celebrated Modern Actors and Actresses…*(London, 1866), pp. 17–18.
72 *Bartholomew, Frost and Suburban Fairs: Consisting of Portraits, Rare Views, Cuttings, Music etc., 1718–1890*, Guildhall Library.
73 See Vanessa Toulmin, *A Fair Fight: An Illustrated Review of Boxing on British Fairgrounds* (Oldham, 1999).
74 Harvey, *Commercial Sporting Culture*, p. 174.
75 Classified advertisement, *World*, 19 Jan. 1790, p. 1.
76 Classified advertisement, *The Morning Post*, 7 Sept. 1822, p. 1.
77 Harvey, *Commercial Sporting Culture*, p. 170.
78 Anon., 'Sparring', *The Morning Chronicle*, 24 Mar. 1819, p. 3.
79 Sheard, *Boxing in the Civilising Process*, p. 142.
80 Anon., News, *World*, 22 May 1789, p. 2.
81 Peter M. Briggs 'Daniel Mendoza and Sporting Celebrity: A Case Study', in Tom Mole (ed.) *Romanticism and Celebrity Culture, 1750–1850* (Cambridge, 2009), p. 112.
82 Classified advertisement, *The Morning Post*, 7 Sept. 1822, p. 1.
83 Cunningham, *Leisure in the Industrial Revolution*, p. 36.
84 Prince Miller, *The Life of a Showman*, p. 17.
85 Anon., 'Life in the Prize Ring', *Bell's Life in London and Sporting Chronicle*, 1 Aug. 1824, p. 246.
86 Harvey, *Commercial Sporting Culture*, p. 180.
87 Ibid.
88 Holt, *Sport and the British*, p. 91.
89 J.A. Mangan, *Athleticism in the Victorian and Edwardian Public School* (London, 1986), pp. 22–28.
90 Ibid, p. 142.
91 Donald E. Hall, 'On the Making and Unmasking of Monsters: Christian Socialism, Muscular Christianity, and the Metaphorization of Class Conflict', in Donald E. Hall (ed.), *Muscular Christianity: Embodying the Victorian Age* (Cambridge, 1994), p. 56.
92 Jacques DeFrance, 'The Making of a Field with a Weak Autonomy', in Philip S. Gorski (ed.) *Bourdieu and Historical Analysis* (Durham, NC, 2013), p. 307.
93 Mike Huggins, *The Victorians and Sport* (London, 2004), p. 51.
94 Holt, *Sport and the British*, p. 84.
95 Bailey, *Leisure and Class*, p. 138.
96 Pierre Bourdieu, *The Rules of Art: Genesis and Structure of the Literary Field*, trans. Susan Emanuel (Cambridge, 1996), p. 292.
97 Tony Mason, *Association Football and English Society 1863–1915* (Brighton, 1980), p. 223.
98 Neil Tranter, *Sport, Economy and Society in Britain 1750–1914* (Cambridge, 1998), p. 38.
99 Anon., 'Amateur Athletic Club', *Sporting Gazette Saturday*, 28 Mar. 1868, p. 247.
100 Pierre Bourdieu, *Practical Reason: On the Theory of Action* (Cambridge, 2001), pp. 10–11.

101 Ibid.
102 Mason, *Association Football*, p. 230.
103 Wray Vamplew, *Pay Up and Play the Game: Professional Sport in Britain, 1875–1914* (Cambridge, 1988), p. 197.
104 Brailsford, *Bareknuckles*, p. 98.
105 Ibid., p. 95.
106 Stan Shipley, 'Boxing', in Tony Mason (ed.), *Sport in Britain: A Social History* (Cambridge, 1989), p. 81.
107 Andrew Horrall, *Popular Culture in London c.1890–1918* (Manchester, 2001), p. 127.
108 Dan Streible, *Fight Pictures: A History of Boxing and Early Cinema* (Berkeley, CA, 2008), pp. 36–37; Horrall, *Popular Culture*, p. 128.
109 Huggins, 'Regular Re-invention', p. 43.
110 Ibid.
111 Walter Armstrong, *Wrestliana; or the History of the Cumberland and Westmoreland Wrestling Society in London Since the Year 1824* (London, 1870), p. 213.
112 Anon., 'The Wrestling Art: Can the Ancient Sport be Revived?', *Daily Mail*, 1 Jan. 1898, p. 6.
113 Ibid., p. 6.
114 Vamplew, *Pay Up and Play the Game*, p. 197.
115 Holt, *Sport and the British*, p. 282.
116 Tranter, *Sport, Economy and Society*, pp. 60–61.
117 Vamplew, *Pay Up and Play the Game*, pp. 77–78.
118 Holt, *Sport and the British*, p. 281.
119 Matthew Taylor, *The Leaguers: The Making of Professional Football in England, 1900–1939* (Liverpool, 2005).
120 Martin Polley, *Moving the Goalposts: A History of Sport Since 1945* (London, 1998), pp. 116–118.
121 Tony Collins, *Rugby's Great Split: Class, Culture and the Origins of Rugby Football League* (London, 1998).
122 Pierre de Coubertin, *Olympism: Selected Writings, 1863–1937* (Lausanne, 2000), p. 299.
123 Anon., 'Wrestling', *Bell's Life in London and Sporting Chronicle*, 5 Mar. 1864, p. 6.
124 Cumberland and Westmoreland Wrestling Society, *Famous Athletic Contests*, p. 119. CRO, DSO 48/156.
125 Ibid, pp. 115–116.
126 Tripp, *Persistence of Difference*, p. 175.
127 Ibid.
128 Anon., 'The Wrestling Art: Can the Ancient Sport be Revived?', *Daily Mail*, 1 Jan. 1898, p. 6.
129 Ibid.
130 Ben Cooper, *The Science of Wrestling* (Carlisle, 1886), p. 1.
131 Huggins, 'Regular Re-Invention', p. 39.
132 Lyn Murfin, *Popular Leisure in the Lake Counties* (Manchester, 1990), p. 109.
133 Tripp, *Persistence of Difference*, p. 176.
134 Ibid., pp. 176–177.
135 Anon., 'The Wrestling Art: Can the Ancient Sport be Revived?', *Daily Mail*, 1 Jan. 1898, p. 6.
136 Similar processes can be seen in wrestling styles across other international wrestling styles. See Katrin Bromber, Birgit Krawietz and Petar Petrov, 'Wrestling in Multifarious Modernity', *The International Journal of the History of Sport*, 31(4), (2014), pp. 391–404.

Bibliography

Armstrong, Walter, *Wrestliana; or the History of the Cumberland and Westmoreland Wrestling Society in London Since the Year 1824*, London, Simpkin, Marshall, & Co., 1870.

Assael, Brenda, *The Circus and Victorian Society*, Charlottesville, VA, University of Virginia Press, 2005.

Bailey, Peter, *Leisure and Class in Victorian England: Rational Recreation and the Contest for Control, 1830–1885*, London, Routledge & Kegan Paul, 1978.

Baker, Norman, 'Whose Hegemony? The Origins of the Amateur Ethos in Nineteenth Century English Society', *Sport in History*, 24(1), (2004), pp. 1–16.

Bakhtin, Mikhail, *Rabelais and His World*, trans. Helene Iswolsky, Bloomington, IN, Indiana University Press, 1984.

Barry, Edward, *A Letter on the Practice of Boxing*, London, A. Grant, 1789. Borlase, William, *The Natural History of Cornwall*, Oxford, W. Jackson, 1758.

Bourdieu, Pierre, *The Rules of Art: Genesis and Structure of the Literary Field*, trans. Susan, Emanuel, Cambridge, Polity, 1996.

Bourdieu, Pierre, *Practical Reason: On the Theory of Action*, Cambridge, Polity, 2001.

Briggs, Peter M., 'Daniel Mendoza and Sporting Celebrity: A Case Study', in Tom Mole (ed.), *Romanticism and Celebrity Culture 1750–1850*, Cambridge, Cambridge University Press, 2009.

Bromber, Katrin, Krawietz, Birgit and Petrov, Petar, 'Wrestling in Multifarious Modernity', *The International Journal of the History of Sport*, 31(4), (2014), pp. 391–404.

Burke, Peter, 'The Invention of Leisure in Early Modern Europe', *Past & Present*, 14(1), (1995), pp. 136–150.

Calhoun, Craig, 'For the Social History of the Present: Bourdieu as Historical Sociologist', in Philip S. Gorski (ed.), *Bourdieu and Historical Analysis*, Durham, NC, Duke University Press, 2013, pp. 36–67.

Collins, Tony, *Rugby's Great Split: Class, Culture and the Origins of Rugby Football League*, London, Frank Cass, 1998.

Collins, Tony, and Vamplew, Wray, *Mud, Sweat and Beers: A Cultural History of Sport and Alcohol*, Oxford, Berg, 2002.

Cooper, Ben, *The Science of Wrestling*, Carlisle, Stewart of Botchergate and Scotch Street, 1886.

Cunningham, Hugh, *Leisure in the Industrial Revolution c. 1780–c.1880*, New York, St. Martin's Press, 1980.

Cunningham, Hugh, 'Leisure and Culture', in F.M.L. Thompson, *The Cambridge Social History of Britain, 1750–1950*, vol. 2: *People and their Environment*, Cambridge, Cambridge University Press, 1993.

de Coubertin, Pierre, *Olympism: Selected Writings, 1863–1937*, Lausanne, International Olympic Committee, 2000.

DeFrance, Jacques, 'The Making of a Field with a Weak Autonomy', in Philip S. Gorski (ed.), *Bourdieu and Historical Analysis*, Durham, NC, Duke University Press, 2013, pp. 303–326.

Dunning, Eric, and Sheard, Kenneth, *Barbarians, Gentlemen and Players: A Sociological Development of Rugby Football*, New York, New York University Press, 1979.

Easton, Susan, Howkins, Alun, Laing, Stuart, Merricks, Linda, and Walker, Helen, *Disorder and Discipline: Popular Culture from 1550 to the Present*, Aldershot, Temple Smith, 1988.

Egan, Pierce, *Boxiana; or Sketches of Modern Pugilism*...vol. 2, London, Sherwood, Jones & Co.,1824.

Ford, John, *Prizefighting: The Age of Regency Boximania*, Devon, David and Charles, 1971.

Golby, J. M. and Purdue, A.W., *The Civilisation of the Crowd: Popular Culture in England 1750–1900*, London, Batsford Academic and Educational, 1984.

Griffin, Emma, 'Popular Culture in Industrializing England', *The Historical Journal*, 45(3), (2002), pp. 619–635.

Guttmann, Allen, 'English Sports Spectators: The Restoration to the Early Nineteenth Century', *Journal of Sport History*, 12(2), (1985), pp. 103–125.

Hall, Donald E., 'On the Making and Unmasking of Monsters: Christian Socialism, Muscular Christianity, and the Metaphorization of Class Conflict', in Donald E. Hall (ed.), *Muscular Christianity: Embodying the Victorian Age*, Cambridge, Cambridge University Press, 1994, pp. 45–65.

Harris, Michael, 'Sport in the Newspapers before 1750: Representations of Cricket, Class and Commerce in the London Press', *Media History*, 4(1), (1998), pp. 19–28.

Harvey, Adrian, *The Beginnings of a Commercial Sporting Culture in Britain, 1793–1850*, Aldershot, Ashgate, 2004.

Harvey, Adrian, *Football: The First One Hundred Years, The Untold Story*, London, Routledge, 2005.

Hazlitt, William, *William Hazlitt: Selected Writings*, ed. by Jon Cook, Oxford, Oxford University Press, 2009.

Holt, Richard, *Sport and the British: A Modern History*, Oxford, Clarendon Press, 1989.

Horrall, Andrew, *Popular Culture in London c.1890–1918*, Manchester, Manchester University Press, 2001.

Huggins, Mike, *Flat Racing and British Society, 1790–1914*, London, Routledge, 1999.

Huggins, Mike, 'The Regular Re-invention of Sporting-Tradition and Identity: Cumberland and Westmorland Wrestling c.1800–2001', *The Sports Historian*, 21(1), (2001), pp. 35–55.

Huggins, Mike, *The Victorians and Sport*, London, Bloomsbury, 2004.

Hyde East, Edward, *A Treatise of the Pleas of the Crown*, vol. 1, London, A. Strahan, 1803. Judd, Mark, '"The Oddest Combination of Town and Country": Popular Culture and the London Fairs, 1800–1860', in John K. Walton and James Walvin (eds), *Leisure in Britain 1780–1939*, Manchester, Manchester University Press, 1983.

Kete, Kathleen, 'Animals and Ideology: The Politics of Animal Protection in Europe', in Nigel Rothfels (ed.) *Representing Animals*, Bloomington, IN, Indiana University Press, 2002, pp.19–34.

Malcolmson, Robert W., *Popular Recreations in English Society 1700–1850*, Cambridge, Cambridge University Press, 2007.

Mangan, J. A., *Athleticism in the Victorian and Edwardian Public School*, London, The Falmer Press, 1986.

Marfany, Joan-Lluis, 'Debate: The Invention of Leisure in Early Modern Europe', *Past & Present*, 156(1), (1997), pp. 174–191.

Mason, Tony, *Association Football and English Society 1863–1915*, Brighton, The Harvester Press, 1980.

Mendoza, Daniel, *Memoirs of the Life of Daniel Mendoza Containing a Faithful Narrative of the Various Vicissitudes of his Life and an Account of the Numerous*

Contests in Which he has Been Engaged, with Observations on Each, London, Hayden, 1816.

Moody, Jane, *Illegitimate Theatre in London, 1770–1840*, Cambridge, Cambridge University Press, 2007.

Murfin, Lyn, *Popular Leisure in the Lake Counties*, Manchester, Manchester University Press, 1990.

Oldfield, Samantha-Jayne, 'Running Pedestrianism in Victorian Manchester', *Sport in History*, 34(2), (2014), pp. 223–248.

Polley, Martin, *Moving the Goalposts: A History of Sport Since 1945*, London, Routledge, 1998.

Poole, Robert, 'Oldham Wakes', in John Walton and James Walvin (eds), *Leisure in Britain 1780–1939*, Manchester, Manchester University Press, 1983, pp. 71–98.

Prince Miller, David, *The Life of a Showman and the Managerial Struggles...With Anecdotes and Letters of Some of the Most Celebrated Modern Actors and Actresses...* London, Thomas Hailes Lacy, 1866.

Reid, Douglas A., 'The Decline of Saint Monday 1766–1876', *Past & Present*, 71(1), (1976), pp. 76–101.

Rule, John Graham, 'The Labouring Miner in Cornwall c. 1740–1870', unpublished doctoral thesis, Warwick University, 1971.

Sheard, Kenneth Gordon, 'Boxing in the Civilising Process', unpublished doctoral thesis, Anglia Polytechnic, 1992.

Shipley, Stan, 'Boxing', in Tony Mason (ed.), *Sport in Britain: A Social History*, Cambridge, Cambridge University Press, 1989.

Steinmetz, George, 'Bourdieu, Historicity, and Historical Sociology', *Cultural Sociology*, 5(1), (2011), pp. 45–66.

Stoddart, Helen, *Rings of Desire: Circus History and Representation*, Manchester, Manchester University Press, 2000.

Storch, Robert D., 'Persistence and Change in Nineteenth-Century Popular Culture', in Robert D. Storch (ed.), *Popular Culture and Custom in Nineteenth-Century England*, London, Croom Helm, 1982.

Strutt, Joseph, *The Sports and Pastimes of the People of England*, London, Methuen & Co., 1801.

Taylor, Matthew, *The Leaguers: The Making of Professional Football in England, 1900–1939*, Liverpool, Liverpool University Press, 2005.

Toulmin, Vanessa, *A Fair Fight: An Illustrated Review of Boxing on British Fairgrounds*, Oldham, World's Fair Publications, 1999.

Tranter, Neil, *Sport, Economy and Society in Britain 1750–1914*, Cambridge, Cambridge University Press, 1998.

Tripp, Michael, 'Persistence of Difference: A History of Cornish Wrestling', unpublished doctoral thesis, University of Exeter, 2009.

Vamplew, Wray, *Pay Up and Play the Game: Professional Sport in Britain, 1875–1914* Cambridge, Cambridge University Press, 1988.

Walton, John K. and Poole, Robert, 'The Lancashire Wakes in the Nineteenth Century', in Robert D. Storch (ed.), *Popular Culture and Custom in Nineteenth-Century England*, London, Croom Helm, 1982, pp. 100–124.

Walton, John K. and Walvin, James (eds), *Leisure in Britain 1780–1939*, Manchester, Manchester University Press, 1983.

Ward, Ian, 'Lakeland Sport in the Nineteenth Century', unpublished doctoral thesis, University of Liverpool, 1985.

Yeo, Eileen and Yeo, Stephen, 'Ways of Seeing: Control and Leisure versus Class and Struggle', in Eileen Yeo, and Stephen Yeo (eds), *Popular Culture and Class Conflict, 1590–1914: Explorations in the History of Labour and Leisure*, Sussex, The Harvester Press, 1981, pp. 128–154.

Chapter 2

'Are the bouts rigged?'

The enduring possibility of sporting entertainment

Assessing the extent to which sport can or should be considered 'entertainment' is not as easy as it may first appear. Clearly, millions of people around the world watch and play sport for a multitude of reasons, of which entertainment is one. Yet, as Garry Whannel has claimed, 'it has always been a very particular form of entertainment'.[1] Both before and after the emergence of its field, sport has entertained spectators, yet in terms of form, economic structure and audience perception, it is something different to cultural forms like theatre or cinema, and it has very deliberately set itself apart from these fields.[2] The best sportsmen and women have often been entertaining in themselves, but their primary purpose has usually been to win the game. When trying to outline the fundamental functions between an entertainer and a footballer, Raich Carter, the former Sunderland, Derby and Hull association footballer, used such variations to illustrate that point:

> An actor ... sets out with the full knowledge that he has to hold and entertain a public audience. With the exception of one or two who deliberately play to the gallery, a footballer is never consciously entertaining his spectators. His business is to win the match with the help of his ten colleagues.[3]

Drawing on Carter's autobiography, Matt Taylor's conclusion that entertainment should be considered 'not as the essence but a by-product of sporting competition' is a useful starting point for understanding how entertainment in sport operates and is understood.[4] By the turn of the twentieth century, the sporting field's key conflicts and terrain had been set, and most sports had settled upon some form of compromise between professionalism and amateurism. Professional wrestling, however, developed differently to other sports, and this chapter examines how and why that was the case.

Tempting though it may be to think so, professional wrestling is not merely an anomaly in an otherwise pure history of athletic games. Many sports had relationships with the stage and other commercial entertainments, as was described in Chapter 1, and after the genesis of the sporting field some attempted to continue these associations. Between the 1880s and 1910s, wrestling (or at least a variation of wrestling) embraced professionalism and continued performances as a fairground and theatrical entertainment. Drawing on newspaper reports and showmen autobiographies, the first section of this chapter analyses the continued influence that the music hall had on the sport. Although wrestlers remained as athletes who competed in legitimate competitions, they also embraced exhibitions and performances, and the chapter details the narrative devices, non-legitimate matches, and wrestler characterisations that emerged in this intersection between the theatrical and sporting fields.

Professional wrestling is the clearest example of sports experimenting with theatricality, but there are other cases. After summarising the role of showpeople, the chapter analyses other sporting relationships with the music hall stage, particularly experiments at the Olympia in presenting football as a theatrical event. Building on Pierre Bourdieu's notion of 'discarded possibles', the chapter posits that professional wrestling served as an enduring possibility. Where a discarded possibility forces a type of counterfactual history, enduring possibilities remain on the terrain of the field, operating as a visible reminder of what could have been, and still could be. In so doing, enduring possibilities structure and legitimize the choices that have been made, and act as a marker and warning for those who resist broader power structures. Wrestling's development came at a time when the role of entertainment in sport was being debated, and consequently offered a very real possibility for how sport might have developed. Where wrestling's appearances on the stage were a success, the football experiments were quickly curtailed due to the Football Association (FA). Key to professional wrestling's development was its lack of sporting organisation that had the power to enforce the wider values of the sporting field. Without a sporting organisation, by the 1920s and 1930s, professional wrestling had become an outright performed spectacle.

Professional wrestling was frequently used in wider debates by rival sporting bodies, local and national government, and concerned commentators in the press, all of whom declared wrestling as an example of all that was wrong with outright professionalism. More importantly, there were repeated attempts by these groups to establish control over the sport. As an enduring possibility, professional wrestling remained a threat to the somewhat precariously negotiated hegemonies of the field which balanced limited forms of professionalism with amateur ideals. Because of this, it has often been positioned as a threat and a warning to other sports where entertainment is embraced too eagerly, or where operating outside of the control of established sporting organisations is considered. In response, there have been long-standing attempts to establish responsible leaders who will be able to 'rescue' the sport from the excesses of performance and entertainment. Out of these debates professional wrestling promoters and others formed the Mountevans Committee in 1947 to help bring the sport in line with the field. Though successful in curbing some of the more colourful aspects of wrestling, notably the violence, the committee merely served as a springboard for the establishment of Joint Promotions and the domination of television contracts. Studying professional wrestling then reveals tensions and anxieties about professionalism and entertainment as they were experienced on the terrain of the sporting field.

Theatrical athletes

Between the 1880s and the 1920s, professional wrestling operated in a manner like prize-fights earlier in the century (see Chapter 1), freely moving between the field and the stage. Big competitions took place: in fields, sporting arenas and theatres, with the terms of the fight agreed upon by the competitors and backers beforehand, but wrestlers also frequently appeared in fairgrounds, circuses and music hall. In so doing, many of the social actors involved with professional wrestling operated across two different fields, the sporting field and the theatrical field, and those intersections, often in conflict with one another, shaped how professional wrestling developed during this period.

Legitimate competition remained a feature of professional wrestling, at least until the 1920s. Wrestlers competed, often for purses or other prizes, at both local meets, in tournaments and in one-off events, and to do so continued to train at the highest levels to remain competitive. Not unlike boxing's 'global ring' during the same period,[5] the competition circuit was international, spanning the globe,[6] but London, Paris and New York were the unofficial centres. The manner of many competitions, however, encapsulated the lack of organisation that wrestling more generally often displayed.[7] Matches were contested under a hodgepodge of styles and rules. Collar and Elbow had been the preferred wrestling style in America, but Lancashire fighters brought their form of Catch wrestling with them, Japanese wrestlers added their own judo holds to the sport, and Graeco-Roman remained the most popular style of wrestling on continental Europe. Other wrestlers, like Jack Carkeek, visited English counties to fight in the local style. When matches took place, Beekman argues, 'Matches occurred in seemingly endless combinations of catch, Graeco-Roman, collar-and-elbow, side hold, back hold, and sumo.'[8]

When not wrestling on the international circuits, the top wrestlers were also attracted to the other commercial opportunities of display and performance on the stage. As it had been for prize-fighters one hundred years earlier, the allure of the stage was powerful: it offered relative safety from injury, its money was more consistent, and theatrical tours aided the distribution of a wrestler's celebrity. William Brady exhibited matches at theatres in New York[9] and William Muldoon starred in a wrestling sequence in *The Gladiator* on stages across America.[10] Other wrestlers found it profitable to offer other entertainments: Farmer Burns had a fairground sideshow where he could display wrestling and his other act of whistling 'Yankee-doodle-dandy' while being hanged by a rope round his neck.[11] Wrestling troupes also toured the fairgrounds and circuses across America and England.[12] William Muldoon toured, for example, with his own troupe for much of the 1880s. More generally, a plethora of wrestlers doubled as circus and vaudeville strongmen.

Never to be outdone, P.T. Barnum and his Greatest Show on Earth added wrestling to his already large ensemble of attractions. The tour accounts only list two wrestlers, Ed Decker and John McMahon.[13] Primary evidence is lacking about the form and manner of the wrestling that took place. Morton and O'Brien, though, argue that the wrestlers wore brightly coloured costumes. Crucially, their matches were pre-arranged and over the course of their two-year tour they did not fight a legitimate contest.[14] Further humbuggery was added to challenge matches. Promoters and circus owners sent wrestlers ahead of schedule, an old Barnumian trick used to whip up local anticipation, have them make a name for themselves in the local community, and then '[generate] excitement over a match … when the athletic company arrived'.[15] At other times, members of the troupe pretended to be local, fought an exciting match lasting the full amount of time, making it seem an easier task than it was, and allowing other audience members feel they were in with a chance. Edward Van Every, a biographer of William Muldoon, claimed the practice:

> [W]as merely by way of setting the stage for the appearance of the champion, and also, in the event of no local champion being able to screw up sufficient courage to go against the great Muldoon, that there would be some sort of opponent.[16]

It is hard to argue that the practice was not a carefully constructed performance designed to entertain an audience and profit performers and cultural entrepreneurs. For the first time, crucially, fighting exhibitions were not being used to demonstrate and perform celebrity with audiences aware that the exhibition was a performance. Instead, audiences were now apparently led to believe that the fight was legitimate.

Music hall and variety had a great affinity with the circus and fairgrounds, and it is unsurprising that successful entertainments from the fairground found their way onto their stages.[17] In the 1890s and the 1900s, the presentation of professional wrestling performances swept the stages of British music halls, partly fuelled by tours of American wrestlers or returning British wrestlers from America. In 1895, the Alhambra exhibited a wrestling tournament that lasted for the week and included famed wrestlers from across England and Europe, including Antonio Pierri and Tom Cannon.[18] In 1897, *The Sporting Mirror and Dramatic Music Hall Record* described the arrival of Strangler Lewis:

> [F]resh arrivals … continue to flock from the States. This time it is a famous wrestler; but regardless of recent attempts to give wrestling a fillip by variety managers, it has fallen back into its old groove. Whether the appearance of amongst us F. Lewis … will infuse fresh life into the sport remains to be seen.[19]

Whether we can attribute Strangler Lewis's tour as the driving force is difficult to say with any certainty, but names that had dominated the professional wrestling circuit in America began more frequently to appear on the English music hall stage. Jack Carkeek in 1900 provided an exciting and popular music hall turn. *The Era* promoted the performance in a celebratory manner, guaranteeing the show 'be a new London sensation … He offers a £10 note to any man he fails to defeat in fifteen minutes.'[20] Challenge matches were a feature of earlier fairground booths, as we have seen, and remained a popular attraction in seaside and fairground wrestling and boxing booths throughout much of the twentieth century.[21] In these contests, members of the audience were invited onto the stage to last a set time with a wrestler, and if they succeeded they would be given some form of (usually cash) prize. Trained athletes often had very little difficulty in tackling the often drunk and boisterous men willing to submit themselves to such trials. In fact, the problem with such bouts was often that members of the public were not equipped to last an amount of time with a wrestler.

On the London or urban stages with their large audiences and press contingent happy to report on the latest gossip, the challenge match also provided ways for wrestlers and managers to promote themselves. A favourite promotional technique for wrestlers eager for fame and fortune was dramatically revealing themselves in the auditorium and then accepting the open challenge posed by the wrestler on the stage. This was how George Hackenschmidt presented himself to the British public. After winning many contests, tournaments and competitions on the continent, Hackenschmidt moved to England in 1902, and made a name for himself by dramatically accepting one of Carkeek's open challenges at the Alhambra music hall. On this night, Hackenschmidt entered the stage, stripped from his evening clothes to reveal his wrestling costume and muscular body.[22] Carkeek refused to accept the challenge, declaring that Hackenschmidt was a professional from Europe and that Carkeek wanted to fight fair contests with Englishmen. Hackenschmidt was eventually removed from the stage by the police.

Unsuccessful in gaining the desired match, the kerfuffle generated the publicity that it was intended to. More importantly, the publicity stunt caught the attention of a theatrical and music hall entrepreneur, Charles B. Cochran. Cochran became Hackenschmidt's manager and a monumental influence in Hackenschmidt's career and the subsequent development of professional wrestling as performance. Hackenschmidt, however, was initially not a popular performer in his first months as a music hall turn. According to him, 'The English public took but scant interest in wrestling, or at any rate, in the Greco-Roman branch of the Art, since few first-class exponents of this system had as yet visited Great Britain.'[23] More probable is Cochran's suggestion that, after inviting individuals to last a specific amount of time in the ring, audiences 'got bored with seeing mountains of men put with their shoulders to the carpet in anything from thirty to forty or fifty seconds'.[24] It was not until Hackenschmidt learnt showmanship, toying with competitors to make it seem like they had a chance, that his fame and popularity accelerated.

Similarly, just as with sparring earlier in the century, professional wrestlers were willing to provide other skills or entertainments, and these were rooted in the theatrical, fairground or circus traditions. According to Cochran, Jack Carkeek's initial successes on the music hall stage could be attributed to the fact that he was an 'experienced and clever showman with a most convincing line of talk and a quick and often witty response to remarks [from the audience]'.[25] Hackenschmidt posed and displayed his muscles, reminiscent of the physical culture shows performed by Sandow the Magnificent. During the 1880s and the 1890s, Sandow had become an international celebrity for his weightlifting routines. Sandow's claim, that he and other strongmen of the era were 'theatrical athletes', is probably an apt description for professional wrestlers.[26] Wrestling troupes, with particular wrestlers adopting villainous personas against the heroics of the lead wrestlers, were also retained from the fairground. Chapter 3 will look in more detail at the legacies and influences of these performances in wrestling throughout the twentieth century, and Chapter 4 will assess the hero/villain dynamic.

A successful professional wrestler's life, then, was not dissimilar to that of a prize-fighter earlier in the century: regular employment as music hall turns mixed intermittently with big fights at sports grounds (football stadiums in Britain and baseball stadiums in America),[27] sports halls or even the Royal Albert Hall. Throughout the 1900s, a series of high profile international matches took place between a group of international professional wrestling stars, often beginning their promotion on the music hall stage before ultimately fighting a legitimate match. The most anticipated match of the period at the Royal Albert Hall between Hackenschmidt and Madrali highlights these tendencies. The match began life, as it had done with Hackenschmidt's debut on the English stage, with a wrestler appearing in the stalls of the Canterbury to agree to the open challenge. In this case, the roles were reversed: Antonio Pierri, The Terrible Greek, who had thrilled audiences in the 1880s and the 1890s, shouted at Hackenschmidt. He claimed that he had found someone who could easily beat him, his protégé, the Terrible Turk. The lead-up to the match culminated in one report coining the term 'the wrestling craze' to describe the eager anticipation with which audiences awaited the fight.[28]

Legitimate sporting contests continued to have complications, though. Problems, for those concerned at least, lay in the difficulty of establishing an agreed-upon set of rules, the pervasive influence of managers looking to control their interests, and the showmanship and excited press reporting what happened in the lead-up to big fights. Rules were inconsistently applied, matches between competitors were dodged, and controversies repeatedly circulated around contests when they did take place. Wrestlers, more concerned with their reputations, avoided fights, and when they did happen, there was a general distrust that they were fixed for the advantage of promoters, bookies or both.

The issues outlined are best demonstrated by the biggest series matches of this period, fought between George Hackenschmidt and Frank Gotch. In 1908, Hackenschmidt was regarded by the English press as the best wrestler in Europe. While he had toured America on one occasion before in 1905, defeating Tom Jenkins at Madison Square Garden, he had, depending on which account you believe, deliberately avoided or had never been matched with Frank Gotch.[29] Gotch's career mirrored Hackenschmidt's on the other side of the Atlantic, emerging at the turn of the century before finally being almost universally recognised as the 'best wrestler in the world' by their respective country's newspapers. Finally, the two were matched at Dexter Park Pavilion, Chicago, in front of a crowd of 20,000. The contest was disappointing. Gotch was overly defensive and used moves that were banned. The first fall lasted two hours. Following a short break, Hackenschmidt refused to restart the match and conceded the contest. He later accused Gotch of greasing his body to gain an unfair advantage.[30]

Similar problems materialised in the 1911 rematch between Hackenschmidt and Gotch which took place in Chicago at Comiskey Park baseball ground in front of 25,000 spectators. Countless newspaper articles were written about the match, and moving pictures of the fight were made to be sent around America and to be played back in England.[31] If the first match had been disappointing, then the return match did significant harm to professional wrestling's respectability.[32] Hackenschmidt wrestled with an injury. There were calls in the American press that Hackenschmidt did not intend to wrestle the match properly and planned to forfeit as quickly as possible.[33] The English responded by claiming the match was not fought in the spirit of the game.[34]

Similar problems materialised throughout legitimate contests during the period. In another match, Stanislaus Zbysco caused outrage among commentators and wrestling fans. One letter to a magazine went as far as to call the match a 'farce'.[35] A newspaper report claimed the match to be a *reductio ad absurdum* of the catch-as-catch-can game in its present form'.[36] In a contest for the championship of the world, a title that had little but decorative value, Zbysco spent almost the entirety of the two-and-a-half-hour match on his belly refusing to fight.[37] In the rematch a week later, Zbysco simply failed to turn up and Gama was awarded the contest. In another match that lasted two minutes, Cochran joked that he had lost count of the number of spectators who had missed the whole match because they 'were just stooping down to pick something up when they found the match was over'.[38] Here were the problems of legitimate wrestling contests: they could end abruptly, sometimes in a matter of seconds, with paying audiences furious about the lack of drama; or matches could last for hours on end, with holds and counter-holds not providing any drama at all.

Amid these controversies, other issues about legitimacy and authenticity circulated. Cochran went so far as to suggest that when a sincere competition did take place, the crowd felt they were being fleeced by the slow-moving action, believing that the wrestlers had fixed the match for a draw. Referring to a match between Pederson and Aberg, he described how:

> The audience cried 'fake' ... Now this match was entirely genuine ... the public knew so little about wrestling that they thought it was a *fake*. I found this was generally the case where straight matches were concerned; whereas, when a good exhibition wrestler would allow his opponent to slip away, and get out of dangerous-looking holds, with extraordinary head-spins and all sorts of monkey tricks which were nothing more or less than showmanship, the audience would go mad with excitement.[39]

Addressing criticisms head-on, he claimed that with regards to exhibition matches or fixed challenge matches, 'the public did not want straight wrestling – they wanted a "show" and a "show" they were given'.[40] Further, he reminded those 'who would condemn this deception that it was only, after all, a music-hall show ... The audience wanted thrills, even though they were artificial.'[41] In Cochran's descriptions, there is a demonstration of the tensions between the theatrical field and the sporting field. While the establishment of the sporting field had restricted some older forms of playing and restricted the control of publicans, showpeople and others, sports were continuing to negotiate their relationship with the theatrical and entertainment fields.

Manly Christian men

While the establishment of the sporting field had restricted sport's development as a theatrical entertainment, sportspeople retained *some* form of relationship with the stage. Professional wrestling is the obvious example, but it was far from the only sport which continued, or at least attempted to continue, relationships with the stage and screen. Cricket and baseball provided entertaining games and spectacles whose sole purpose was amusement, often featuring stars from the wider theatrical entertainment stage, usually, if not always, under the guise of 'charity' contests.[42] Sport continued to be a popular topic on the music hall stage, with players sometimes appearing in skits.[43] Finally, boxing and wrestling proved to be one of early cinema's most popular topics, with 'performed' boxing matches serving audiences where footage of fights was not recorded.[44] Analysing those boxing films, Dan Streible has argued:

> It is a fallacy to think of the film industry, boxing world, and theatrical business as autonomous entities ... they inhabited a common sociological world, where men (almost always) involved in all manner of amusement, entertainment, promotion, and popular presentation operated within and saw themselves as part of a shared endeavour.[45]

This is partly true, but applying Simmel's conception of intersecting social circles with Bourdieu's fields provides some insights. As set out in the Introduction, social circles are loose and informal social organisations experienced by individuals, and modernity is produced by sitting across numerous circles.

Fields, on the other hand, are autonomous social spaces with their own discrete values and logical. While people exist across multiple fields, it is in social circles where everyday conflicts and negotiations between fields are enacted. 'Proximity in social space', furthermore, is partly generated by shared coordinates across fields and subfields. Film, sport, and the stage were all distinct fields, with their own values and capitals, but certain groups and individuals existed across all three. Those intersections helped to create the terrain of the field, and they also account for some of conflicts in the sporting field (see Chapter 1). Tracking who won and lost these conflicts often reveals the relative power of the intersecting fields in the wider social field. Those who continued to view sport as an entertainment-orientated spectacle, often with intersections in the theatrical field, were met with wide-ranging resistance from sporting organisations, amateur purists and those connected with public schools, universities and the medical field. Sporting organisations that won control during the formation of the sporting field were especially prominent in policing these conflicts.

Importantly, though, it did not have to be this way. An important aspect of fields, as Calhoun stresses, is 'the definition of each field embodies a cultural arbitrary, a historically achieved demarcation that did not have to exist in that form'.[46] The continuities and intersections between sport and stage demonstrate that 'sport' was not and is not universal and timeless, and that its values are constructed from the conflicts and compromises existing in the broader sporting field. A field's 'direction of change depends on the state of the system of possibilities ... inherited from history. It is these possibilities which define what it is possible or not possible to think or do at a given moment.'[47] A (re)examination of history can be one of the more productive ways in which we might rediscover these lost potentials:

> by bringing back into view the conflict and confrontations and therefore all the discarded possibles, it retrieves the possibility that things could have been (and still could be) otherwise. And, through such a practical utopia, it questions the 'possible' which, among all others, was actualized.[48]

Professional wrestling might appear to be a corruption of a purer notion of sport, but it might have been a path that any number of sports might have taken, alongside other competing versions of sport ranging from the purest forms of amateurism, to different rules, to national set-ups. As Gavin Kitching warns, 'The writing of good history requires us to treat this "might" as more than a mere logical formality.'[49]

A particularly intriguing case study for assessing how these intersections and battles played out, and a good illustration of the notion of discarded possibilities, is Olympia's 'Winter Club' football experiments in the winter of 1905/1906.[50] Pa Payne, managing director of London's Olympia, hired Edwin Cleary, a popular if not especially prominent London showperson, to create a series of sporting events to fill the cavernous indoor arena in the usually empty winter season. Cleary set about transforming Olympia into simulacrum sporting arena, but with the material comforts of the theatre. Stands surrounded a grand, artificial playing field, a feature which generated the most advance publicity.[51] Electrical lighting illuminated the pitch, and 'glass roof was draped in white and pale green, and the galleries in red and gold'.[52] One report claimed that the 'vast building [had] completely transformed' with 'nothing of the usual bareness of the Olympia was left'.[53] Another offered that the space was now 'a magnificent place – a resort for all and sundry'.[54] Much like other circus, theatre and variety entertainments of the late nineteenth century, this was a performance that stressed novelty and spectacle, of which the electric lights and carpet played an important role.[55]

Numerous sports were played in the arena, including 'whippet racing, fencing, rifle shooting, tennis, wrestling … Schroyer's great diving trick from his bicycle, and a score of other sports'.[56] By far the biggest attraction of the Winter Club season, however, was a series of football games scheduled to take place on the carpet. Given the successes of professional wrestling outlined above, Cleary and Payne saw a serious opportunity for applying those same conditions to one of industrial capitalism's most popular entertainments, association rules football.[57] *Football Chat* commented that 'Football promises to be the legitimate successor of the wrestling displays which have held the music-hall stage for the past few years.'[58] Rather than 'competition football' contributing towards a league or cup, the events sought to offer 'a very interesting exhibition of an hour's duration, showing the finer points of the game'.[59] Such a description is supported by Cochran's claim that the central purpose of the event was offering 'attractive' football matches.[60] The lack of competitive spirit, despite the advertised £25 purse, was identified by Alfred Davis who observed that while the 'veterans were as lively as kittens', the tackles in the game demonstrated a 'considerable regard for each other'.[61] The exhibition and performed nature of the games were apparently identified by the footballing papers who tellingly did not provide scores or match reports as they did for league, cup and amateur games.

The Winter Club came at a timely period in which the role of 'entertainment' in sport generally was being debated, and boundaries with entertainment institutions delineated. If sporting bodies had been formed in the nineteenth century as a type of bourgeoisie boys club, concerned with codifying games, offering moral guidance to competitors, and arranging matches for university and public school graduates, the role of those organisations was beginning to change in the early twentieth century. As sports came to be recognised as an important part of the leisure provision industry, many sporting bodies, especially those that had allowed some form of professionalism, increasingly saw their role to 'maximise revenue by improving the product offered for sale'.[62] In some sports, sometimes surreptitiously, rules and regulations were adopted by associations to appeal to audiences.[63] In the dedicated sport press, the relationship between sport and entertainment was openly debated and discussed, even if the vast majority of writers sought to distance the two.[64] At the same time, sporting entrepreneurs were experimenting with indoor sporting spectacles: at Madison Square Garden in New York City in the same period, entrepreneurial promoters of the six-day cycling races 'provided a promotional model … to use indoor arenas as sporting venues rather than as generic performance and storage locations'.[65] Across the field, the value and purpose of sport were debated, tested and new models of display were experimented with. These models sought to make games unpredictable, fluid in action, contained, and comfortable to watch.

Changes to rules and regulations were permitted, but an outright embrace of entertainment threatened the highly precarious balance that had been reached. The Winter Club experiment was a direct challenge to the negotiated settlements that had been found in the footballing subfield, itself a reflection of broader compromises in the field. Since the formal allowance of professionalism in 1885, many members of the FA had been concerned about such developments, '[foreseeing] dangers of many kinds … and [visualizing] clubs playing outside the pale of the Association'.[66] The FA had been pragmatic in their compromises around professionalism two decades earlier, partially because they felt they did not have the capital to sustain an all-out battle, but for many of the Football Association's members, they had *already* ceded too many compromises and too much power to the Football League, the professional competition that allowed negotiated forms of professionalism. Exhibitions stressing entertainment and showmanship above all else were at odds with the existing structure. To squash the Olympia experiments, the FA were firm: all players who took part were permanently disbarred from playing for any FA affiliated clubs. Without the players or backing of the FA, the event folded mere months after it had begun. The FA's ominous show of power demonstrated the strength of the association and the security of the subfield as it stood: the institution had direct control over a vast amount of economic capital and could wield that power to resist outside challenges. 'Uncontrolled professionalism,' Wall continued, with a sly reference to professional wrestling, 'is the bane of any sport. The game has been firmly controlled in England.'[67]

The role of the FA is vital here, and key to understanding professional wrestling's development as a sporting entertainment is its lack of obvious and clearly defined sporting organisation. Sporting bodies and institutions were key markers on the field's terrain, policing conflicts and managing compromises. In sport, as Mike Huggins claims, 'a key mark of any authoritative sport regulatory body is its ability to formulate rules and impose them on the sport as a whole'.[68] Wrestling, as we saw in Chapter 1, was bereft such an institution, and without such a group, the sport could neither discipline wrestlers or outside forces who sought to embrace entertainment outright, but nor did they have a group who could tweak and enforce rules that might have made legitimate contests more entertaining. This lack of organisation, and the flagrant display contrary to the values of the field, disturbed commentators. In 1904, the *Daily Mail* wrote a scathing piece about the professional wrestling craze.

> [O]rganisations, with a firm grip of the sport, can be the only road to a proper recognition of wrestling as a sport and pastime. The present boom, started by rival music halls and rival sporting newspapers with no central authority of control, and leaving the competitors to practically make their own rules, possesses no real elements of prosperity.[69]

In reply, a Westmorland clergyman and writing under the fantastic pseudonym of 'clerical collar', and still reasonably enamoured with muscular Christian belief, agreed.

> Are there not enough manly Christian men, be they Westmorland, Cumberland, Lancashire, Cornwall, or Devonshire men, ready to form an 'Amateur Wrestling Association'[?] ... It will be a miserable weakness on the part of our universities, public schools, and other amateur athletic clubs if wrestling is allowed to become dubbed the 'music hall' sport from sheer want of energy to take this wholesome recreation in hand under a properly-qualified and strong-minded committee.[70]

There was some stirring to answer the clerical collar's request. In 1904, the London Amateur Wrestling Society was formed with an aim to 'arrest the decay of wrestling in England'.[71] Likewise, in 1906, the National Amateur Wrestling Association was formed and provided some wrestling competitions in conjunction with other amateur sporting bodies.[72] Finally, in 1906, there was a proposal for a central governing body to control the numerous and informal wrestling organisations scattered around the northern counties: 'The idea was to have an authority similar to the Football Association,' they were quoted as saying, 'if they suspended a wrestler in one ring he would be debarred from wrestling in the ring of any other club or association affiliated with the governing body.'[73] The groups, however, met with limited success. The local organisations, by their very remit, were resistant to embracing a national set of rules controlled by a centralised bureaucracy. Their very survival as a local tradition proceeded on their active resistance to such a movement. In Cornwall, in fact, no such group was established until the 1920s.[74]

Another obvious place for wrestling to be 'rescued' as a 'respectable' amateur sport was in the newly formed Olympic movement. The initiation of the Olympics was both a testament to the ideologies of amateurism and its acceptance and dissemination to the Western world. When the modern Olympics were introduced in 1896, wrestling was included out of a dutifulness to a preconceived idea of the Greeks rather than a passionate desire to involve the sport. The history of the Greek Olympics clearly stressed the involvement of wrestling, and the Victorians often went to great lengths to find validation for their interests in the 'classics'. Despite its obviousness for inclusion, many of the difficulties which had stalled the creation of a national amateur wrestling group were replicated in the creation of an international sporting body. The best and most talented wrestlers across Europe had already competed for prize-money: the allure of professionalism remained strong for wrestlers. Where boxing had done all it could to establish international agreement, there was no agreed set of international wrestling rules controlled by a single governing body. French wrestling, known as Graeco-Roman, and popular across Europe, had failed to catch on in America and England.[75] Compounding these problems, no rules were published until 1937. According to Leyshon, 'All Olympic competition up to 1948 was held under any rules that the host country could foist off on the visitors.'[76]

The slow process of creating an amateur international wrestling organisation began in 1911, taking a full decade to crystallise as Fédération Internationale des Luttes Associées (FILA) in 1921. That FILA's own official history can only speculate about the exact year that an official international wrestling body was formed, detailing the different groups and affiliations that preceded it, probably serves as a testimony to how confused the central organisation of wrestling remained at the beginning of the twentieth century, at a local, national and international level.[77] On the one hand, professional wrestlers, of course, were not welcome at the games. On the other, wrestlers proficient in their local styles were discouraged from entering a competition with alien rules, and the best had all competed for cash prizes at one point or another, deemed professional in the Olympic organisers' strict definitions of 'amateur'. At the first Olympic Games, only five men entered and in 1900 wrestling was not competed at all. In short, the Olympics and their national and international bodies demonstrated little control over the sport.

Removed from the purer amateur interpretations, a professional body was established to at least police the international competitions that continued to cause disappointment. The Professional Wrestling Board of Control was created in 1908 with an aim to 'arrange and govern' the sport, creating matches and hoping to force wrestlers into legitimate contests with one another.[78] The board sat three times, writing to Hackenschmidt and Gotch, whom they had apparently matched with Zbysco and Lemm. Hackenschmidt and Gotch failed to even reply. The group disbanded three weeks after its first meeting claiming it had 'found it impossible to perform the duty for which it was elected – viz, the promotion of straightforward matches'.[79] It was an understatement. As they had done with amateur sporting and wrestling bodies in the preceding years, wrestlers, promoters and showmen were able to resist outside agents and groups looking to alter the subfield of professional wrestling. The failures of traditional organisations to gain control of professional wrestling left a mark on the field. Without a sporting body, legitimate professional wrestling matches were eternally disappointing. Fights were too long or too short, wrestlers cheated, if they turned up at all, and the real money was in the theatrical exhibitions. After failing to attract much of an audience, a 1911 match at the Crystal Palace between Bux and de Riaz summoned the following reaction from the press: 'evidently professional wrestling will not regain its popularity yet awhile'.[80] Celebrations about professional wrestling's demise were premature and short-lived, however. Promoters in the 1920s found a way of addressing the myriad problems that the sport faced: fixing matches to eliminate disappointments.

Rather than a discarded possibility, then, professional wrestling served as a type of *enduring possible*, a stark reminder of the potential and legitimacy of sporting entertainments, and a very real set of counterfactual directions along which the sporting field might have continued. Furthermore, it retained sporting's longer history with publicans, showpeople and other entrepreneurs, and Chapter 5 examines in more detail the continued role professional wrestling plays in debates about sport on television. The enduring possibility of professional wrestling has shaped, and continues to shape, the terrain of the sporting field in numerous ways: providing alternative models of conducting sport, being utilised as a warning to other sports about the dangers of adopting entertainment as a wholesale value. In being positioned in this manner, though, professional wrestling has faced extensive confrontation from existing sporting and governmental bodies.

If anyone can do anything if there be money in it

While relationships between sport and the stage had been mostly restricted, debates about the role of entertainment in sport continued throughout the twentieth century. Though boxing had established some form of negotiated values linked to sport, like wrestling, it had never entirely severed its links with the theatrical and film fields. When, in the late 1910s and the early 1920s, the sport looked like it might eschew the values of the sporting field entirely, the enduring possibility of wrestling always figured heavily in press criticisms. In a 1919 fight, suspicions were raised that the finish might have been arranged by promoters to book a financially beneficial return match. After all, boxing could also suffer from some of the problems – short matches, disappointing finishes – that wrestling did. The *Daily Mail* offered:

> May I call to the minds of any boxers who may be inclined to take liberties the wretched fate which befell professional wrestling? That sport is dead, never to rise again, and the same doom awaits professional boxing if those who live by it fall into the same bad habits as did the wrestlers.[81]

During this time, the first British Boxing Board of Control was established (beginning in 1919 before fully being constituted in 1928), in part as a response to these challenges. At this time, an American attempting to promote a fight at the Royal Albert Hall outside the group garnered this response from *The Times*:

> All that is best among the professionals themselves and all that is in the best interests of the boxers and their craft will, automatically almost, range itself on the side of control. Even the promoters, or anyway those who

have a vision extending beyond the pay boxes of today and tomorrow, will realise that, in the end, professional boxing will fizzle out like professional wrestling and all other uncontrolled sports if anyone can do anything if there be money in it.[82]

Boxing's flirtations with such solutions were countered by the British Boxing Board of Control's (BBBC) objections and the interjections of the press. The remarks made clear that sport pursued simply in the name of profit and spectatorship was a habit that needed to be curbed. A controlling body's role was to upkeep the rules and regulations while discouraging the excesses of commercialisation. In other words, institutions maintained, or at the very least managed, the sporting field's precarious and negotiated structures of power. Commercialism was gaining traction within the field, but it almost always had to be in a limited and controlled form.

During the 1910s, professional wrestling, as we have seen, found itself caught between the field and the stage. After failing to establish an organisation to negotiate and discipline the field as boxing had done, promoters embraced its theatricality. Understandably, given the protectiveness that promotors felt towards presenting wrestling as 'real', archival records with extensive details of who, why and when this happened in exact terms are often difficult to locate. With that said, this history is often tracked to America and credited to 'the gold dust trio', composed of Ed 'Strangler' Lewis, Billy Sandow and Toots Mondt.[83] While taking their influence from the showpeople who had laid the groundwork for theatrical sporting entertainments earlier in the century, the gold dust trio addressed the problems of disappointing matches not with rule changes but by fixing the presentation of fully performed sporting spectacles. This involved controlling wins and losses for maximum dramatic effect, and keeping control over champions. In turn, matches offered more exciting and entertaining wrestling holds, throws and counters; according to a rather excited journalist's contemporary account, the trio were looking to 'take the best features of boxing and the holds from Graeco-Roman, combine these with the old time lumber camp style of fighting and call it "Slam Bang Western Style Wrestling"'.[84]

Given the transnational cultural networks that had grown throughout the nineteenth century, developments in theatrical entertainments that were selling out vaudeville and variety theatres in America were likely to find their way to English stages.[85] Again, details are sketchy about how this version of professional wrestling debuted in Britain. According to Atholl Oakeley's autobiography, after a chance encounter and impromptu match between Oakeley and the American Ben Sherman, the former and Henry Irslinger felt there would be a significant opportunity to offer such contests to English audiences.[86] On 15 December 1930, all-in wrestling, the name professional wrestling was billed as, because 'all' wrestling moves were 'legal', was introduced to the English public in two cities on the same evening: at the Olympia in London and at Belle Vue in Manchester.[87] All-in wrestling became immensely popular throughout the 1930s and Oakeley and Irslinger were just one set of promoters in a competitive market. All-in wrestling exhibitions toured and made use of the growing commercial venues and boxing halls around the country. Places like the Turton Street Stadium in Bolton, the White City Stadium in Hull, the Winter Gardens in Clapham, and St James Hall in Newcastle could all provide boxing and wrestling exhibitions while occasionally doubling-up as other places of leisure (particularly dancing halls and bingo halls).

Pre-arranged wrestling contests were immensely popular with urban, working-class audiences. Drawing inspiration from the theatrics of music hall and fairground, by the 1930s virtually all matches were pre-arranged by promoters, presenting fluid, exciting and engaging sporting spectacles, controlling wins and losses for maximum dramatic effect, and keeping control over who would be named champion. Matches offered quicker combinations of wrestling holds compared to drawn-out legitimate contests, throws and counters, and removed the possibility of long, boring matches. Moreover, promoters added clear narratives grounded in moralistic and melodramatic characters, often featuring excessive violence, the use of weapons in matches, blood, violence towards referees, fighting in the audiences, and gimmick matches like mud wrestling. Chapter 3 examines in more detail the audience's pleasures and responses to these characters and events. Though pre-arranged, matches continued to be presented as legitimate sporting contests. Running counter to the ideology of sporting competition, this shift in style certainly solved many of the issues faced by legitimate contests in the 1910s.

As an enduring possible, professional wrestling's outright rejection not just of the amateur ideal, but of one of sport's defining pillars, competition, meant that it continued to serve as threat to and an example of how the rest of the field might advance. Wrestling was met with significant resistance, from within the sporting field and wider social field. Critiques were common, particularly in the 1930s and the 1940s, from the press, from local and national government, sporting bodies, and concerned citizens. In the decades that followed Oakeley's and other wrestling promoters' adoption of 'all-in' wrestling in Britain, there were significant attempts to restrict this version of sporting competition and to reinstate 'legitimate' contests. The London County Council, responsible for licensing sport and entertainments in the capital, kept an extensive log of their criticisms – including first-hand accounts, complaints, letters and internal memos. Significant attempts were made to restrict or limit the new sporting entertainment, and while care should be given in not assuming that sports meanings and ideologies are fixed, we should also be careful not to assume that once professional wrestling became a sporting entertainment, it was destined to stay that way. There was a very real possibility that professional wrestling might have been restricted just as quickly as it had begun.

Given the importance of sporting bodies in disciplining theatrics, key to the council's worries was the lack of control or accountability in how the sport was governed. In a 1934 letter to the House of Commons, for example, an LCC clerk argued: 'Unlike other forms of public entertainment … "all-in" wrestling or any other form of wrestling is at present uncontrolled either by the council or any other authority.'[88] The British Wrestling Association, set up by Henry Irslinger, was the closest the sport came to a central body in the 1930s, but for all intents and purposes this was merely a business organisation that operated under the grandiose guise of a respectable ruling organisation. Oakeley claims, for example, anyone who applied for a licence to wrestle was granted one from the association.[89] More obviously, rival wrestling companies produced shows without a licence from the group, despite the protestations from Oakeley to the Home Secretary.[90]

The lack of a licence was the primary and over-arching criticism of many aspects of the sport. Professional wrestlers were often not trained to a high standard and in many cases were not trained at all. The lack of training became most apparent in tragic circumstances, and two cases caught the attention of the press. On 3 March 1933 at the Attercliffe Central Hall, Sheffield, George 'Strangler' Johnson collapsed in a dressing room and died in a taxi en route to the local hospital. At this point, the coroner's jury described that all-in was 'not a clean sport and ought to be prohibited'.[91] Four years later, another wrestler died after a contest. According to the promoter, 'Flack was not sufficiently strong or healthy to wrestle … Flack had not been wrestling under Mr Gregory for some months, but it was believed that he had been augmenting his income by wrestling on his own account.'[92] It appeared to critics that Flack's death might have been prevented if a central organisation had existed to license a wrestler's involvement with some consideration made about their health. It was a task that the BBBC was then undertaking in professional boxing. At the very least, the deaths continued to add negative publicity that had been circulating around all-in for most of the decade, with a strong sense of the sport being violent, anarchic and out of control. This was not helped by the sport's maintenance that it was a legitimate competition, only serving to highlight the apparent violence critics assumed the sport embraced.

In a similar vein, the use of women wrestlers, whether against men or other women,[93] also fuelled the feeling among local and national government that professional wrestling was not properly controlled. Women have a complicated place in the history of professional wrestling, and if archives reproduce the values of a field, then women have been neglected in many of the institutions consulted by this book. Further research may very well reveal a more central role in the history of British wrestling. Women were often unfairly side-lined or positioned as secondary entertainment, particularly in America's World Wrestling Federation in the 1980s and the 1990s. Then again, compared to other sports, women have been placed prominently on shows at a time when other sports were banning or restricting women's involvement, and wrestlers like Mildred Burke, Judy Grable and the Fabulous Moolah were important characters in wrestling's expansion on television, whether in America or on Pay-TV in Britain (see Chapter 5).

Central to this ambivalence were ideologies about gender across the sporting field. Since its genesis, intensely held beliefs about gender and sport had been perpetuated, intersecting with ideologies about gender from industry, the church, or medicine, which positioned, or even excluded, women as subordinate in virtually every field in which they operated. The sporting field restricted access for women to certain sports, particularly those that were seen to be violent, overly exerting, or competitive,[94] or even banned them altogether as the FA did from 1921 to the 1970s. Where women's participation was encouraged in the sporting field, it was under very specific logics that insisted women were obviously and always separate to men, a system Bourdieu calls 'symbolic violence'.[95] These logics encouraged women to participate in gentle exercise that prepared them for their roles in the home, producing the labour often unattached to fields and therefore with a poor exchange rate to other fields. In some regards, and as we will see in further detail in Chapter 3, professional wrestling offered an alternative model of gender relations, parodying hegemonic masculinity, and appealed to female audiences.

Wrestling's more permissive approach to women as performers operated against the values of the sporting field, reflecting its theatrical, fairground embrace of novelty. Moreover, the fact of women wrestling against men was enough for other fields to enact their combined regulatory power, demonstrating the ways in which fields link and coordinate to enforce meta-capitals. In the House of Commons, the Home Secretary was asked to comment on the growing tendency of women to wrestle on all-in cards. He responded by saying, 'In my view public exhibitions of what is called "all-in" wrestling between women are open to the strongest objection.'[96] Reactions like these indicate how entrenched sport and masculinity were in most of the public's minds. Even the slightest deviation from the established rules of the field in a fringe sport was enough to warrant a question in Parliament.

For those in government, the lack of a sporting organisation was dangerous, and efforts were made to remedy this situation. In a series of correspondence, the London County Council (LCC) requested that sporting bodies take over the control and running of all-in wrestling. The National Amateur Wrestling Association, a group that had been conceived decades after other amateur sporting groups, had neither the desire nor jurisdiction to take control over the professional circuit. In 1933, the LCC asked the National Amateur Wrestling Association, who had previously written to the council asking for all-in to be banned,[97] whether they would be willing to undertake control of all-in. They refused.[98] In April 1934, the LCC asked the BBBC to regulate professional wrestling. They also refused. Considering that the BBBC had banned all-in wrestling from its cards in 1933,[99] this seems to have been wishful thinking on the part of the LCC rather than a realistic offer.

Some popular histories, and even the contemporary press, have suggested that the LCC ultimately banned wrestling. The *Picture Post*, for instance, claimed:

> The proposal by certain county councils to ban all-in wrestling in their areas will be welcomed by a large number of wrestling fans who have steadily grown sick of the degenerate trend that this sport has taken ... the introduction of buffeting and limb-twisting (with all mock heroics well rehearsed), has turned all-in wrestling from a sport to a music-hall act.[100]

There is no evidence to suggest this, however. Rather, the LCC applied the Lord's Day Observance Act in the hope of curtailing the successes of the sport. After 1935, boxing and wrestling halls that disobeyed the Act found themselves in court facing summons and prosecutions.[101] Further immediate responses were made unnecessary with the outbreak of the Second World War, where Oakeley withdrew his business, citing that 'if strong men could wrestle in public for money, they could also fight for their country',[102] though other promotions continued to exhibit wrestling, albeit with reduced numbers and in a less flamboyant manner.[103] When all-in wrestling was reintroduced after the war, problems that had plagued the sport throughout the 1930s resurfaced.

The bad days are over

Operating in a hostile media climate, with heavy restrictions from local government, the last proper attempt at 'saving' professional wrestling was made in the 1940s. The British Wrestling Board of Control was formally launched on 10 January 1947, and they were much more successful than the Professional Wrestling Board of Control had been 40 years earlier. Headed by the Admiral Lord Mountevans, the board featured the Member of Parliament, Maurice Webb; Commander Campbell, a respected broadcaster on the BBC; and Norman Morrell, an amateur wrestler who had appeared at the Olympics.[104] Thirty years later, Norman Morrell wrote that the board was formed 'with a view to establishing a style of wrestling acceptable to public and local authorities free from the excesses of the so-called "all-in" style prevalent before the war'.[105] In a newspaper report published at the time, according to Webb, the board wished to help assist 'the "ancient and honourable sport"'.[106] In less grand tones, the group set out a list of rules that would be abided by all competitors, it streamlined championships, created stricter weight categories and awarded Mountevans championships, not dissimilar to the Lonsdale belts. At the first press conference for the board they also indicated that they would help to arrange permits for visiting international wrestlers and would be initiating a benevolent fund for retired wrestlers.[107]

The Mountevans rules garnered positive press – the first of its kind since the early 1930s – and offered a semblance of control that had been lacking in professional wrestling since the mid-nineteenth century. It is difficult to establish whether every member was aware that the board's role was about restoring confidence to the press and the public rather than reforming performed aspects of the sport. Legitimate competition was certainly not restored under

Mountevans, and entertainment remained a primary attraction for audiences. Importantly, when asked, promoters could claim the Mountevans group as symbolising a fresh start. Professional wrestling promoters distanced themselves from the all-in moniker and were adamant that the Mountevans wrestling was a world away from the unfettered violence, spectacle and performance that had characterised the sport before the war. Bill Best, a Joint Promotions manager, was asked by a *Guardian* reporter in 1960, 'Do you fix the results?'. He replied, 'The bad days are over.'[108] The article, following Best's suggestion, continued, 'Since 1946, when Lord Admiral Mountevans gave his name to a code of rules now accepted nationally, Mr Best felt that the sport had begun to become respectable and appeal to family audiences.'[109]

Insofar as the Mountevans Committee set out to provide a sense of control, the group were a success. The committee's most lasting impact, though, was 'the framing of regulations to protect existing promoters against unfair and uncontrolled competition'.[110] The rationale was that a free market had led to a rapid increase in violence and gimmicks during the 1930s, and therefore a sanctioning 'controlling body' offered protection and respectability enjoyed by other sports. The recommendations, however, merely allowed a monopolistic syndicate, Joint Promotions, to emerge and dominate the sport until the 1980s. Joint Promotions was made up of constituent wrestling promotions who ran regional shows via the protection of a national group. Broadly speaking, the South was run by Dale Martin Promotions;[111] Lancashire and Merseyside were run by Bill Best; operating out of Bradford and running Yorkshire and the Midlands was Norman Morrell, the amateur wrestler who had served on the Mountevans Committee,[112] and Ted Beresford; and Relwyskow and Green Promotions ran the Midlands and the North.

For those involved in the creation of Joint Promotions, a monopoly was precisely what was needed to secure professional wrestling's respectability, especially because that was how other sports operated. *The Guardian* summarised Norman Morrell's argument as it was presented to them:

> [T]he syndicate had put British wrestling on a controlled and workable basis. 'Until [Joint Promotions] came along, wrestling was an utter farce.' During their fifteen years' management of one of the biggest arenas the referee had never once been struck by a wrestler.[113]

For those on the outside of Joint Promotions, the group had simply used the Mountevans Committee as a springboard to set up a monopoly on buildings and wrestlers for financial gain. Oakeley, who, it must be remembered, had his own reasons to dislike the new group, contended that, 'Wrestling was now being run as a closed shop, with rights of admission strictly reserved, so eliminating outside challenges.'[114] Wrestlers and promoters outside of the Joint Promotions syndicate were unhappy with the arrangement. In 1958, a collection of wrestlers, complaining of low pay and unfair working conditions, formed a union to campaign against the monopoly system. Gentleman Jim Lewis described the situation: 'A wrestler's got to go on his knees to some of these promoters if he wants a square deal.'[115] The response from Joint Promotions argued that the group 'had enough proficient wrestlers on their books without needing to call upon the trade unionists'.[116] Wrestlers, as Oakeley rightly claimed, were prohibited from '"working" for any promoter who was not a member of this organisation'.[117]

The problem was not that there were insubstantial numbers of non-cartel promotions. Nor were there insufficient locations in which to tour. Professional wrestling continued its long and rich history with the fairground, offering performances in boxing and wrestling booths. When the BBBC tightened regulations about members performing in the booths on the fairgrounds in 1947, professional wrestling became ever-more present in such entertainments.[118] Similarly, holiday towns and camps continued to exhibit professional wrestling in the summer seasons. Butlin's provided weekly wrestling exhibitions as part of their broad entertainments. The central problem for wrestlers and promoters not associated with Joint Promotions was that the group, with the ability to claim they were the heirs to the Mountevans rules and the general feeling that the group were a sporting body like the BBBC, were in a prime position to dominate television contracts when ITV began seeking sporting contracts in the 1950s.

Chapter 5 explores in more detail the relationship between commercial television and wrestling, but for now it is enough to say that the exclusive contract held by Joint Promotions and its members caused several complaints from other wrestling organisations *without* access to a television audience. Throughout the 1960s and the 1970s, organisations not affiliated to Joint Promotions complained to the ITA about the monopoly. In a 1967 letter, Tom Charles Wrestling and Boxing Promotions wrote:

> Ever since the Independent Television began to present professional wrestling twice weekly in their programmes it has been very difficult, at times almost impossible for the independent Promoter in this Country to make a living owing to the fact that weekly television appearance of the few wrestlers has made them Stars and household favourites and their services are denied to the Independent Promoters due to the monopoly conditions created by a group of promoters who are for some reason or other chosen by your television Authority.[119]

The response from Lew Grade, the charismatic show business mogul, was blunt: 'The exposure of wrestling on television has done an enormous amount to make this a popular form of entertainment … I fail to understand why the popularity … precludes the smaller promoter from capitalising [on this].'[120]

Smaller promotions were precluded in a variety of ways. Howard Thomas at the Independent Television Authority (ITA) claimed, 'televised wrestling has become a sort of "shop window"'.[121] Having weekly exposure on national television allowed its performers to become popular cultural icons whose names could be used on touring posters. Their closed shop deal, which had been in operation since the Mountevans Committee, meant the group had exclusive contract rights over these popular performers. *The Guardian* reported that 'a wrestler who fights on Joint Promotions bills is most unlikely to appear on anyone else's'.[122] Using television as a shop window, and dividing the country into distinct touring locales, Joint Promotions were 'promoting wrestling in a big way, with sometimes 70 or 80 shows a week'.[123] By any measurement, wrestling was big business, but those on the outside of Joint Promotions did not profit from this version of control.

Nor did the presentation of wrestling on television detract critics of the sport. If anything, its prominent placement in the schedules merely served to attract further attention. Intriguingly, Norman Morrell, who had played such a pivotal role in the creation of the Lord Mountevans style and Joint Promotions, found himself increasingly disillusioned with professional wrestling on television and was one of the most prominent of critics. In a long series of letters to the Independent Broadcasting Authority (IBA) from 1975 to 1980, Morrell, who was always quick to point out his previous involvement with the sport, decried the current situation: 'TV originally paid lip service to … Mountevans and Joint Promotions Ltd [exercised] a degree of uniformity of control amongst their members.'[124] He further added: 'The necessity of presenting ITV wrestling to look like a sport in the world of sport is both common sense and good business.'[125] He also drew attention to the perennial problem of sporting control, now nearly a century old:

> As it is with no effective Board of Control – Promoters, officials and wrestlers conduct themselves as they like without fear of penalty. Good Television presentation is the easiest way to attain an acceptance of high standard wrestling presentation around the halls in the absence of Control.[126]

The sense that professional wrestling still did not adhere to the wider logics of the sporting field continued to circulate around the sport, and the lack of a proper sporting body was still seen to be of central import in this regard.

In the mid-1960s, ITA and Joint Promotions exchanged an increasingly frustrated series of memos and letters. Upon extensive internal correspondence, the ITA settled on a set of five questions to which they demanded answers:

1   Is there a controlling body for wrestling not connected with the promotion of individual matches, e.g., BBBC, FA?
2   Who investigates charges of malpractice? How many investigations were there in 1965?

3   The point was made that there was no gambling associated with wrestling. All other professional sports seem to attract the gambling industry, why not wrestling?
4   Are the bouts rigged?
5   What are the qualifications of referees? Do they pass any practical or written tests? Is there a central governing body who appoints referees? Are they, as in other sports, subject to regular reports?[127]

These were questions that had ultimately plagued the sport since its inception in the late nineteenth century. Lew Grade was wrong, knowingly or not, when he claimed that Joint Promotions was 'a group of small independent promoters who formed themselves into one Association, just as the football companies have combined under the banner of the football association'.[128] Joint Promotions had never had full control over professional wrestling in any commonly understood sense. Several major promotions operated outside of their control, more if we include promotions from overseas, and there was no uniform application of rules or any form of disciplinary procedures for wrestlers who broke rules. The only similarity is that Joint Promotions looked increasingly like a sporting organisation because its central position in the field gave the directors a monopoly of selling sporting content to television. As we will see in Chapter 5, television radically altered the terrain of the sporting field, and wrestling's status as an enduring possible continued to be a defining characteristic.

Conclusion

At the turn of the twentieth century, performed professional wrestling entertainments became a celebrated attraction of the music hall stage. In many ways, such performances continued older legacies of the stage which had been resisted during the genesis of the sporting field. Though there were attempts to launch other theatrical sporting entertainments, these were strongly resisted by sporting bodies. Without a sporting body to enforce the values of the field, showpeople and other entrepreneurs gained power and influence over professional wrestling. There was no group with the relevant power to discipline competitors who indulged in theatricality, and without this, wrestlers were drawn to the stage. Sporting organisations and institutions were key in both establishing the sporting field's autonomy but also in (re)producing the values and ideologies of the field as established in Chapter 1.

Central to these confrontations was the notion of entertainment, a complex value in the sporting field. It was never embraced as a defining ideology of the field, yet it sat as an important feature of the field, and throughout the twentieth century multiple sporting organisations have tweaked rules for their sports to be more enjoyable for paying audiences. Without a sporting organisation, professional wrestling developed in two related but separate ways. There was no person or group to tweak sporting rules to be more entertaining, and therefore legitimate competitions were usually disappointing for audiences. Promoters found a solution to this problem: fixing professional wrestling contests entirely, and presenting those contests to an eager paying public. Critically, other sports might have developed in this manner if not for the terrain of the field. Wrestling's development, then, served as an enduring possibility, often being utilised as a warning to other sports. Because of its status, it has been actively confronted and opposed, by local and national government, television producers, and by sporting bodies. Promoters and wrestlers, overall, have been able to resist such interactions. Conflicts are powerfully shaped by the fields in which they operate, but they are never set in stone. The field's terrain was intensely powerful in producing ideas about what sport was, and who it was for. That terrain, furthermore, expanded beyond sporting organisations and into the everyday lives of all involved, including audiences who were watching. Chapter 3 explores in details the ways in which that terrain influenced audiences, and their pleasures and displeasures.

Notes

1 Garry Whannel, *Fields in Vision: Television Sport and Cultural Transformation* (London, 1992), p. 79.
2 Richard Holt, *Sport and the British: A Modern History* (Oxford, 1989), p. 282; Wray Vamplew, *Pay Up and Play the Game: Professional Sport in Britain, 1875–1914* (Cambridge, 1988).
3 Matthew Taylor, *The Leaguers: The Making of Professional Football in England, 1900–1939* (Liverpool, 2005), p. 252.
4 Ibid.
5 Matthew Taylor, 'The Global Ring? Boxing, Mobility, and Transnational Networks in the Anglophone World, 1890–1914', *Journal of Global History*, 8(2), (2013), pp. 231–255.
6 John Griffiths, 'All the World's a Stage: Transnationalism and Adaptation in Professional Wrestling Style c. 1930–45', *Social History*, 40(1), (2015), pp. 38–57.
7 Gerald W. Morton and George M. O'Brien, *Wrestling to Rasslin': Ancient Sport to American Spectacle* (Bowling Green, OH, 1986), p. 37.
8 Scott M. Beekman, *Ringside: A History of Professional Wrestling in America* (Westport, CT, 2006), p. 24.
9 William A. Brady, *Showman* (New York, 1937), p. 219.
10 'Bruisers in Buskin', *The Era*, 16 May 1891, p. 12.
11 Marion Wrenn, 'Managing Doubt: Professional Wrestling Jargon and the Making of "Smart Fans"', in Craig Calhoun and Richard Sennett (eds), *Practicing Culture* (London, 2007), p. 165.
12 Ibid.
13 Alvaro Bentancourt, *My Diary or Route Book of P. T. Barnum's Greatest Show on Earth and The Great London Circus for the Season of 1883*. Available at: www.circushistory.org/History/PTB1883.htm (accessed 7 June 2013).
14 Morton and O'Brien, *Wrestling to Rasslin'*, p. 29.
15 Beekman, *Ringside*, pp. 25–26.
16 Quoted in Beekman, *Ringside*, pp. 25–26.

17 Lois Rutherford, '"Managers in a Small Way": The Professionalisation of Variety Artistes, 1860–1914', in Peter Bailey (ed.) *Music Hall: The Business of Pleasure* (Milton Keynes, 1986).
18 Classified advertisement, *The Standard*, 4 July 1895, p. 4.
19 Anon., 'Boxing', *The Sporting Mirror and Dramatic Music Hall Record*, 31 May 1897, p. 3. F. Lewis should refer to E. Lewis.
20 Anon., 'Music Hall Gossip', *The Era*, 22 Dec. 1900, p. 18.
21 Vanessa Toulmin, *A Fair Fight: An Illustrated Review of Boxing on British Fairgrounds* (Oldham, 1999), pp. 22–23.
22 Charles B. Cochran, *Showman Looks On* (London, 1945), p. 273; George Hackenschmidt, *The Way to Live: Health and Physical Fitness* (London, 1908), p. 145.
23 Hackenschmidt, *The Way to Live*, pp. 144–145.
24 Charles B. Cochran, *Cock-A-Doodle-Do* (London, 1941), pp. 175–176.
25 Cochran, *Showman Looks On*, p. 273.
26 David L. Chapman, *Sandow the Magnificent: Eugen Sandow and the Beginnings of Bodybuilding* (Urbana, IL, 2006), p. 67.
27 Matthew Lindaman, 'Wrestling's Hold on the Western World Before the Great War', *The Historian*, 62(4) (2000), p. 786.
28 'The Wrestling Craze: The Great Match at the Royal Albert Hall', *Illustrated London News*, 9 July 1904, p. 51.
29 Charles B. Cochran, *The Secrets of a Showman* (London, 1925), p. 117.
30 Beekman, *Ringside*, p. 47.
31 Lindaman, 'Wrestling's Hold on the Western World', p. 791.
32 Beekman, *Ringside*, p. 49.
33 Ibid.
34 Anon., 'Toe Screwing', *Penny Illustrated Paper*, 16 Sept. 1911, p. 1.
35 Anon. letter, *Penny Illustrated Paper*, 24 Sept. 1910, p. 410.
36 Anon., 'Wrestling: Gama v Zbysco', *The Times*, 19 Sept. 1910, p. 15.
37 Anon., 'Wrestling: Gama v Zbysco', *The Times*, 12 Sept. 1910, p. 14.
38 Cochran, *Cock-A-Doodle-Do*, p. 199.
39 Cochran, *Secrets of a Showman*, p. 114.
40 Ibid., p. 110.
41 Ibid., p. 111.
42 Andrew Horrall, *Popular Culture in London, c.1890–1918* (Manchester, 2001).
43 Keith Gregson and Mike Huggins, 'Sport, Music-Hall Culture and Popular Song in Nineteenth-Century England', *Culture, Sport, Society*, 2(2), (1999), p. 82.
44 Streible, *Fight Pictures*. Luke Stadel, 'Wrestling and Cinema, 1892–1911', *Early Popular Visual Culture*, 11(4), (2013), pp. 342–364.
45 Dan Streible, *Fight Pictures: A History of Boxing and Early Cinema* (Berkeley, CA, 2008), p. 49.
46 Craig Calhoun, 'For the Social History of the Present: Bourdieu as Historical Sociologist', in Philip S. Gorski (ed.), *Bourdieu and Historical Analysis* (Durham, NC, 2013), p. 51.
47 Pierre Bourdieu, *The Rules of Art: Genesis and Structure of the Literary Field*, trans. Susan Emanuel (Cambridge, 1996), p. 206.
48 Pierre Bourdieu, 'Rethinking the State: Genesis and Structure of the Bureaucratic Field', in George Steinmetz (ed.), *State/Culture: State-Formation After the Cultural Turn* (New York, 1999), p. 57.
49 Gavin Kitching, '"Old" Football and the "New" Codes: Some Thoughts on the "Origins of Football": Debate and Suggestions for Further Research', *The International Journal of the History of Sport*, 28(13), (2011), p. 1742.

50 I have explored this example in further detail in Benjamin Litherland, 'Sporting Entertainments, Discarded Possibilities and the Case of Football as a Variety Sport, 1905–1906', *Sport in History*, 35(3), (2015), pp. 391–418.
51 'Football at Olympia', *Football Chat*, 12 Dec. 1905, p. 2; 'Winter Delights at Olympia', *The Penny Illustrated Paper and Illustrated Times*, 6 Jan. 1906, p. 7.
52 'Football at Night: Opening of the Winter Club at Olympia', *The Observer*, 24 Dec. 1905, p. 3.
53 Ibid.
54 'The World of Pastime: Football', *The Penny Illustrated Press and Illustrated Times*, 30 Dec. 1905, p. 294.
55 Michael R. Booth *Victorian Spectacular Theatre 1850–1910* (London, 1981).
56 'Winter Delights at Olympia', *The Penny Illustrated Paper and Illustrated Times*, 6 Jan. 1906, p. 7.
57 'Olympia's Novel Winter Programme', *Daily Mail*, 2 Nov. 1905, p. 8.
58 'Football as a Variety Sport', *Football Chat*, 12 Sept. 1905, p. 2.
59 'Olympia's Novel Winter Programme', *Daily Mail*, 2 Nov. 1905, p. 8.
60 Cochran, *The Secrets of a Showman*, p. 135.
61 Alfred Davis, 'Football at Olympia', *Daily Mail* 28 Dec. 1905, p. 6.
62 Vamplew, *Pay Up and Play the Game*, p. 112.
63 Wray Vamplew, 'Playing with the Rules: Influences on the Development of Regulation in Sport', *The International Journal of the History of Sport*, 24(7), (2007), pp. 843–871.
64 Taylor, *The Leaguers*, pp. 250–254.
65 Ari de Wilde, 'Six-Day Racing Entrepreneurs and the Emergence of the Twentieth Century Arena Sportscape, 1891–1912', *Journal of Historical Research in Marketing*, 4(4), (2012), p. 533.
66 Frederick Wall, *Fifty Years of Football* (London, 1935), p. 19.
67 Ibid., p. 19.
68 Mike Huggins, *Flat Racing and British Society, 1790–1914* (London, 1999), p. 179.
69 Anon., 'A Neglected English Sport: Need of a Controlling Power in the Wrestling Pastime', *Daily Mail*, 13 Jan. 1904, p. 6.
70 Anon., 'A Neglected English Sport: Clerical Proposal to Form a Wrestling Association', *Daily Mail*, 15 Jan. 1904, p. 6.
71 John E. McLachlan, 'A London Amateur Society', *Daily Mail*, 15 Jan. 1904, p. 6.
72 Anon., 'The World of Pastime', *The Penny Illustrated Paper and Illustrated Times*, 2 Jun. 1906, p. 340.
73 Reproduction of 'A Governing Body Formed', taken from *The Carlisle Journal*, in Roger Robson, *Cumberland and Westmorland Wrestling: A Documentary History* (Carlisle, 1999), p. 57.
74 Michael Tripp, 'Persistence of Difference: A History of Cornish Wrestling', unpublished doctoral thesis (Exeter, 2009), p. 44.
75 Donald Sayenga, 'The Problem of Wrestling Styles in the Modern Olympic Games – A Failure of Olympic Philosophy', *Citius, Altius, Fortius*, 3(3), (1995), p. 19.
76 Glynn A. Leyshon, 'Capricious Rules and Arbitrary Decisions', *Citius, Altius, Fortius*, 2(2), (1994), p. 24.
77 Rayko Petrov, *100 Years of Olympic Wrestling* (Lausanne, 1997), p. 61.
78 Anon., Untitled note, *Daily Mail*, 20 Nov. 1908, p. 9.
79 Anon., 'Wrestling', *Daily Mail*, 8 Dec. 1908, p. 9.
80 Anon., 'Wrestling: Ahmud Bux v. De Riaz', *The Times*, 25 May 1911, p. 17.
81 Berkley, 'The "No-Contest" Boxing Match', *Daily Mail*, 10 Oct. 1919, p. 7.
82 Kenneth Gordon Sheard, *Boxing in the Civilising Process* (Cambridge, 1992), p. 303.

83 See Beekman, *Ringside*, p. 57.
84 Marcus Griffin, *Fall Guys: The Barnums of Bounce* (Chicago, 1937), p. 27.
85 Griffiths, 'All the World's a Stage'.
86 Ibid., p. 30.
87 Ibid., p. 36.
88 Clerk's letter to Hyde, 21 Mar., 1934, LCC, box CL/PC/01/026.
89 Atholl Oakeley, *Blue Blood on the Mat*, Chichester, Summersdale Publishers, 1996, p. 86.
90 Letter from Atholl Oakeley to the Home Secretary, 11 Nov. 1950, National Archives, HO box 45/24142.
91 Anon., '"All-in" Wrestling Condemned', *The Times*, 16 Mar. 1933, p. 16.
92 Anon., 'Wrestler's Death in Hospital', *The Times*, 30 Dec. 1937, p. 5.
93 'Man vs Woman Wrestling Match Called Off', newspaper clipping from *Daily Herald*, National Archives, HO box 45/24142.
94 Jennifer Hargreaves, *Sporting Females: Critical Issues in the History and Sociology of Women's Sport* (London, 2002).
95 Pierre Bourdieu, *Masculine Domination* (Stanford, CA, 2001).
96 Anon., 'Women and "All-in Wrestling"', *The Times*, 31 Mar. 1933, p. 7.
97 Letter from The National Amateur Wrestling Association, Mar. 1933, LCC, box CL/PC/01/026.
98 Letter from The National Amateur Wrestling Association, May 1933, LCC, box CL/PC/01/026.
99 Anon., 'Boxing: Board of Control Meeting', *The Times*, 7 Oct. 1933, p. 7.
100 R. Wardle, 'Let's Have "All-Out" Wrestling' *Picture Post*, 3 Feb. 1945, p. 26.
101 Anon., 'All-in Wrestling Match: Summons Under Sunday Observance Act', *The Times*, 16 Nov. 1935, p. 7.
102 Oakeley, *Blue Blood on the Mat*, p. 147.
103 Anon., 'Only Slight Drop in Entertainments', *The Daily Mirror*, 5 Feb. 1940, p. 5.
104 N. F. Berry, *Wrestling: The Lord Mount Evans Style* (Halifax, 1951), p. 2.
105 Letter from Norman Morrell to Mr Rook, 9 Nov. 1975, Sporting Events "Wrestling", vol. 4, IBA, box 01097.
106 Anon., 'Wrestling Board's Aims', *The Guardian*, 11 Jan. 1947, p. 5.
107 Ibid.
108 Anon., untitled, *The Guardian*, 3 Nov. 1960, p. 19.
109 Ibid.
110 Anon., 'Wrestling Board's Aims', *The Guardian*, 11 Jan 1947, p. 5.
111 Doddy Hay, 'Sport or a Crude Burlesque?', *The Observer*, 18 Mar. 1962, p. 18.
112 Kent Walton, *This Grappling Game* (London, 1967), p. 20.
113 Anon., 'Wrestlers Approach Problems the Trade Union Way: Dealing with Promoters' Syndicate', *The Guardian*, 21 Oct. 1958, p. 2.
114 Oakeley, *Blue Blood*, p. 148.
115 Anon., 'Wrestlers Approach Problems the Trade Union Way', p. 2.
116 Ibid.
117 Oakeley, *Blue Blood*, p. 148.
118 Toulmin, *A Fair Fight*, pp. 22–23.
119 Letter from Tom Charles to ITA chairman, 15 Mar. 1967, Sporting Events "Wrestling", vol. 1, IBA, box 01097.
120 Letter from Lew Grade to Bernard Sendall, 28 Mar. 1967, Sporting Events "Wrestling", vol. 1, IBA, box 01097.
121 Letter from Howard Thomas to Bernard Sendall, 21 Jan., 1966, Sporting Events "Wrestling", vol. 1, IBA, box 01097.
122 Arthur Hopcraft, 'Black and Blue Wrestlers', *The Guardian*, 10 May 1962, p. 9.

123 Letter from Howard Thomas to Bernard Sendall, 21 Jan., 1966, Sporting Events "Wrestling", vol. 1, IBA, box 01097.
124 Letter from Norman Morrell to Mr Rook, 5 Nov. 1975, Sporting Events "Wrestling", vol. 4, IBA, box 01097.
125 Ibid.
126 Ibid.
127 Internal notes for a meeting between Mr. Sendall, Mr. Copplestone and Howard Thomas, 15 July 1966, vol. 1, IBA, box 01097.
128 Letter from Lew Grade to Bernard Sendall, 28 Mar. 1968, Sporting Events "Wrestling", vol. 1, IBA, box 01097.

Bibliography

Beekman, Scott M., *Ringside: A History of Professional Wrestling in America*, Westport, CT, Praeger, 2006.
Bentancourt, Alvaro, *My Diary or Route Book of P. T. Barnum's Greatest Show on Earth and The Great London Circus for the Season of 1883*. Available at: www.circushistory.org/History/PTB1883.htm (accessed 7 June 2013).
Berry, N.F., *Wrestling: The Lord Mount Evans Style*, Halifax, Wrestling News and Views, 1951.
Booth, Michael R., *Victorian Spectacular Theatre, 1850–1910*, London, Routledge, 1981.
Bourdieu, Pierre, *The Rules of Art: Genesis and Structure of the Literary Field*, trans. Susan Emanuel, Cambridge, Polity, 1996.
Bourdieu, Pierre, 'Rethinking the State: Genesis and Structure of the Bureaucratic Field', in George Steinmetz (ed.), *State/Culture: State-Formation After the Cultural Turn*, Ithaca, NY, Cornell University Press, 1999.
Bourdieu, Pierre, *Masculine Domination*, Stanford, CA, Stanford University Press, 2001.
Brady, William A., *Showman*, New York, Curtis Publishing, 1937.
Calhoun, Craig, 'For the Social History of the Present: Bourdieu as Historical Sociologist', in Philip S. Gorski (ed.), *Bourdieu and Historical Analysis*, Durham, NC, Duke University Press, 2013, pp. 36–67.
Chapman, David L., *Sandow the Magnificent: Eugen Sandow and the Beginnings of Bodybuilding*, Urbana, IL, University of Illinois Press, 2006.
Cochran, Charles B., *The Secrets of a Showman*, London, William Heinemann Ltd, 1925.
Cochran, Charles B., *Cock-A-Doodle-Do*, London, J.M. Dent & Sons Ltd, 1941.
Cochran, Charles B., *Showman Looks On*, London, J.M. Dent & Sons Ltd, 1945. De Wilde, Ari, 'Six-Day Racing Entrepreneurs and the Emergence of the Twentieth Century Arena Sportscape, 1891–1912', *Journal of Historical Research in Marketing*, 4(4), (2012), pp. 532–553.
Gregson, Keith and Huggins, Mike, 'Sport, Music-Hall Culture and Popular Song in Nineteenth-Century England', *Culture, Sport, Society*, 2(2), (1999), pp. 82–102.
Griffin, Marcus, *Fall Guys: The Barnums of Bounce*. Chicago, Reilly and Lee, 1937.
Griffiths, John, 'All the World's a Stage: Transnationalism and Adaptation in Professional Wrestling Style c. 1930–45', *Social History*, 40(1), (2015), pp. 38–57.
Hackenschmidt, George, *The Way to Live: Health and Physical Fitness*, London, Health and Strength Limited, 1908.
Hargreaves, Jennifer, *Sporting Females: Critical Issues in the History and Sociology of Women's Sport*, London, Routledge, 2002.

Holt, Richard, *Sport and the British: A Modern History*, Oxford, Clarendon Press, 1989.
Horrall, Andrew, *Popular Culture in London, c.1890–1918*, Manchester, Manchester University Press, 2001.
Huggins, Mike, *Flat Racing and British Society, 1790–1914*, London, Routledge, 1999.
Kitching, Gavin, '"Old" Football and the "New" Codes: Some Thoughts on the "Origins of Football": Debate and Suggestions for Further Research', *The International Journal of the History of Sport*, 28(13), (2011), pp. 1733–1749.
Leyshon, Glynn A., 'Capricious Rules and Arbitrary Decisions', *Citius, Altius, Fortius*, 2(2), (1994), pp. 24–28.
Lindaman, Matthew, 'Wrestling's Hold on the Western World Before the Great War', *The Historian*, 62(4), (2000), pp. 779–797.
Litherland, Benjamin, 'Sporting Entertainments, Discarded Possibilities and the Case of Football as a Variety Sport, 1905–1906', *Sport in History*, 35(3), (2015), pp. 391–418.
Morton, Gerald W. and O'Brien, George M., *Wrestling to Rasslin': Ancient Sport to American Spectacle*, Bowling Green, OH, Bowling Green State University Press, 1986.
Oakeley, Atholl, *Blue Blood on the Mat*, Chichester, Summersdale Publishers, 1996.
Petrov, Rayko, *100 Years of Olympic Wrestling*, Lausanne, International Federation of Associated Wrestling Styles, 1997.
Rickard, John, '"The Spectacle of Excess": The Emergence of Modern Professional Wrestling in the United States and Australia', *The Journal of Popular Culture*, 33(1), (1999), pp. 129–137.
Robson, Roger, *Cumberland and Westmorland Wrestling: A Documentary History*, Carlisle, Bookcase, 1999.
Rutherford, Lois, '"Managers in a Small Way" The Professionalisation of Variety Artistes, 1860–1914', in Peter Bailey (ed.), *Music Hall: The Business of Pleasure*, Milton Keynes, Open University Press, 1986, pp. 93–117.
Sayenga, Donald, 'The Problem of Wrestling Styles in the Modern Olympic Game: A Failure of Olympic Philosophy', *Citius, Altius, Fortius*, 3(3), (1995), pp. 19–30.
Sheard, Kenneth Gordon, 'Boxing in the Civilising Process', unpublished doctoral thesis, Anglia Polytechnic, 1992.
Stadel, Luke, 'Wrestling and Cinema, 1892–1911', *Early Popular Visual Culture*, 11(4), (2013), pp. 342–364.
Streible, Dan, *Fight Pictures: A History of Boxing and Early Cinema*, Berkeley, CA, University of California Press, 2008.
Taylor, Matthew, *The Leaguers: The Making of Professional Football in England, 1900–1939*, Liverpool, Liverpool University Press, 2005.
Taylor, Matthew, 'The Global Ring? Boxing, Mobility, and Transnational Networks in the Anglophone World, 1890–1914', *Journal of Global History*, 8(2), (2013), pp. 231–255.
Toulmin, Vanessa, *A Fair Fight: An Illustrated Review of Boxing on British Fairgrounds*, Oldham, World's Fair Publications, 1999.
Tripp, Michael, 'Persistence of Difference: A History of Cornish Wrestling', unpublished doctoral thesis, University of Exeter, 2009.
Vamplew, Wray, *Pay Up and Play the Game: Professional Sport in Britain, 1875–1914*, Cambridge, Cambridge University Press, 1988.
Vamplew, Wray, 'Playing with the Rules: Influences on the Development of Regulation in Sport', *The International Journal of the History of Sport*, 24(7), (2007), pp. 843–871.
Wall, Frederick, *Fifty Years of Football*, London, Cassell, 1935.

Walton, Kent, *This Grappling Game*, London, Compton Printing Ltd, 1967.
Whannel, Garry, *Fields in Vision: Television Sport and Cultural Transformation*, London, Routledge, 1992.
Wrenn, Marion, 'Managing Doubt: Professional Wrestling Jargon and the Making of "Smart Fans"', in Craig Calhoun and Richard Sennett (eds), *Practicing Culture*, London, Routledge, 2007, pp. 149–170.

Chapter 3

'Equally vociferous both for and against'

Compromise, conflict and pleasure

In 1933, in his report for the Metropolitan Police, Stanley John Bisnell described all-in wrestling's apparent attractiveness to audiences: 'the sport is so popular with public, that at 8pm the house was sold out, with no seats or standing room available'.[1] Attendances ebbed and flowed over the century, the notion of eternal absolute sell-outs the stuff of promoters' dreams, but Bisnell's documentation captured a general reality: since its inception as performed entertainment, professional wrestling has remained consistently, enthusiastically appealing. In the halls, crowds flocked to see the grapple and grunt game, and on television professional wrestling remained one of Independent Television's most watched programmes. Though likely apocryphal, on the day of the 1963 FA Cup final, reports suggested that the match between Jackie Pallo and Mick McManus would have more viewers than the football, an event by then established as one of the great national sporting occasions.[2] This chapter begins by examining the types of audiences that professional wrestling appealed to, particularly the young, the working class, and women, commercial television's attitude to popular culture, and the relationship between ITV and the sport.

In part, because of the audiences that it attracted, since its emergence as 'all-in', in the 1930s, police, magistrates, licensing councils, sporting bodies, journalists, television controllers, and others, have all expressed forms of anxiety about wrestling, and its presumed influence on audiences. This echoed, moreover, wider debates about the commercial popular cultures more generally, including those that could be seen on ITV. Fans of the sport, on the other hand, have been vocal in expressing their pleasures, whether to promoters, Mass Observers, television controllers or simply by live attendance or television viewership. In the debates, there is often a misunderstanding about what types of pleasures audiences derive from the sport. In these sets of articulations, the chapter suggests, we can see a type of battle about the values and capitals of the sporting field, battles reflecting the wider structures of the field. It was on these everyday expressions of fandom or frustration, where the everyday conflict and compromise, sustainment or challenge, of the sporting field played out. Given the types of audiences attracted to wrestling, combined with its fringe status in the field, responses were especially heated and give another view of the changing ideologies, beliefs and values about sport's purpose. Unlike the very real conflicts outlined in Chapter 2, where institutions and agents could be directly named, these battles were more imagined and phantasmagorical. Though more difficult to trace, understanding audiences and the texts they enjoy is key to understanding how the field's tensions were experienced, articulated and managed.

Finally, the chapter explores many of the points of contention that circulated about professional wrestling. Often, the things that audiences appeared to like most of all caused the greatest complaints. This included performances of violence, the display of bodies, comedy, and subversions of gender. These pleasures, furthermore, were laced with questions about wrestling's authenticity, and audience's understanding of that performativity. The question of authenticity has been discussed in relation to kayfabe, a concept that concludes the chapter. In these debates, there are echoes of the tensions created by professional wrestling's intersection with the sporting and theatrical fields, particularly borrowing theatricality from the music hall, the fairground and circus. To explore these tensions, the analysis draws on archival research – Home Office and council records; fan letters explaining pleasures to the Mass Observation archives; letters, both for and against, to the Independent Broadcasting Authority and the Independent Television Authority (IBA/ITA); and audience research conducted for ITV – alongside forms of textual and semiotic analysis of professional wrestling texts. What audiences like or do not like, and their expressions of those pleasures or displeasures, reflect, refract and reverberate wider tensions in the field, and are of central importance in understanding the broader history of sport.

What the public wants, it's going to get

By the 1960s, professional wrestling was one of commercial television's most popular programmes. Chapter 5 assesses in more detail the fundamental changes produced by television's intersections with the sporting field. For now, it is enough to say that professional wrestling and commercial television were well matched in tone and the types of audiences they attracted. This contrasted with the public service broadcaster, the British Broadcasting Corporation (BBC). Since its nationalisation in 1927, the BBC's output continued 'a notion of cultural improvement that had been developed in the nineteenth century by intellectuals such as Matthew Arnold, and which had since then been at the root of many concerns expressed about the nature of popular leisure'.[3] Lord Reith's 'long shadow',[4] the notion that a public broadcasting should uphold cultural values and stress morally uplifting programming, loomed over radio and then television, and wrestling simply did not meet these standards. Aside from early experiments in the 1930s and a single BBC broadcast in May 1965, BBC controllers remained 'adamant that professional wrestling was not a suitable sport for the BBC'.[5]

Independent Television (ITV), on the other hand, was expected to provide a range of programming for a diverse, 'mass' audience. When Associated Rediffusion (AR) started officially broadcasting in September 1955, it was clear from the start that the channel was going to be different in its tone, style and content. 'The new channel gave notice', Bernard Sendall writes in the official history of Independent Television, that its 'approach to the viewing public was to be different from that of the BBC.'[6] Given the channel's reliance on advertising revenue, ITV sought populist programming that could attract and sustain large audiences. One sceptical BBC employee described ITV programming as 'wiggle dances, give-aways, panels and light entertainment'.[7] Roland Gillet, an ITV programme controller at AR, states what became a kind of shorthand for the types of programming offered on the channel:

> Let's face it once and for all. The public likes girls, wrestling, bright musicals, quiz shows and real-life drama. We gave them the Halle orchestra, Foreign Press Club, floodlit football and visits to the local fire station. Well, we've learned. From now on, what the public wants, it's going to get.[8]

Building on the popularity of professional wrestling before television, the sport was an immensely successful programme for the channel. Professional wrestling was well received across certain demographics, most notably those who could be described as one or more of the following: working classes, young people and women. Moreover, often complaints about the sport were constructed around anxieties about these groups.

From the time of its emergence as a pre-arranged entertainment in the 1930s, wrestling had catered, if not exclusively, then predominately, for the lower-middle and working classes. As we saw in Chapter 2, during the formation of the sporting field in the nineteenth century 'respectable' middle-class groups never fully gained control over professional wrestling, and some showpeople were more concerned with offering entertainments that were popular than they were in accruing cultural or symbolic capital. Wrestling was embedded in working-class cultures and geographies. Venues that displayed wrestling often featured other working-class entertainments: boxing and bingo being two obvious examples. In addition, these venues were often in working-class, urban areas, as the Mass Observation ethnographers found in their classic Worktown project in Bolton.[9] Likewise, after attending several shows in 1969, an ITV programmer described the live audience as being composed of 'decent working/lower middle class'.[10] Dobie and Wober found a similar class make-up when they examined the television audience a decade later.[11]

Between the 1930s and the 1960s, young people grew as an important demographic for the newly forming mass entertainments, and professional wrestling was no different. Wrestling actively attracted youths, and this continued onto television. In a 1935 meeting of the London County Council's (LCC)

Entertainment Committee, one representative summarised a particular view, arguing that

> It is a performance we think it is degrading; we have seen queues outside and the class of person who attends there in many cases are adolescent people, who we feel are likely to be influenced by this and influenced for the worse.[12]

While Joint Promotions often failed to attract younger audiences in the 1970s, the notion of 'young people', and the threat popular culture posed to them, remained a key discourse in writings about wrestling and commercial popular cultures more broadly.

Perhaps less obvious was the role gender played in constructing wrestling audiences. After the monumental changes to society that followed the First World War, Robert James has identified women, notably working-class women, as being the 'main beneficiaries of … changes to society's consumption patterns'.[13] Sporting consumption habits of working-class women in this period have been less documented, in part because of an inaccurate assumption that sport remained the sole domain of men.[14] Some sports promoters recognised this emerging market, and in Manchester, speedway and greyhound racing offered discounted ticket prices to female spectators.[15] All-in promoters were part of this wider campaign to attract female spectators. In Bolton, women were offered half-price tickets. One committee at the London County Council described, not without disgust, advertising deliberately targeting female consumers that declared all-in to be 'The Men's Sport Women Adore'.[16] Another commentator to the LCC claimed that 'a good proportion of those present included women who were as voracious in their demands for the all-in system as many of the men present'.[17] Though women were far from the only spectators at the wrestling, compared to other sports, they were significant and visible, and women wrestling audiences continued to be significant on television and beyond, both in America and the UK.[18]

What popular audiences wanted to see was often very different to the notion of sport as a morally uplifting, respectable leisure practice, and professional wrestling was very much categorised as the 'wrong' way to enjoy sports, at least in the mid-twentieth century. Things seen at shows were precisely the types of things that many in the wider sporting field, and indeed many in wider society, did not think sport should include. Professional wrestling revelled in virtually all of the types of pleasures that the field had been trying to reduce: extreme violence, disrespect for authority figures, comedy, audience heckling, raunchiness, and a variety of other visceral entertainments. Clearly, sport had never removed these pleasures from sporting spectatorship or indeed participation, but there had been some attempt to lessen them, or treat them as a by-product rather than the key attraction. The performed professional wrestling of the twentieth-century, on the other hand, embraced and then embellished these traits, offering a world of carnivalesque mockery.

Commercial television, furthermore, focused debates about the role of mass media in contemporary society, particularly with regards to the supposedly degrading effects it had on the nation.[19] Cultural critics began to fear the materialisation of the worst excesses they had imagined commercial television might bring, and 'ITV had become hugely popular precisely by showing the kinds of programmes which offended its critics'.[20] In some regards, these tensions were the continuation of long-standing criticisms from the nineteenth century. Rational recreation, in various guises, was still an influential ideology in debates about entertainment, popular culture and pleasure.[21] Commercial television appeared to be a continuation of many of the types of popular culture and mass cultures that some groups had been opposed to since the 1920s and the 1930s. Matthew Hilton, summarising the *Scrutiny* editor's view, encapsulates a predominant opinion of the working classes: 'slavish and unthinking followers of commodity capitalism; indeed, mechanization, modernity, America, suburbia and the "adman's civilisation" had promoted their own system of corrupt ethics'.[22]

For many, professional wrestling encapsulated the worst excesses of the channel, and was an exemplar of the candy floss of mass culture. If not in a literal sense, all-in wrestling simply *felt* American. Or, to put it another way, one critic posited that the spectacle was 'wholly un-English'.[23] Similarly, *The Mirror* claimed in a report about all-in wrestling: 'I don't like the game AND I HOPE IT DOES NOT CATCH ON OVER HERE.'[24] Worse, some viewers were concerned that it influenced certain audiences to follow unhealthy actions, values and beliefs. Despite Joint Promotion's intentions to keep wrestling more 'family-friendly' than it had been in the interwar years, these antics continued onto television. The nature of professional wrestling denied it the possibility of ever being an abundantly 'respectable' sport enjoyed by those rich in cultural capital, and this was escalated by the types of audiences that wrestling appeared to attract.

Audiences who were not necessarily familiar with professional wrestling, and who would never have paid to watch wresting in a hall, frequently wrote to the channel to complain about the sport, and we will assess these complaints in further detail later in this chapter. As Jeremy Potter later wrote about wrestling, 'Large numbers of people liked to watch but the serious-minded condemned. Was it innocent fun or an endorsement of savagery? Society was divided between those who wanted more wrestling on television and those who demanded less.'[25] Certainly, a vast swath of those employed by ITA were at best ambivalent and at worst openly hostile to its place as ITV's most-watched sport, and for many at the station it was an embarrassment. University-educated programmers and staff at the ITA were often keen to distance themselves from enjoyment of the show. 'Personally', one member of staff offered, 'I would never watch wrestling unless I had to.'[26] It was an intriguing dynamic in which those employed to regulate the content of the channel had little sense of why and how people enjoyed one of its most popular programmes.

Despite their ambivalence, regulators accepted wrestling's popularity. Indeed, at the end of the 1960s, a letter seemed to sum up the position at which the institution had arrived:

> Admittedly, opinions on professional wrestling are sharply divided and indeed are equally vociferous both for and against. It is a fact, however, that there is a large and enthusiastic audience for these programmes, and while the Authority keeps a watchful eye on all performances so as to ensure that they do not contravene normal programme standards, it considers them acceptable as part of the pattern of television entertainment.[27]

While being cautious to not glibly celebrate the power of consumption, or be too eager to perpetuate the notion that the market gives the audience what they want, many popular or 'mass' entertainments, from the music hall to the cinema screens, found spaces that could flourish, even if they were not to the taste of the ruling classes. From the nineteenth century onwards, popular tastes and entertainments were broadly accepted across cultural and sporting fields, with capitalism somewhat emerging 'as the guarantor of popular sovereignty',[28] even if that sovereignty was subject to a set of complex rules and laws. Because 'the market' protected certain types of popular pleasure, battles about the structure and control of the sporting field often turned towards questions of taste. Beyond the debates at the level of sporting institution, governmental organisation and elsewhere, the sporting field's reproduction of values were sustained and/or challenged in the everyday consumption and discussion of professional wrestling.

Perception and appreciation

Hitherto, this book has been concerned with how the sporting field emerged, and how professional wrestling served as an enduring possible for that field. In so doing, it has analysed the conflicts and compromises between key organisations and institutions, notably sporting bodies, theatrical showpeople, and local and national government. The narrative has been one where sporting bodies have been key to policing sport, and professional wrestling's lack of sporting organisation meant it developed differently to other sports. Undoubtedly, the history of sport and leisure is a history of a variety of groups attempting to define the sporting field, and players, owners and organisations rightfully play central roles in any account. Writing about the many influences on sport, Stephen G. Jones claims:

> Human agents from ruling cliques such as landowners, amateur gentlemen and churchmen to organised labour movements, spontaneous crowds, and players and athletes themselves have been able to bring their own meaning, culture, concerns and emotions to sports. Once again it should be

recognised that certain agents have greater leverage over the structures they have created: football chairmen have had more influence over the game than the average, individual supporter. Also here, the notion of social agency needs to be fragmented to take into account the diversity of interests from class to age and gender, the plurality of issues, and the level of agency – public or private, national or local.[29]

One of problems of field theory is that it can place too much emphasis on production rather than on texts or consumption, and that the role of audiences is too easily obscured. Much of the work on journalistic fields, for example, fails to describe the roles media audiences play in the co-creation and dissemination of meanings and power structures of fields. Erik Neveu offers a robust defence of Bourdieu's field theory and its adequacy in explaining audience's roles, but does not explain how this operates in practice.[30] The most sustained analysis of fields and audiences have come from those working in a Fan Studies perspective. Rebecca William and Elana Shefrin have analysed the relationship between fans and film and media texts, and their works provide useful case studies for the benefits of placing audiences into fields, but their analyses still mostly theorise the relationship between producers and consumers of texts.[31] This is useful, particularly when working in the model of artistic or cultural production, but thinking about how audiences respond to each other, reproducing the terrain of the field, offers another avenue of analysis. Combining this with theories of hegemony and intersection, furthermore, offers a working model for how individuals group and interact, generating conflicts over meaning and practices, at both a micro and macro level, producing historical changes.

As Jones makes clear above, when it comes to sport, spectators and broader participatory cultures have helped shape its history. Building on social history and British cultural studies, we know that participants have never been passive dupes when it comes to watching entertainments, including mass and commercialised sports. While typically far from having the types of social, economic or cultural capital to, say, sit on the board of directors or play a prominent role in legal disputes, the tastes and values of popular audiences have remained important contributors to the terrain of the field. Whether in organised supporters groups and associations or individual fans, what audiences *do* with sports is an important aspect of those histories and one we should be careful not to exclude.

'Audiences', however, are more than just the types of spectators who have a passion for sport, and drawing upon the types of historical evidence outlined above we can see three forms. First, what can loosely be described as a 'fan' position, or audiences that express some form of pleasure or emotional engagement with wrestling. Second, there were audiences who articulated a form of displeasure or concern about wrestling and its influence. At its most basic, simple articulations of liking and disliking professional wrestling, watching on television or not watching on television, reveal one's own investment and stake in the field as it is currently understood. At a more complex level, expressions of pleasure or displeasure – letters to newspapers or channel controllers, live attendance – sought to influence the direction of change in the sporting and media fields. The third distinct form is the regulator's conception of the audience, which was often composed of a type of impression of the first two positions. For the ITA, wrestling was a moral grey area: wrestling was unintelligent and of dubious influence, but audiences were reliably enthusiastic, tuning in each week. The first two groupings, with regulators serving as the crucial feedback loop, have been active in shaping dialogues and debates about the purpose of sport in myriad ways, demonstrating that the conflicts and compromises of the field stretch into everyday consumption and participation. Debates about the right and wrong way to enjoy sport were of vital importance because they were central in reproducing the power structures of the field, which in turn were vital in reproducing wider power dynamics in the social field.

This approach continues to bring together Bourdieu's works about taste and cultural consumption and his works on fields. In this reading, one's reaction to sport, or other entertainments, are subject to one's own intersectional position across multiple fields. As Mike Featherstone's borrowing of Bourdieu's distinctive lexicon suggests, 'Groups, classes and class fractions struggle and compete to impose their own particular tastes as *the* legitimate tastes, and to thereby, where necessary, name and rename, classify and reclassify, order and reorder the field.'[32] Ordering and reordering the field are not as easy it sounds, though. Everyday expressions of sporting pleasure or displeasure to some degree reflected the battles taking place in the broader field, but they are battles and conflicts that were more imagined, ephemeral and fractured. At the core of the field it was quite clear what the key antagonisms were and who they were between, with named and recognisable agents, bodies and institutions. For those belonging to mass media audiences, however, positions were always partially produced by an imagined sense of who and what other audiences were doing and thinking. Battles were more impressionistic and phantasmagorical, directed towards imprints of imagined allies and enemies in structures that one could not entirely see or make sense of. If sporting bodies, government, television controllers, and theatre producers were the generals of a war, then audiences were the everyday soldiers, often unable to see the terrain of the field.

Because of this, many battles were characterised by a misunderstanding of what professional wrestling was, and how imagined oppositional audiences received or understood the sport. In some regards, misunderstandings demonstrate the difficulty in trying to 'construct' audiences, whether historically or contemporaneously. It also establishes the ways in which audiences construct each other, assigning values, pleasures and beliefs to others out of sight. While clearly being linked to class, gender and age, reactions to professional wrestling revealed one's own position and investment in and alongside the sporting field. Maintaining one's position was also partly derived from securing what was the hegemonic response to a text: being 'disgusted' by professional wrestling was not enough, some audiences demanded that disgust be upheld as the common-sense response. Though it is true that audiences can offer 'resistant' readings, such readings are still produced, and reproduced the terrain of the wider field(s) in which they are situated. Expressing one's taste, whether for or against, is actively seeking to maintain or improve one's own position in the field, and we can see similar examples of jockeying and positioning in a variety of fan and audience and practices. Securing dominant reading practices, and securing dominant field positions, involve extensive and continued struggle.

Because professional wrestling could only be defined as a spectator sport, it threatened to devalue types of capital associated with the sporting field. It was designed to be accessible and entertaining to a broad range of audiences, and therefore everyone – men, women and children – could attend a wrestling match and understand the rules, narrative form and structure. Bourdieu has claimed that spectators who have played a sport in the past are privileged watching it insofar as their knowledge provides them with insight. 'The "connoisseur"', he argues, 'has schemes of perception and appreciation which enable him to see what the layman cannot see.'[33] Very few watching wrestling, whether live or televised, could draw on memory or experience to appreciate the subtleties of the game, because those subtleties did not exist, at least in any obvious way. The grand gestures – or 'spectacle of excess',[34] in Barthes' oft-quoted analysis – of wrestling were specifically performed so that the 'layman' could appreciate and understand. 'Connoisseurs', at least in the sense of those who had grown up playing the games at elite public schools, simply did not exist. Though professional wrestling developed its own taste and hierarchical groupings as the century continued,[35] the presentation of wrestling in the halls and on television stripped out types of cultural capital associated with certain sports and certain groups who had grown up playing them.

Similarly, as we have seen and as we will continue to see in Chapter 5, structures of a field are not timeless, and new entrants to a field, whether generationally or via the creation of new intersections, will also threaten older forms of a field's capital, shifting its terrain. Without necessarily disregarding the role of the media or other social forces that underpin the structures of a moral panic, one way of analysing them is to see them as flare-ups between competing groups about tastes, particularly at moments when new fields or sub-fields are established, thus challenging the structure of pre-existing fields. A new cultural form requires new types of knowledge, and its newness is *de facto* challenging to existing types of knowledge. As such, panics have tended to flare up around the emergence of new technologies, the introduction of new styles or groups, and moments during globalisation when new styles or ideas have been imported. Usually, these tastes have been linked to younger people before being incorporated and folded back into the structure of the field. Professional wrestling's links with new commercial entertainments and technologies, and its relative late re-entry into the sporting field in the 1920s and the 1930s, meant that it can be read in this manner, producing unsettled responses from audiences whose pre-existing tastes were threatened.

In a very real sense, then, professional wrestling endangered the types of knowledge and experiences of those who maintained privileged positions in the sporting field, and their position in the sporting field structured them across many intersecting fields. Forms of pleasures and spectacles linked to the sport (performativity, violence, comedy, the display of bodies) and the spaces and places where it was performed and were associated with wrestling (America, commercial television, the music hall stage) meant that audiences posed just as much a challenge to the field's structure as the producers who offered them. Just as professional wrestling remained a threat for sporting organisations, then, it remained a flashpoint for equally invested audiences about what sport was, who it was for, and what its central purposes were. Both the emergence of professional wrestling in the 1930s, and then its broadcasting on commercial television were greeted with a range of complaints and criticisms. In the pages of the press, in local and national government, and in letters to television controllers, there continued a campaign of complaints about professional wrestling, and this can be seen a type of micro debate about the legitimate values and structures of the sporting field. In analysing both the pleasures and displeasures of the sport, combined with articulations about professional wrestling, we reveal underlying tensions in the wider sporting field and how these played out in everyday pleasures and engagements.

We want blood, we want blood

Nominally, wrestling was presented as a legitimate sport for much of the twentieth century. At live events, rules printed on the back of programmes and on television commentaries helped to explain how matches operated. In Britain, a fall was given after a submission or after shoulders were pinned to the mat, a match was given after 'two falls, or two submissions, or one knock out'.[36] Oiled bodies were disallowed, wrestlers were warned to stay in the ring, and the use of foreign objects to hit opponents was banned, as was assaulting the referee. Despite this presentation, there was little respect for the regulations, even if they were printed on the back of programmes. Rather, the publishing and distribution of rules may have in fact served to inform the audiences *which* rules were being broken. Matches often involved brawls, bloodiness and violence. From the 1930s onwards, promoters and wrestlers could control the length and pace of a match, heightening the pleasure for all those present. In so doing, professional wrestling embraced forms of performance: matches were embellished, violence was embraced as a key trait, stories revolved around heroes and villains, and referees were abused, all for the entertainment of audiences. Audiences embraced these aspects of the sport, and in so doing often unsettled many of the types of capitals, values and ideologies that structured the sporting field.

If most popular spectator sports offered the possibility of entertaining moments, there was still a tendency for sport not to deliver on these fronts. The professional wrestling contests of the early twentieth century had proven this: in big fights, there remained a predisposition for long tedious matches that could last for hours or matches that lasted minutes, with audiences feeling short-changed on both counts. Professional wrestling presented a concentrated sporting entertainment, containing and managing the thrills and pleasures of sport while reducing the potential for disappointment, intensifying 'the emotional experience offered by traditional sports'[37] and replicating 'the formula that makes "miracle moments" in sports so miraculous'.[38] Pre-arranged professional wrestling matches contained everything that made an exciting sporting contest and attempted to remove the unknown variables that competitive sporting competitions suffered. One respondent to the Mass Observation Project in the early 1930s claimed that they enjoyed wrestling because it was 'so fast and full that one cannot release attention for a second'.[39] Part of this pleasure grew from the fact that promoters and wrestlers removed many of the complexities of sports. The sport did not get involved in discussions on regional wrestling holds and variations. Technical nuances were removed completely. Gone were the encumbering 'rules and fine points', one audience member claimed in his postcard to the Mass Observation, 'such as in the case in boxing and catch-as-catch can wrestling'.[40]

Wrestling's lack of 'rules or fine points', as the impressed audience member put it, was something of an understatement. Conversely, Bisnell's report for the Metropolitan Police noted, appalled, 'I am still not positive, as to the rules which are laid down, if there are any at all, they are so vague.'[41] A type of exaggerated, performative violence was a key feature of a typical wrestling event, particularly in the 1930s. For example, and with a distance that only a Mass Observer could muster, they described the antics of one match: 'P– still has stool so B– picks up water bowl and with a terrific bang lands it on P–'s head. P– drops almost unconscious.'[42] Percy Longhurst, a former amateur wrestling champion and Olympics Game wrestling judge, wrote an article decrying all-in: 'Is it sporting to spit in your opponent's face, to drag at his hair, and to twist his ears, nose and lips; to kick with the knee or foot or strike with hand at vulnerable parts of the body?'[43] Despite the outrage, audiences apparently loved these moments. One man described that he went to see the wrestling to watch 'the bowl on each other's heads' and wrestlers 'breaking the stool'.[44] A newspaper report described 'gorilla-like wrestlers of superb physique [who] bit, scratched … kicked, gouged while a sensation mad audience cheered them on …"Break his leg!", they shouted, "Break his fingers off!"'[45] In a particularly revealing passage in his autobiography, Athol Oakley, one of those responsible for introducing all-in, summarised how audiences responded to a typical contest:

> [I]n All-in Wrestling it was not done to fall down on the floor of the ring screaming 'Foul' every time anyone got hurt. Nor were the fights stopped because of blood. In fact at Newcastle if the fights did not get rough, the fans used to chant 'We want blood, we want blood.'[46]

It is hard to say for sure how blood was generated in these contests, but in wrestling in the second half of the twentieth century it was produced by concealed razor blades cutting the top of the forehead. Lucy Nevitt captures the multifarious meanings that blood in professional wrestling elicits. Blood 'is striking, noticeable, intriguing, disconcerting ... [it] generates physical, emotional and psychological responses'.[47] Violence and blood, even in the contained and performed context of the all-in wrestling ring, produced an exciting and visceral reaction for those in attendance.

Foregrounding violence to this degree sat in opposition to the wider sporting field. Since its emergence in the nineteenth century, sport had undergone what Norbert Elias and Eric Dunning describe as a 'civilizing process', where outright violence had been restricted and retained, but with sport still serving a social function in offering a release in both players and spectators.[48] In the prize-fights of the Georgian period, fights took place until a competitor could not stand, with fighters often left bloodied and disfigured. Such fights, held in semi-legality, were challenged, and then ultimately replaced, by gloved fights with time limits and imbued with the values of amateurism. These new rules stipulated that boxing gloves should be worn always, introduced timed rounds, and finally banned wrestling holds; they privileged the 'scientific' style of boxing rather than the brute strength and endurance; gloves allowed respectable men to compete without the worry of bloodied and bruised faces.[49] Professional wrestling openly embraced the types of visceral pleasures about violence, and as such posed a challenge to the sporting field's 'scientific' style and skill, and which claimed violence as a by-product rather than central pleasure of sport.

If, as according Dunning, sport is 'a form of non-scripted, largely non-verbal theatre and emotional arousal',[50] it could be possible to locate professional wrestling as an exemplar of the civilizing process; continuing to offer a facsimile of violence and escape without many of the underlying dangers. Yet this was not how it was understood in the sporting field or indeed in wider society. Unsurprisingly, perhaps, the antics at all-in captured the attention and imagination of moral reformers throughout the 1930s, and they frequently took the shape of complaints that television controllers 30 years later faced. The National Amateur Wrestling Association expressed it thus:

> A real service to sport will be done if the present 'all-in' be done away with. It admits most fouls, it is brutal and crude, not scientific, it panders to the 'blood lust' and it is everything but sport ... it is a disgusting and degrading dog-fight.[51]

Correspondingly, a recurrent theme in the condemnations of writers was that the violence pandered to an animalistic enjoyment of participants' pain that could destroy empathy and civility. Another writer complained:

The attempts to gull the public by throwing their opponents out of the ring and continuing the fight on the floor of the hall, and the usual tricks on the mat to the create the appearance of bloodthirstiness, succeeded to a great extent, and it is in this connection that the present 'all-in' systems gives rise to unhealthy and sadistic satisfaction.[52]

In these accounts, two things become clear. First, the types of (imagined) audiences who watched and enjoyed wrestling were seen to be at 'risk' from the violence they witnessed, and in so doing certain types of pleasure were positioned as lesser and even damaging. Related to this, those pleasures were in direct contrast to the types of uplifting and morally good role sport was supposed to play in society.

Key to understanding professional wrestling's embrace of performative violence was its continued relationship with the music hall stage between 1880 and 1910. Chapter 2 outlined in detail the control that showpeople continued to have on wrestling, and these influences extended into professional wrestling's development throughout the rest of the twentieth century. In so doing, it was infused with values more in keeping with the theatrical stage rather than the sporting field. The music hall was a space in which dominant systems and everyday life were critiqued, gently mocked and 'chronicled'.[53] Even in the more 'respectable' variety theatres, performances pushed questions of 'taste', celebrated the everyday lives of the working classes, and gently mocked and parodied the aristocracy and upper middle classes.[54] One of the main things to consider in this regard was the music hall's opposition to the supposed 'respectable' culture of rational recreation. Kift explains:

> The values propagated in the music hall – hedonism, ribaldry, sensuality, the enjoyment of alcohol, the portrayal of marriage as a tragi-comic disaster, and the equality of the sexes at work and leisure ... were dramatically opposed with those propagated by and attributed to the Victorian middle-class: asceticism, prudery, refinement, abstinence, a puritanical work ethic, marriage and the family as the bedrock of social order.[55]

Andy Medhurst has described the influence of the 'music hall tradition' on English popular culture and the multiple ways in which this tradition manifests itself in film and television,[56] and professional wrestling can be added to this tradition. Wrestling promoters understood the promotional appeal of having wrestlers antagonise the public. At the height of his acclaim, Hackenschmidt toured with a troupe of wrestlers. One was specifically designated as the villain who would fight Hackenschmidt. Cochran describes how 'a German named Shackmann played the role of a brutal wrestler, who would not listen to the referee though repeatedly warned about foul tactics'.[57] Another wrestler in the troupe 'threw the referee ... into the orchestra'.[58] Like other music hall performances, this aspect of professional wrestling parodied and satirised the discourses that had circulated during the codification of sports. Not unlike the master of ceremonies who took up the image of the middle-class gentleman while gently mocking his affectations,[59] wrestling acts followed a similar pattern, exaggerating, mocking and laughing at the seriousness and pretentiousness of the amateur ideal. Stage performances took beliefs that circulated in the Victorian and Edwardian period about professionals, that they were cheats who were willing to do anything to win, and embellished them. Core amateur ideals – respecting the referee, style and grace, playing for the love of the game, and gentlemanly sportsmanship – were inverted for both comic and dramatic effect.

Open disrespect to referees continued both in thehalls and on television. One writer to the MO study excitedly, and not without glee, described wrestlers 'tearing the referee's shirt off, jumping on it, and then throwing the referee out of the ring'.[60] Another commentator explained with frustration that matches were frequently returning 'a verdict of "no contest". Why? Because the referee has been unable to find one, he has been "out" himself struck by one of the contestants, or thrown of the ring.'[61] The standards of refereeing were also a continued topic of conversation, particularly to those who wrote to ITA to complain about the standards of wrestling. Referees generally failed to discipline villainous wrestlers, and repeatedly missed fouls. This was part of the narrative structure, but those watching on television were appalled:

> Realising the difficulties to which the referees are subjected I am reluctant to criticise their actions but surely it is time their rulings should be obeyed immediately. Contestants should be required to remain in their corners and await the signal for the bout to begin and failure to obey the ruling of the referee should call for an immediate warning and, if repeated, disqualification.[62]

That referees seem to have taken the brunt of abuse in both sports is telling: the opportunity granted to disenfranchised members of society to laugh at, mock, and shout insults at an authority figure without recourse must have been, and remains, part of the appeal of some organised spectator sports. Ross McKibbin explains English football crowds were well known for being 'contemptuous of the … referee's eyesight, hearing and mental capacity'.[63] Though it remained part of the appeal of football games, moralists and amateur purists frequently complained, and assigned such antics to the dark side that professionalism could unleash. Professional wrestling formalised and embellished those pleasures, and it was unlikely for a night of wrestling to pass without the referee falling victim to physical violence.

The brutal and bullying wrestler who refused to follow the rules became a central wrestling archetype, and by the 1930s professional wrestling had developed a specific moral dualism with wrestlers retaining the roles of villains or blue-eyes (heroes). Chapter 4 explores these histories and promotional systems in more detail. Villains continued to be easily identifiable throughout the twentieth century, indulging in excessive violence, cheating, disobeying the referee, and antagonising the crowd. A talented villain had any number of techniques to generate a hostile reaction from the crowd. An audience respondent to the MO similarly described the pre-match rituals that took place: 'Wrestlers [refused] to fight until their opponents nails have been but cut, or grease wiped off his back, this latter act causing intense excitement before the fight has commenced.'[64] Other correspondents described wrestlers, 'challenging and spitting on the audience, dancing, shouting and gurning across the ring in a temper'.[65]

Where attempts by Mountevans to 'legitimize' and clean up the sport had led to a reduction in the more obvious display of weapons and blood (see Chapter 2), televised professional wrestling continued to pose many problems to television regulators and audiences appalled by the spectacle. The model of villainous wrestlers cheating continued, and audiences continued to be appalled by the effects such displays had on younger audiences. An impassioned but indicative complaint about the behaviour of Mick McManus claimed:

> Continual deliberate fouling seems to be his chosen policy. He gives many indications that he thinks cheating is clever. He swings his opponent around to unsight, so that he may handicap that opponent by deliberate fouling and if possible weaken him so that McManus may win. Under the auspices of the Authority sheer swinedom is being paid substantial sums for cheating endlessly .... No person, young or not so young, who thinks savagely of others can be uninfluenced by this behaviour ... This can do nothing but harm the state of the nation where already so much violence lurks near the surface.[66]

It is easy to claim these type of performances as mere moral tales where the villains always got their comeuppance, but this is not the case. In many matches, cheaters *did* prosper. If anything, villains and cheating were often more successful, because, as a promotional device, a long-reigning villain was more attractive to audiences. As before, the type of responses such antics generated was telling. Audiences apparently enjoyed the villains. One promoter claimed that the crowd 'want a dirty wrestler and though they shout "foul" and boo a lot ... it is dirty wrestling which gives them a thrill, makes the excitement and brings them back'.[67] According to Hargreaves, 'sport ... gives convincing substance to the ideology that the ambitious, hardworking, talented individual ... may achieve high status and reward'.[68] In professional wrestling this ideology was turned on its head, and the sport served as the ultimate subversion of those qualities that common-sense notions about what sport was supposed to be for.

What frightful needs are satisfied there?

Whether on television or in the boxing halls of the interwar years, the display of men's bodies, half-naked, (sometimes) muscular and oiled, were another a key attraction of professional wrestling. Responses to the Mass Observation project in Bolton, for example, highlight this. One respondent suggested she attended 'to see *real* men'.[69] Another offered that 'no other sport has such fine husky specimens of manhood as wrestling. I find it such a change to see real he-men after the spineless and insipid men one meets ordinarily.'[70] Similarly, in their study of television audiences, Dobie and Wober recorded that four out of ten viewers liked to 'admire the strength and power of the wrestlers' bodies'.[71] Women sitting watching in the wrestling crowd have become what Tom Phillips has described as synecdochic fandom, a dominant image that was often linked to the sport.[72] One controller at ITA exclaimed, 'I'm at a complete loss to understand a person such as the pleasant, gentle elderly [woman] … who claimed wrestling as her favourite TV entertainment! What frightful needs are satisfied there?'[73]

The type of masculine wink-nudge jokiness exhibited by programmers is revealing. Female sporting spectators have often been characterised as merely being in the stands or stadiums for the erotic pleasures that sport might provide. Dismissing women in this manner has then been used to build barriers between 'authentic' male fans and 'inauthentic' female fans, where men are there to watch sport in the proper manner and women are there to watch for frivolous reasons.[74] Clearly, this is incorrect: women enjoy sports for a variety of reasons, including an appreciation of skill and an understanding of nuanced tactics, systems and formations. More importantly, watching sport because of the pleasures of seeing flesh is a perfectly legitimate enjoyment to take, and we should not deny audiences who express these pleasures their agency or validity. Sport has historically provided displays of men's bodies in a culture that usually only displays 'incidental bits and pieces',[75] but those bits and pieces have been a by-product and not a central aim and are generally devalued in the wider field. Building on Bourdieu's notion of connoisseurship, where sporting knowledge was often derived from playing, the spectacle of bodies is an immediate pleasure, and one that can be enjoyed by any number of groups. Professional wrestling's open embrace of the body, not as a by-product but as a key attraction, helps explain some of the resistance the sport faced.

Like the music hall's influence regarding violence and the role of the referee, the centrality of the body in professional wrestling can partly be explained by its theatrical legacies and intersections. From the earliest circus and fairground boxing and wrestling exhibitions, emphasised and framed by stage lighting and costume, bodies had been placed as something pleasurable to be admired. At the Five Courts, the African-American boxer Bill Richmond sparred, for example, with his shirt off 'in order that the spectators might admire the muscular development of the fighters'.[76] In his circus tours, Jem Mace posed in Grecian statue routines, a form of display perfected by Andrew Ducrow that shifted emphasis from the strength of strongmen to simply the display of bodies.[77] On the music hall stage, variations of physical culture display were borrowed from these older performance traditions. Hackenschmidt, for example, posed and displayed his muscles in what he referred to as the 'Famous and Renowned POSES PLASTIQUES',[78] reminiscent of Sandow the Magnificent's world-renowned weightlifting and display. In these exhibitions, theatricality and straightforward displays of the body were foregrounded over the types of sporting displays that encouraged more valued sporting appreciation.

The types of bodies that could be seen in professional wrestling retained an uneasy relationship with the wider sporting field. Wrestlers like Hackenschmidt often espoused a very particular form of physical culture not dissimilar to that of muscular Christianity, in which the Hellenistic ideal was displayed as an antidote to many aspects of modernising industrialism. Writing about these 'theatrical athletes',[79] the phrase Sandow once used to describe his craft, Broderick Chow has claimed Hackenschmidt, and professional wrestlers more broadly, perpetuated a 'dominant, normative, masculine ideal'.[80] Certainly, for much of the twentieth century, many of the bodies in professional wrestling were a performance of masculinity, with muscles connoting strength, power and discipline, and some audiences no doubt enjoyed these displays in this reading. One 1930s man, for instance, enjoyed the show because it took him back to his 'young days when men were men! and not the namby-pamby … artificial-hair-curling variety that is most prevalent in the present generation'.[81] Placing professional wrestlers' bodies as unproblematically normative, though, fails to capture many of the tensions that the professional wrestling body encapsulates. Like other ideologies and capitals, hegemonies about bodies and gender were field-specific, and subject to struggles over definitions and meanings.

In many regards, professional wrestlers' bodies were the antithesis to the amateur ideal. Where music hall, the fairground and the circus all placed an 'emphasis on the materiality of the body' that 'traded in excess',[82] professional wrestling was no different. The Victorian and Edwardian professional wrestler's body was big and bulky, often barrel-chested and broad-shouldered, built to be hard to pin to the ground.[83] This materiality meant that it was denied the respectability of bodies that trained for the amateur ideal. As Richard Holt notes, the amateur sporting body was a 'neo-classical norm of human proportion, balancing height, weight, muscle development and mobility … neither too tall nor too small, too thin nor too fat'.[84] The amateur sporting body, at least in its Victorian and Edwardian idealised model, should excel at a variety of sports; the professional wrestler's body, built to win and display, was often subversive to some of the values of the wider sporting field. The hegemonic masculinity of muscularity described by Chow, then, was more complex, and professional wrestlers' bodies were more transgressive, offering an alternative model of masculinity on the fringes of the sporting field.

This subversive body reached its complete embellishment with some of the types of bodies seen on television in the 1970s. Super-heavyweights, most famously Big Daddy and Giant Haystacks, so called because of their weight, encapsulated the anxieties of the professional body. Once again, such bodies can be traced to an older performance tradition, the freak show, and these forms of display had been embraced in wrestling and prize-fighting exhibitions. Fat ladies, and to a lesser extent fat men, had been a regular feature of the Victorian fairground as well as being an attraction on the music hall stage,[85] serving to eroticize fatness in a manner that wider society often disdained, and at the same time mocking the stoic and restrained attitudes of the Protestant work ethic. Following a tour of America in the 1840s, for example, Ben Caunt, a popular English prize-fighter, returned with Charles Freeman, who had been displayed as a giant at Barnum's American Museum. Upon arrival in England, he performed as a sparring partner for Caunt in Manchester, Liverpool and London. This type of extreme display of bodies, with little people being utilized as wrestlers or ring announcers, continued in wrestling promotions in the 1930s, and post-Mountevans in the fairground and in America. As stated in the above section, wrestling continued to gently mock the seriousness of the wider sporting field, and in attracting audiences drew concern from commentators who were otherwise invested in the field.

Any claims to seriousness were further undermined by what bodies *did* in the ring. While it would never have been openly discussed in this manner, wrestling promoters were keen to offer the variety of an evening's entertainment that could compete with rival leisure venues, and comedy was an important part of an all-in wrestling performance. Luke Stadel has claimed that 'the representational norms of early cinema came to serve as the central organizing force in the business of wrestling', claiming that wrestling continued a legacy of early cinema slapstick and physical comedy.[86] That is partly true, but this analysis misses the fact that both professional wrestling and early cinema progressed from a shared history of physical clowning and comedy on the variety and music hall stage. Wrestling cards contained an element of the variety theatre, incorporating different performance styles and traditions into matches. Most wrestling cards had one 'comedy bout between a couple of lightweights',[87] and, on television, professional wrestling's inherent comedy continued. Tellingly, Dobie and Wober found that nine out of ten audience members enjoyed the sport because it was 'funny and amusing' and watched it for its 'comic character'.[88] Barthes acknowledges this in his work, but does not dwell on it, suggesting that, all-in wrestling is akin to pantomime: 'some wrestlers, who are great comedians, entertain as much as a Molière character'.[89] Indeed, wrestlers had a specific role, and indeed talent, in playing the clown. Les Kellett was the most famous and enduring character in this mould.[90] A typical Kellett match involved him toying with his opponent, staggering around the ring wildly missing punches, and interacting with the referee and audience. In some cases, rather than bodies being trained for peak sporting perfection, some professional wrestlers were trained to entertain.

The playfulness in comedy matches, finally, was ultimately matched by a playfulness with regards to gender. Sharon Mazer argues that, 'to some degree, a professional wrestler is always in drag, always enacting a parody of masculinity at the same time that he epitomizes it'.[91] Ricki Starr, a former ballet dancer, wore pointe shoes and pirouetted before, during and after matches. He garnered a mixed reaction of both laughter and derision, the comedy in the situation derived from the juxtaposition between the hyper-masculine and popular cultural world of contact sport and the supposedly feminine and 'high art' (ballet) dancing. Ballet dancing seemed mild in comparison to Adrian Street who debuted in the 1970s. Street drew equal influence from America's first television professional wrestling star, Gorgeous George, and glam rock. With long, bleached blonde hair, and wearing a combination of make-up, glitter, feather boas, and sequins (he never wore the same outfit twice, naturally), his entrances drew audible gasps, laughter and catcalls. In an interview with the *Daily Mirror*, Street outlined his (in character) reasoning for the mixed reaction he often received: 'I'm hated because I am so lovely. Some think I'm a poof, but I'm not really. I'm just very conceited … Women do fancy me. Maybe they're curious or want to convert me.'[92] Away from the world of *Top of the Pops*, Street offered a radical representation of gender in the hyper-masculine *World of Sport*.

Professional wrestling's embrace of displaying bodies, comedy, and its playful attitude to gender, betrayed the influences of the stage and challenged the values and capital of the wider sporting field. Norman Morrell, who had played such a pivotal role in the creation of the Lord Mountevans style and Joint Promotions, found himself increasingly disillusioned with professional wrestling on television. In a long series of letters to the IBA from 1975 to 1980, Morrell, who was always quick to point out his previous involvement with the sport, decried the current situation: 'the necessity of presenting ITV wrestling to look like a sport in the world of sport is both common sense and good business'.[93]

All were cynical about wrestling

In February 1989, Vince McMahon, chairman of the World Wrestling Federation, testified to the New Jersey Senate that professional wrestling was just an 'entertainment'.[94] In so doing, McMahon removed himself from the auspices of the Athletic Control Board while simultaneously being able to avoid paying the taxes of televised sports. Fans and wrestlers have often positioned McMahon's reveal as marking the end of *kayfabe*. An old carnival term reflecting professional wrestling's fairground and circus roots, kayfabe refers to the practice of sustaining the in-diegesis performance into everyday life. At its most basic, kayfabe fundamentally means the presentation of wrestling as a legitimate sporting competition rather than theatrical entertainment. As a concept, however, kayfabe sits centrally as one of wrestling's defining pleasures and modes of engagement, complicating many of the above pleasures and complaints, and '[eluding] moral and academic authority'.[95]

Central to kayfabe is the discussion and debate of authenticity and fakery. From its emergence in the 1920s to the 1990s, and on both sides of the Atlantic, wrestlers, promoters and virtually all connected with the sport remained adamant that the contests in the ring were not dissimilar to other sporting events, and often went to great lengths to 'protect' the sport's apparent secrets. If a performed injury was sustained in the ring, then performers had to show the consequences of the injury on the street. Wrestler's auto-biographies between 1930 and 1990, for example, generally offer a fictionalised first-person account of how someone might have felt if engaged in a legitimate sporting contest. Those connected to Joint Promotions often claimed that all-in, the type of wrestling seen in the 1930s, might have been crooked, but after the post-Mountevans committee, the sport had been reclaimed. In an article about wrestling in the sport annual *Grandstand Sport*, the author Bob Findlay joked:

> 'Ah ha!' you say, 'I KNOW wrestling is phony. Everybody knows the fights are fixed. You win this week and I'll win next week.' Maybe it used to be that way, but it isn't now. Proof lies in the fact that two wrestlers seldom meet more than once in six months.[96]

This position was also maintained to controllers at ITA, who remained steadfast in their concerns about the performative aspect of the sport, what it said about ITV's attitude to sport more broadly, and their own roles in offering wrestling to audiences.

Because of its presentation as a 'legitimate sport', many complaints felt that wrestling's presentation was a dishonesty, a kind of cheating and duplicity more akin to a confidence trick than either a sporting contest or theatrical performance. Reflecting wider concerns about the effects of mass cultures, spectators at professional wrestling were seen to be at risk from conmen seeking a quick profit. Concern had to be expressed in a way where audiences did not understand or comprehend what they were seeing at the wrestling. Audiences, in such readings, were cultural dupes, uninterested or even unable to separate fact from fiction, intoxicated by the spectacle before them, and 'gulled' by the 'burlesque athletics'.[97] In London, one critic complained:

> I know about it in Chelsea and there the people of Chelsea object to this class of sport going on and the reason why they object to it is that they don't consider it a genuine sport at all … They consider that it is really a kind of performance and it is rehearsed before and it is not really a bona fide sport and so much of it is a performance. The whole point of these shows is to display cruelty and I do not think much in fury takes place to people who are wrestling.[98]

These grievances hinted at one of the contradictions of claiming professional wrestling as 'fake', at least when it combined with other criticisms outlined above. If the violence was simulated, then opposing the sport on the grounds of concern for the wrestlers themselves, and even the concern for the public, was more difficult to sustain. In the terms laid out in the sporting field, it was safer than virtually all combat sports, and safer than many contact sports. One could in fact position it as the logical conclusion of the civilizing process, continuing to offer the thrills of sport with many of the actual threats of sustained injury being curbed. Evidently, in both the above account and in others, this was not the position taken. Rather, writers sought to bring those positions together. In the press, Percy Longhurst suggested that he was 'very willing ... to agree that very often these brutalities are but fake pure and simple ... such deception is nothing than a further insult to the public, an impudent assertion that spectators prefer brutality to honest contention.'[99] Similarly, in a report for the Metropolitan Police, an inspector offered:

> To the ordinary lay-man the above methods, kneeing, kicking, and rabbit punching etc., look extremely brutal but to the experienced eye they are cleverly faked attacks, and combined with the expression of pain make a very real impression upon the audience.[100]

To manage these contradictions, then, critics had to propose that simulations of violence remained dangerous precisely because audiences struggled to disentangle one from the other. If the violence was fake, it was not fake to the audiences watching, and it was only those with relevant forms of cultural capital imbued from the wider sporting field who could untangle the performance.

Yet in these descriptions there was an uneasiness in articulating in exact terms what professional wrestling is, how it operates, and the mechanisms by which it operated. Those producing reviews for the Home Office, for example, were often willing to claim the sport as pre-arranged, but it was almost always couched in qualifiers of informed speculation. A good proportion of those working at the ITA during the 1960s could not say for certain whether professional wrestling displayed legitimate sporting contests. After a meeting with Joint Promotions, one of many, one controller tentatively offered that 'these wrestlers are as much showmen as athletes ... [and] they have to give the spectators a show for their money. This doesn't mean rigging a result.'[101] In general terms, often those condemning professional wrestling as 'fake' struggled to understand how audiences could enjoy something that seemed to them so obviously fabricated.

Such confusion ultimately stemmed from a false assumption that audiences believed wrestling to be a real sport, an assumption for which there is very little supporting evidence. Though Vince McMahon's testimony in 1989 created a candidness in talking about the form and structure of professional wrestling's performances, it is hard to sustain the idea that before then kayfabe was 'alive' in the sense audiences fully believed the performances as it was presented to them. How could they? From the moment wrestling became a sporting entertainment, the press regularly ran reports about wrestling's nature. Whether in explanations for why they did not feature reports in the sporting pages, pulp magazines about con tricks, descriptions of wrestlers joining theatrical trade unions,[102] or 'exclusive' exposures from disgruntled former referees,[103] wrestling being 'fake' was repeated throughout the twentieth century, and audiences would have seen this. This background noise combined with the extravagant characters, comedy matches, gymnastics and a range of tricks to keep audiences entertained, described throughout this chapter. The apparent performativity identified by governmental observers was just as obvious, if not more so, for regular attendees. In their study, Dobie and Wober found that 'nearly three quarters of the whole sample (and a greater proportion among those interested in wrestling) considered that results of matches are fixed'.[104] As valuable as much of Dobie and Wober's analysis is, even the questionnaire's wording could not adequately describe professional wrestling's presentation: might the results have been higher if the question claimed pre-determined rather than fixed? Given how kayfabe helps to structure audience's pleasures, encouraging audience to play along, some of these responses might likewise have been answered with tongues in cheeks.

General critiques and criticisms of the 'duplicitous' nature of wrestling reflected a misunderstanding of how audiences engaged with the sport. Generally, audiences did not care that it was performed because it was entertaining, and their participation was a vital part of the event. For engaged audiences, as well as enjoying the athleticism, showmanship and storytelling of a good wrestling match, the text, live or televised, was examined for pockets of 'authenticity' or moments where kayfabe and its own internal logic bend or break.[105] In other words, for some audiences there is a pleasure in looking for the underlying performance techniques, and seeking to explore how authenticity or performance were produced. A *Guardian* article, written at the height of professional wrestling's popularity in 1960, captured this complicated relationship:

> All were cynical about wrestling: to come and remain undeceived by the most extravagant antics seems to be an attraction in itself. Too much showmanship – when a fighter falls as if struck by a steam-hammer when he has obviously not been touched – leaves the Belle Vue connoisseur amused but undismayed.[106]

Wrestling's shared history with the stage is once again important in understanding this. In many of sideshows, P.T. Barnum placed debates about authenticity as a key attraction. Performers were introduced from fictional locations, clearly embellished narratives were offered, and sizes and weights were exaggerated. That such narratives were obvious ballyhoo was not important: Barnum understood that deception could be entertaining because an audience's enjoyment could be found in dissecting where performance and reality met.[107] It did not matter whether audiences believed the stories they were being told, Neil Harris writes, audiences 'delighted in debate'. He continues, 'amusement and deceit could coexist; people would come to see something they suspected might be an exaggeration or even a masquerade'.[108] This performance tradition, and we should remember showpeople's key role in professional wrestling development, was a key attraction for the sport.

Despite this cynicism, it is perhaps understandable that some commentators felt that wrestling audiences believed everything they were seeing. Crowds were eager and excited to play along with the performance, and those present in the arena became part of the spectacle and narrative of the performance in the ring. Annette Hill has described contemporary professional wrestling as a form of 'co-production' between fans, wrestlers and promoters,[109] and this appears to have been the case historically. Before the contests began there would be cries of 'bring out the bulls'.[110] Throughout the matches there were shouts and cat-calls from the audience. Wrestlers often indulged in 'gouging, punching and kicking whilst on the floor amongst the audience'.[111] Finally, much to chagrin of one writer to MO who took the opportunity to complain that, 'women should not be allowed in at half price. They take much of the enjoyment out of the bouts with their "cat-calls".'[112] Live audiences, then, were part of the performance. As Broderick Chow has explained, 'While the spectacle is fake, its affective dimension is surely real.' He continues that kayfabe, and fundamentally the spectatorship of wrestling, are based upon 'opening oneself up to be swept away in the spectacle while, simultaneously, acknowledging its constructed nature'.[113] One observer in the 1930s struggled to make sense of the animated crowds who were also in absolute control: 'the crowd appeared very excited, and threatening, but nothing untoward happened outside the ring … and the crowd left very orderly'.[114] In striving not to be duped by the performance in the ring, he had been duped by the performance by the crowd.

Kayfabe, therefore, was fundamental to the enjoyment of professional wrestling. It folded audiences into the text, while excluding those who were inclined not to like it. It framed the comedy, violence, excessive bodies and all the other pleasures described above: it did not matter that Big Daddy could clearly not wrestle because that was part of the joke. Kayfabe's centrality, furthermore, was the ultimate challenge to the sporting field. Competition and uncertainty of outcome, key markers of sport, and their ideologies about sportsmanship and amateurism, were entirely undersold. Audiences continued to flock to professional wrestling, knowing that what they were watching was pre-arranged. For many, this fakery was more enjoyable than other sporting contests could ever be. As an explanatory term, kayfabe might also help explain responses to contemporary commodity culture, in which cynical audiences allow themselves to be swept up.[115] It certainly also provides a useful term in which to interrogate contemporary celebrity culture, as we will see in Chapter 4.

Conclusion

Professional wrestling, this chapter has argued, offered obvious forms of pleasure: performative violence, displays of both muscular and non-muscular bodies, comedy and critiques of hegemonic masculinity, audience participation, and a playfulness with regards to 'authenticity'. Some of these pleasures were embellishments of those that could be found in other sports, and other pleasures can be directly traced to the fairgrounds, circuses and music hall. Regardless, they almost always subverted or parodied dominant values as they existed in the sporting field. Despite claims to the contrary, professional wrestling posed no direct threat to the social order, but the types of tastes it elicited did pose a direct threat to the structure of the sporting field. Criticisms were quite specific: wrestling did not look or feel or present itself like other sports, and it openly flaunted its opposition to the amateur ideal. Wrestling very much threatened the wider values of sport, and in so doing threatened the complex positions occupied by those in the sporting field, and indeed the sporting field's wider position in society. Between 1930 and 1980, professional wrestling serves as an especially good example of the ways in which a field's structures, conflicts and compromises are experienced for everyday audiences. A field's directions, capitals and ideologies shape genres and cultural forms, but the securing of those values and directions, at least in advanced capitalist economies, is partially produced by the active involvement of audiences, fans and consumers.

Notes

1 Report by Stanley John Bisnell for Metropolitan Police, National Archives, HO box 45/24142.
2 Martin Johnes and Gavin Mellor, 'The 1953 FA Cup Final: Modernity and Tradition in British Culture', *Contemporary British History*, 20(2), (2006), pp. 263–280.
3 Jeffrey Hill, *Sport, Leisure and Culture in Twentieth Century Britain* (Basingstoke, 2002), p. 98.
4 Richard Holt and Tony Mason, *Sport in Britain 1945–2000* (Oxford, 2000), p. 98.
5 Garry Whannel, *Fields in Vision: Television Sport and Cultural Transformation* (London, 1992), p. 49.
6 Bernard Sendall, *Independent Television in Britain*, vol. 1: *Origin and Foundation, 1946–62* (London, 1982), p. 319.
7 Asa Briggs in John Mundy, 'Spreading Wisdom', *Media History*, 14(1), (2008), p. 59.
8 Quoted in Sendall, *Independent Television in Britain*, vol. 1, p. 328.
9 James Hinton, *The Mass Observers: A History, 1937–1949* (Oxford, 2013).
10 Internal memo from J.E. Harrison, 17 Mar. 1969, Sporting Events "Wrestling", vol. 2, IBA, box 01097.
11 Ian Dobie and Mallory Wober, *The Role of Wrestling as a Public Spectacle: Audience Attitudes to Wrestling as Portrayed on Television* (London, 1978), p. 3.
12 Entertainments Committee's discussion with representatives from the Met standing joint committee, 11 Dec. 1935, LCC, box CL/PC/01/026.
13 Robert James, *Popular Culture and Working-Class Taste in Britain, 1930–39: A Round of Cheap Diversions?* (Manchester, 2010), p. 15.
14 Martin Polley, *Moving the Goalposts: A History of Sport Since 1945* (London, 1998), p. 89.
15 Stephen G. Jones, 'Working-Class Sport in Manchester Between the Wars', in Richard Holt (ed.), *Sport and the Working Class in Modern Britain* (Manchester, 1990), p. 73.

16 Entertainments Committee's discussion with reps of the Met Standing Joint Committee, 11 Dec. 1935, LCC, box CL/PC/01/026.
17 Confidential statement sent to Captain Bertram Mills, May 1933, LCC, box CL/PC/01/026.
18 Chad Dell, *The Revenge of Hatpin Mary: Women, Professional Wrestling and Fan Culture* (New York, 2006); Catherine Salmon and Susan Clerc, '"Ladies Love Wrestling, Too": Female Wrestling Fans Online', in Nicholas Sammond (ed.), *Steel Chair to the Head: The Pleasure and Pain of Professional Wrestling* (Durham, NC, 2005).
19 Jonathan Bignell, 'And the Rest Is History: Lew Grade, Creation Narratives and Television Historiography', in C. Johnson and R. Turnock (eds), *ITV Cultures: Independent Television Over Fifty Years* (Maidenhead, 2005), p. 61; Janet Thumim, *Inventing Television: Men, Women and the Box* (Oxford, 2004), p. 17.
20 Jeffrey Milland, 'Paternalists, Populists and Pilkington: The Struggle for the Soul of British Television, 1958–1963', unpublished thesis (Bristol, 2005), p. 4.
21 Hill, *Sport, Leisure and Culture*, pp. 61–62.
22 Matthew Hilton, 'The Legacy of Luxury: Moralities of Consumption Since the 18th Century', *Journal of Consumer Culture*, 4(1), (2004), pp. 101–123.
23 Letter from the National Amateur Wrestling Association to the LCC Entertainments Council Committee, Mar. 1933, LCC, box CL/PC/01/026.
24 Atholl Oakeley, *Blue Blood on the Mat* (Chichester, 1996), p. 67.
25 Jeremy Potter, *Independent Television in Britain*, vol. 4: *Companies and Programmes, 1968–80* (London, 1990), p. 282.
26 Internal memo from J.E. Harrison, 17 Mar. 1969, Sporting Events "Wrestling", vol. 2, IBA, box 01097.
27 Letter from F.H. Copplestone to Mr. Coombs, 12 Jun. 1967, Sporting Events "Wrestling", vol. 1, IBA, box 01097.
28 F.M.L. Thompson, *The Rise of Respectable Society: A Social History of Victorian Britain, 1830–1900* (London, 1988), p. 289.
29 Stephen G. Jones, *Sport, Politics, and the Working Class* (Manchester, 1988), p. 10.
30 Erik Neveu, 'Bourdieu, the Frankfurt School, and Cultural Studies: On Some Misunderstandings', in Rodney Benson and Erik Neveu, *Bourdieu and the Journalistic Field* (Cambridge, 2005), pp. 195–213.
31 Rebecca Williams 'Good Neighbours? Fan/Producer Relationships and the Broadcasting Field', *Continuum*, 24(2), (2010), pp. 279–289; Elana Shefrin, 'Lord of the Rings, Star Wars, and Participatory Fandom: Mapping New Congruencies Between the Internet and Media Entertainment Culture', *Critical Studies in Media Communication*, 21(3), (2004), pp. 261–281.
32 Mike Featherstone, *Consumer Culture and Postmodernism* (London, 2007), p. 85.
33 Pierre Bourdieu, 'Sport and Social Class', *Social Science Information*, 17, (1978), p. 829.
34 Roland Barthes, *Mythologies*, trans. Annette Lavers (Reading, 1993), p. 15.
35 Lawrence B. McBride and Elizabeth Bird, 'From Smart Fan to Backyard Wrestler: Performance, Context, and Aesthetic Violence', in Jonathan Alan Gray, Cornel Sandvoss, and C. Lee Harrington (eds), *Fandom: Identities and Communities in a Mediated World* (New York, 2007), pp. 165–176.
36 'Rules of "Free Style" Wrestling', reproduced in Archie Potts, *Headlocks and Handbags* (Sunderland, 2005), p. 8.
37 Henry Jenkins, '"Never Trust a Snake": WWF Wrestling as Masculine Melodrama', in Nicholas Sammond (ed.), *Steel Chair to the Head: The Pleasure and Pain of Professional Wrestling* (Durham, NC, 2005), p. 40.

38 Laurence De Garis, 'The "Logic" of Professional Wrestling', in Nicholas Sammond (ed.), *Steel Chair to the Head: The Pleasure and Pain of Professional Wrestling* (Durham, NC, 2005), p. 201.
39 Correspondence, MO, box SxMOA1/5/E/8.
40 Ibid.
41 Report by Stanley John Bisnell for the Metropolitan Police. HO box 45/24142.
42 Report, MO, box SxMOA1/5/E/8.
43 Percy Longhurst, 'Stop This Burlesque Sport', *Daily Mail* 15 April 1933, p. 8.
44 Correspondence, MO, box SxMOA1/5/E/8.
45 *Daily Herald* press clipping, HO box 45/24142.
46 Oakeley, *Blue Blood*, p. 38.
47 Lucy Nevitt, 'Popular Entertainments and the Spectacle of Bleeding', *Popular Entertainment Studies*, 1(2), (2010), pp. 78–92.
48 Norbert Elias and Eric Dunning, *Quest for Excitement: Sport and Leisure in the Civilizing Process* (Oxford, 1986).
49 Kenneth Gordon Sheard, 'Boxing in the Civilising Process' unpublished doctoral thesis, 1992.
50 Eric Dunning, *Sport Matters: Sociological Studies of Sport, Violence and Civilisation* (London, 1999), p. 3.
51 Letter from the National Amateur Wrestling Association to the LCC Entertainments Council, Mar. 1933, LCC, box CL/PC/01/026.
52 Confidential statement sent to Captain Bertram Mills, May, 1933, LCC, box CL/PC/01/026.
53 Andy Medhurst, *A National Joke: Popular Comedy and English National Identity* (London, 2007), p. 65.
54 Hugh Cunningham, *Leisure in the Industrial Revolution c. 1780–c.1880* (New York, 1980), p. 173.
55 Dagmar Kift, *The Victorian Music Hall: Culture, Class and Conflict* (Cambridge, 1996), p. 176.
56 Andy Medhurst, 'Music Hall and British Cinema', in Charles Barr (ed.), *All Our Yesterdays: Ninety Years of British Cinema* (London, 1986), p. 168.
57 Charles B. Cochran, *The Secrets of a Showman* (London, 1925), p. 110.
58 Ibid., p. 120.
59 Kift, *The Victorian Music Hall*, p. 22.
60 Correspondence, MO, box SxMOA1/5/E/8.
61 Ibid.
62 Letter from Lancelot Keay to ITA, 19 Feb. 1968, Sporting Events "Wrestling", vol. 1, IBA, box 01097.
63 Ross McKibbin, *Classes and Cultures, England, 1918–1951* (Oxford, 1998), p. 343.
64 Correspondence, MO, box SxMOA1/5/E/8.
65 Ibid.
66 Letter from J.S. Malloch to Lord Aylestone, 3 Apr. 1968, Sporting Events "Wrestling", vol. 2, IBA, box 01097.
67 Robert Snape, 'All-in Wrestling in Inter-War Britain: Science and Spectacle in Mass Observation's "Worktown"', *The International Journal of the History of Sport*, 30(12), (2013), p. 1427.
68 John Hargreaves, *Sport, Power and Culture* (Oxford, 1986), p. 111.
69 Emphasis in original, correspondence, MO, box SxMOA1/5/E/8.
70 Correspondence, MO, box SxMOA1/5/E/8.
71 Dobie and Wober, *The Role of Wrestling*, p. 3.
72 Tom Phillips, '"Angry False-Teeth-Chattering Mayhem": Synecdochic Fandom, Representation and Performance in Mature Woman Fandom of British

Professional Wrestling', in Paul Booth (ed.), *Wiley Companion to Media Fandom and Fan Studies* (Oxford, 2017), pp. 227–241.
73 Internal memo from J.E. Harrison, 17 Mar. 1969, Sporting Events "Wrestling", vol. 2, IBA, box 01097.
74 Garry Crawford and Victoria K. Gosling, 'The Myth of the "Puck Bunny": Female Fans and Men's Ice Hockey', *Sociology*, 38(3), (2004), p. 486.
75 van Zoonen, quoted in Salmon and Clerc, '"Ladies Love Wrestling, Too"', p. 75.
76 John Ford, *Prizefighting: The Age of Regency Boximania* (Devon, 1971), p. 138.
77 David L. Chapman, *Sandow the Magnificent: Eugen Sandow and the Beginnings of Bodybuilding* (Chicago, 2006), p. 138; Maria Wyke, 'Herculean Muscle!: The Classicizing Rhetoric of Bodybuilding', *Arion*, 4(3), (1997), p. 54.
78 John Rickard, '"The Spectacle of Excess": The Emergence of Modern Professional Wrestling in the United States and Australia' *The Journal of Popular Culture*, 33(1), (1999), p. 130.
79 Chapman, *Sandow*, p. 67.
80 Broderick D.V. Chow, 'A Professional Body: Remembering, Repeating and Working out Masculinities in Fin-de-Siècle Physical Culture', *Performance Research*, 20(5), (2015), p. 35.
81 Correspondence, MO, box SxMOA1/5/E/8.
82 Brenda Assael, *The Circus and Victorian Society* (Charlottesville, VA, 2005), p. 8.
83 Anon., 'Wrestling: Gama v Zbysco', *The Times*, 12 Sept. 1910, p. 14.
84 Richard Holt, 'The Amateur Body and the Middle-Class Man: Work, Health and Style in Victorian Britain', *Sport in History*, 26(3), (2006), p. 361.
85 Anne Hole, 'Fat History and Music Hall', *Women's History Notebooks*, 7(1), (2000), pp. 3–7.
86 Luke Stadel, 'Wrestling and Cinema, 1892–1911', *Early Popular Visual Culture*, 11(4), (2013), p. 356.
87 Correspondence, MO, box SxMOA1/5/E/8.
88 Dobie and Wober, *The Role of Wrestling*, pp. 3, 6.
89 Barthes, *Mythologies*, p. 19.
90 Simon Garfield, *The Wrestling* (London, 2007), p. 38.
91 Sharon Mazer, *Professional Wrestling: Sport and Spectacle* (Jackson, MS, 1999), p. 100.
92 'Why Wrestling Has a Stranglehold on Women', *Daily Mirror*, 21 Nov. 1970, p. 9.
93 Letter from Norman Morrell to Mr Rook, 5 Nov. 1975, Sporting Events "Wrestling", vol. 4, IBA, box 01097.
94 Peter Kerr, 'Now It Can Be Told: Those Pro Wrestlers Are Just Having Fun', *New York Times*, 10 Feb. 1989, p. B2.
95 Sharon Mazer, '"Real Wrestling"/"Real" Life', in Nicholas Sammond (ed.), *Steel Chair to the Head: The Pleasure and Pain of Professional Wrestling* (Durham, NC, 2005), p. 68.
96 Report by Stanley John Bisnell for the Metropolitan Police. HO box 45/24142.
97 Percy Longhurst, 'Stop This Burlesque Sport', *Daily Mail*, 15 April 1933, p. 8.
98 Entertainments Committee's discussion with reps of the Met Standing Joint Committee, 11 Dec. 1935, LCC, box CL/PC/01/026.
99 Longhurst, 'Stop This Burlesque Sport.'
100 Report by Stanley John Bisnell for the Metropolitan Police. National Archives, HO box 45/24142.
101 Letter from Dale Martin Promotions to Howard Thomas, 6 Apr., Sporting Events "Wrestling", vol. 1, IBA, box 01097.
102 Clifford Davies, 'Ring Stars Join Variety Union: Wrestlers Fight for Bigger TV Purse', *Daily Mirror*, 23 Apr. 1962, p. 11.

103 Michael Gabbert, 'The Great Wrestling Fiddle: Now Referees Admit It…"We DID Fake the Bouts!"', *The People*, 1 Aug. 1965, p. 4.
104 Dobie and Wober, 'The Role of Wrestling', p. 5.
105 Mazer, 'Real Wrestling'.
106 Anon., no title, *The Guardian*, 13 Nov. 1960, p. 19.
107 Marion Wrenn, 'Managing Doubt: Professional Wrestling Jargon and the Making of "Smart Fans"', in Craig Calhoun and Richard Sennett (eds), *Practicing Culture* (London, 2007), p. 165.
108 Neil Harris, *Humbug: The Art of P.T. Barnum* (Chicago, 1981), p. 62.
109 Annette Hill, 'Spectacle of Excess: The Passion Work of Professional Wrestlers, Fans and Anti-Fans', *European Journal of Cultural Studies*, 18(2), (2014), p. 3.
110 Report, MO, box SxMOA1/5/E/8.
111 Letter from Peter Gotz to Clyde Wilson, 20 March 1933, LCC, box CL/PC/01/026.
112 Correspondence, MO, box SxMOA1/5/E/8.
113 Broderick D.V. Chow, 'Parterre: Olympic Wrestling, National Identities, and the Theatre of Agonism', in Tony Fisher and Eve Katsouraki (eds), *Performing Antagonism: Theatre, Performance & Radical Democracy* (London, 2017), p. 75.
114 S. Mews Inspector Report: Wrestling Match, Madeley St. Baths, 25 March 1933. HO box 45/24142.
115 Wrenn, 'Professional Wrestling Jargon'.

Bibliography

Assael, Brenda, *The Circus and Victorian Society*, Charlottesville, VA, University of Virginia Press, 2005.

Barthes, Roland, *Mythologies*, trans. Annette Lavers, Reading, Vintage Press, 1993.

Bignell, Jonathan, 'And the Rest is History: Lew Grade, Creation Narratives and Television Historiography' in Catherine Johnson, and Rob Turnock (eds), *ITV Cultures: Independent Television Over Fifty Years*, Maidenhead, Open University Press, 2005.

Bourdieu, Pierre, 'Sport and Social Class', *Social Science Information*, 17, (1978), pp. 819–840.

Chapman, David L., *Sandow the Magnificent: Eugen Sandow and the Beginnings of Bodybuilding*, Urbana, IL, University of Illinois Press, 2006.

Chow, Broderick D.V., 'A Professional Body: Remembering, Repeating and Working out Masculinities in Fin-de-Siècle Physical Culture', *Performance Research*, 20(5), (2015), pp. 30–41.

Chow, Broderick D.V., 'Parterre: Olympic Wrestling, National Identities, and the Theatre of Agonism', in Tony Fisher and Eve Katsouraki (eds), *Performing Antagonism: Theatre, Performance & Radical Democracy*, London, Palgrave. 2017, pp. 61–79.

Cochran, Charles B., *The Secrets of a Showman*, London, William Heinemann Ltd, 1925.

Crawford, Garry, and Gosling, Victoria K., 'The Myth of the "Puck Bunny" Female Fans and Men's Ice Hockey', *Sociology*, 38(3), (2004), pp. 477–493.

Cunningham, Hugh, *Leisure in the Industrial Revolution c. 1780 – c.1880*, New York, St. Martin's Press, 1980.

De Garis, Laurence, 'The "Logic" of Professional Wrestling', in Nicholas Sammond (ed.), *Steel Chair to the Head: The Pleasure and Pain of Professional Wrestling*, Durham, NC, Duke University Press, 2005, pp. 192–212.

Dell, Chad, *The Revenge of Hatpin Mary: Women, Professional Wrestling and Fan Culture*, New York, Peter Lang, 2006.

Dobie, Ian, and Wober, Mallory, *The Role of Wrestling as a Public Spectacle: Audience Attitudes to Wrestling as Portrayed on Television*, London, Independent Broadcasting Authority, 1978.

Dunning, Eric, *Sport Matters: Sport Matters: Sociological Studies of Sport, Violence and Civilisation*, London, Routledge, 1999.

Elias, Norbert, and Dunning, Eric, *Quest for Excitement: Sport and Leisure in the Civilizing Process*, Oxford, Blackwell, 1986.

Featherstone, Mike, *Consumer Culture and Postmodernism*, London, Sage, 2007.

Ford, John, *Prizefighting: The Age of Regency Boximania*, Devon, David and Charles, 1971.

Garfield, Simon, *The Wrestling*, London, Faber & Faber, 2007.

Gray, Jonathan Alan, Sandvoss, Cornel and Harrington, C. Lee (eds), *Fandom: Identities and Communities in a Mediated World*, New York, New York University Press, 2007, pp. 165–176.

Hargreaves, John, *Sport, Power and Culture*, Oxford, Polity, 1986.

Harris, Neil, *Humbug: The Art of P.T. Barnum*, Chicago, University of Chicago Press, 1981.

Hill, Annette, 'Spectacle of Excess: The Passion Work of Professional Wrestlers, Fans and Anti-Fans', *European Journal of Cultural Studies*, 18(2), (2014), pp. 174–189.

Hill, Jeffrey, *Sport, Leisure and Culture in Twentieth Century Britain*, Basingstoke, Palgrave, 2002.

Hilton, Matthew, 'The Legacy of Luxury: Moralities of Consumption Since the 18th Century', *Journal of Consumer Culture*, 4(1), (2004), pp. 101–123.

Hinton, James, *The Mass Observers: A History, 1937–1949*, Oxford, Oxford University Press, 2013.

Hole, Anne, 'Fat History and Music Hall', *Women's History Notebooks*, 7(1), (2000), pp. 3–7.

Holt, Richard, 'The Amateur Body and the Middle-Class Man: Work, Health and Style in Victorian Britain', *Sport in History*, 26(3), (2006), pp. 352–369.

Holt, Richard, and Mason, Tony, *Sport in Britain 1945–2000*, Oxford, Wiley-Blackwell, 2000.

James, Robert, *Popular Culture and Working-Class Taste in Britain, 1930–39: A Round of Cheap Diversions?*, Manchester, Manchester University Press, 2010.

Jenkins, Henry, '"Never Trust a Snake": WWF Wrestling as Masculine Melodrama', in Nicholas Sammond (ed.), *Steel Chair to the Head: The Pleasure and Pain of Professional Wrestling*, Durham, NC, Duke University Press, 2005, pp. 33–66.

Johnes, Martin and Mellor, Gavin, 'The 1953 FA Cup Final: Modernity and Tradition in British Culture', *Contemporary British History*, 20(2), (2006), pp. 263–280.

Jones, Stephen G., *Sport, Politics, and the Working Class*, Manchester, Manchester University Press, 1988.

Jones, Stephen G., 'Working-Class Sport in Manchester Between the Wars', in Richard Holt, (ed.), *Sport and the Working Class in Modern Britain*, Manchester, Manchester University Press, 1990, pp. 67–83.

Kift, Dagmar, *The Victorian Music Hall: Culture, Class and Conflict*, Cambridge, Cambridge University Press, 1996.

Mazer, Sharon, *Professional Wrestling: Sport and Spectacle*, Jackson, MS, University Press of Mississippi, 1999.

Mazer, Sharon, '"Real Wrestling"/"Real" Life', in Nicholas Sammond (ed.), *Steel Chair to the Head: The Pleasure and Pain of Professional Wrestling*, Durham, NC, Duke University Press, 2005, pp. 67–87.

McBride, Lawrence B. and Bird, Elizabeth, 'From Smart Fan to Backyard Wrestler: Performance, Context, and Aesthetic Violence', in Jonathan Alan Gray, Cornel Sandvossand C. Lee Harrington (eds), *Fandom: Identities and Communities in a Mediated World*, New York, New York University Press, 2007.

McKibbin, Ross, *Classes and Cultures, England, 1918–1951*, Oxford, Oxford University Press, 1998.

Medhurst, Andy, 'Music Hall and British Cinema', in Charles Barr (ed.), *All Our Yesterdays: Ninety Years of British Cinema*, London, BFI Publishing, 1986, pp. 168–188.

Medhurst, Andy, *A National Joke: Popular Comedy and English National Identity*, London, Routledge, 2007.

Milland, Jeffrey, 'Paternalists, Populists and Pilkington: The Struggle for the Soul of British Television, 1958–1963', unpublished doctoral thesis, University of Bristol, 2005.

Neveu, Erik, 'Bourdieu, the Frankfurt School, and Cultural Studies: On Some Misunderstandings', in Rodney Benson and Erik Neveu, *Bourdieu and the Journalistic Field*, Cambridge, Polity, 2005, pp. 195–213.

Nevitt, Lucy, 'Popular Entertainments and the Spectacle of Bleeding', *Popular Entertainment Studies*, 1(2), (2010), pp. 78–92. Oakeley, Atholl, *Blue Blood on the Mat*, Chichester, Summersdale Publishers, 1996.

Phillips, Tom, '"Angry False-Teeth-Chattering Mayhem": Synecdochic Fandom, Representation and Performance in Mature Woman Fandom of British Professional Wrestling', in Paul Booth (ed.), *Wiley Companion to Media Fandom and Fan Studies*, Oxford, Wiley-Blackwell, 2017, pp. 227–241.

Polley, Martin, *Moving the Goalposts: A History of Sport Since 1945*, London, Routledge, 1998.

Potter, Jeremy, *Independent Television in Britain*, vol. 4: *Companies and Programmes, 1968–80*, London, Macmillan, 1990.

Potts, Archie, *Headlocks and Handbags: Wrestling at New St James's Hall*, Sunderland, Black Cat Publications, 2005.

Rickard, John, '"The Spectacle of Excess": The Emergence of Modern Professional Wrestling in the United States and Australia', *The Journal of Popular Culture*, 33(1), (1999), pp. 129–137.

Salmon, Catherine and Clerc, Susan, '"Ladies Love Wrestling, Too": Female Wrestling Fans Online', in Nicholas Sammond (ed.), *Steel Chair to the Head: The Pleasure and Pain of Professional Wrestling*, Durham, NC, Duke University Press, 2005.

Sendall, Bernard, *Independent Television in Britain*, vol. 1: *Origin and Foundation, 1946–62*, London, Macmillan, 1982.

Sheard, Kenneth Gordon, 'Boxing in the Civilising Process', unpublished doctoral thesis, Anglia Polytechnic, 1992.

Shefrin, Elana, '*Lord of the Rings, Star Wars*, and Participatory Fandom: Mapping New Congruencies Between the Internet and Media Entertainment Culture', *Critical Studies in Media Communication*, 21(3), (2004), pp. 261–281.

Snape, Robert, 'All-in Wrestling in Inter-War Britain: Science and Spectacle in Mass Observation's "Worktown"', *The International Journal of the History of Sport*, 30(12), (2013), pp. 1418–1435.

Stadel, Luke, 'Wrestling and Cinema, 1892–1911', *Early Popular Visual Culture*, 11(4), (2013), pp. 342–364.

Thompson, F.M.L., *The Rise of Respectable Society: A Social History of Victorian Britain, 1830–1900*, London, Fontana, 1988.

Thumim, Janet, *Inventing Television: Men, Women and the Box*, Oxford, Oxford University Press, 2004.

Whannel, Garry, *Fields in Vision: Television Sport and Cultural Transformation*, London, Routledge, 1992.

Williams, Rebecca, 'Good Neighbours? Fan/Producer Relationships and the Broadcasting Field', *Continuum*, 24(2), (2010), pp. 279–289.

Wrenn, Marion, 'Managing Doubt: Professional Wrestling Jargon and the Making of "Smart Fans"', in Craig Calhoun and Richard Sennett (eds), *Practicing Culture*, London, Routledge, 2007, pp. 149–170.

Wyke, Maria, 'Herculean Muscle!: The Classicizing Rhetoric of Bodybuilding', *Arion*, 4(3), (1997), pp. 51–79.

Chapter 4

Villains, blue-eyes and the melodrama of celebrity

In the early 1960s, a young Cassius Clay met the professional wrestler Gorgeous George at a radio station in Las Vegas. George was an immensely popular performer in the 1950s, taking advantage of burgeoning television technology to become immediately recognisable throughout America. Accompanied by a valet who sprayed perfume around the ring before the match, his bobby-pinned, bleach blonde hair jumped from the screens of half-tuned TV sets. Audiences both loved and hated George. According to his later retelling of that meeting, Clay's encounter with the grappler would be an important moment in helping to turn the boxer into the brash and cocky Muhammad Ali who mesmerised global audiences, boxing fan or non-boxing fan, in the 1960s, the 1970s and beyond. Though the details of that meeting change depending on the retelling, for Ali, one thing stood out:

> I saw a wrestler once named Gorgeous George and the place was jam packed with people. Cars just lined up for miles. They hated Gorgeous George, they wanted him beat. But they paid $100 for a ringside seat ... I got this from Gorgeous George. I said, 'That was a good idea. He's getting rich.' So I start talking. 'I am the greatest! I cannot be beat! I'm too pretty to be a fighter!'[1]

He is not the only sportsperson, pugilist or otherwise, to recognise the promotional attractions that 'hate' could generate. Whether in recurring figures like the 'diving foreigner' of association football or the downfall of formerly considered greats, sport is an arena in which rich narratives about heroes overcoming adversity, or villains cheating to secure a victory, are propagated.[2] Professional wrestling did not invent this model of reporting, but it is the one sport to have crystallised and institutionalised it as a dominant mode of storytelling, and one that other sports frequently look for inspiration in their narratives and framing.

This chapter begins by describing and then analysing the moral structure of wrestling, outlining the ways in which blue-eyes (or babyfaces) and villains (heels) create narrative structures. In so doing, it examines critical arguments about how stereotypes operate in professional wrestling before assessing existing arguments that professional wrestling can be understood through theatrical genres like morality plays or melodrama. Melodrama is hard to define in absolute terms, but it is a theatrical genre characterised by high emotions and embodiments of good and evil. Critiquing and then building on these arguments, the chapter suggests that professional wrestling can be read as melodramatic not because it serves as an extension of theatrical genres but because wrestlers are versions of celebrity, and all celebrity culture is an expression of a broader melodramatic mode. Celebrity, the chapter proposes, offers cultural spaces where the melodramatic mode is performed, where forms of representation provide flattened-out characters that come to stand for wider ethical forces.

To understand the relationship between melodrama and celebrity, the chapter examines the historical conditions in which they both emerge, and suggests that they are both responses to the fielding of society. Analysing commercial pugilists and the growth of professional wrestling, the chapter points towards the emergence of commercial popular culture in response to new industrial forms of production, and in turn the notion of performativity produced by urban and industrial living. It also describes the growth of the press, a key component in the expansion of both commercial culture and celebrity culture. In so doing, the chapter traces the history of personas and promotion in the boxing booths, theatres and other commercial popular cultures, and the ways in which pugilists and promoters developed star systems in tandem with the sporting press. From there, music hall entrepreneurs helped to further fictionalise and embellish these characters, ultimately leading to the form of quasi-fictionalised, highly performative professional wrestling personas of the twentieth century.

Though wrestling may seem outlandish and especially melodramatic, the chapter concludes by arguing that the form of celebrity in professional wrestling is indicative of much celebrity culture. Many fields and subfields have developed highly codified, invented, fictionalised or performed conventions around fame, comparable in many ways to professional wrestling. Wrestling, however, feels different, but this can be explained by the sport's intersections between sport and the stage. The chapter concludes with a discussion of kayfabe, the competing and often conflicting forms of fame operating in the theatrical and sporting fields, and the resistance from the mainstream (sporting) press to report on wrestling alongside other sports. Celebrities are rooted in the specific logics and structures of fields, and over time become naturalised. Examining celebrities and the histories of their emergence reveals the terrains, conflicts and compromises, and assessing the operation of fame in professional wrestling can reveal broader issues relating to contemporary celebrity culture.

The fans hate him more each time they buy a ticket

Mick McManus was one of British wrestling's most celebrated and long-standing performers. Whether in haranguing referees, executing low blows, headbutts or other illegal moves, brawling after the bell, or throwing competitors after the bell, McManus revelled in breaking rules in the 1960s and the 1970s. As one article described of him, he apparently sought, and was often successful, in making 'the fans hate him more each time they buy a ticket'.[3] McManus was an especially talented performer when it came to generating audience responses, but such antics will not be unfamiliar to those who have seen a wrestling match on either side of the Atlantic.

The defining narrative convention of professional wrestling is its moral structure. In the clear majority of contests, although notably not in *all* contests, drama is produced by 'good guys' wrestling 'bad guys'. In general terms, one wrestler is willing to cheat, is arrogant, disobeys the referee, and does all that they can to win, while the other pays close attention to the rules, is humble in both loss and defeat, and is respectful to all around them, including the audience, referees and other authority figures. Subcultural language, reflecting the theatrical and fairground roots of contemporary professional wrestling, refers to the very specific narrative forms outlined above. In American wrestling parlance, these types are described as (baby)faces and heels. In lucha libre, these types are described as *técnicos* and *rudos*. Though they essentially referred to the same roles and positions, British wrestling developed its own subcultural language during the twentieth century, instead preferring 'blue-eyes' and 'villains'.

For the blue-eye/villain dichotomy to operate, wrestlers should be easily identified: the roles of each participant, according to Barthes, 'expresses to excess the part which has been assigned to the contestant',[4] usually through costume, body language, engagement with audiences, or other clear markers. While this basic model helps structures the narratives, ultimately a range of colourful and memorable characters types have been utilised in the sport. Whether in Adrian Street's glitter and glam rock, Kendo Nagasaki's mysterious and orientalist masks, Ricki Starr's ballet dancing and pre-match pirouettes, Kung Fu, Catweazle (so-called because he looked like a wizard appearing on British children's television), nostalgia sites commemorating British professional wrestling have got a varied cast to choose from. In America, Britain, Mexico or Japan, characters usually adopt a stereotypical or archetypal identity, often from wider popular culture.

One of the clearest and most obvious character types, and often of delineating 'good' from 'bad', and indeed one that has drawn a good degree of critical examination, is 'foreign' wrestlers being positioned as villainous. For Jeffrey Mondak[5] and John W. Campbell,[6] albeit writing about the World Wrestling Federation (WWF) in the 1980s and 1990s, professional wrestling's reliance on stereotypes meant that they were guilty of using national and ethnic caricatures to distinguish their villains from the American heroes. Mondak goes so far to say that the WWF presented 'simplistic, xenophobic interpretation of international [politics]'.[7] Similar forms of representation can be identified in British professional wrestling. In 1930s Bolton, for example, one respondent for the MO described the villainous performers he enjoyed seeing, offering a snapshot of how popular culture and professional wrestling articulated wider political events and tensions: 'a German wrestler giving the "nazi" salute and getting the "raspberry" in return. "Ali Baba" taking out his mat and praying to "Allah"'.[8] When wrestling became a television attraction, it was often these stereotypes that played out on *World of Sport* on ITV on a Saturday afternoon, negotiating Britain's post-colonial legacies in highly dramatized form.[9] As one article explained, professional wrestling featured an array of colourful characters, often exhibiting stereotypical personas of 'Russians, Japs, Greeks, Americans, dressed up in skullcaps, monkey capes, multi-coloured dressing gowns, feathers... anything for a laugh or a snarl'.[10] Similarly, a description by Kent Walton of Sheik El Mansour captured a central appeal of many of these wrestlers: 'a truly exotic figure'.[11] Characters abounded that fit this model: Masambula, who entered the ring wearing the fur of a tiger, performed as an African witch-doctor. Johnny Kwango was described as having 'boiled-egg eyes and "lethal" nut'.[12] Other representations included Zando Zabo, the 'wrestling gypsy'; and Billy Two Rivers, the Native American with full ceremonial headdress. Needless to say, such representations fed on and perpetuated racist and orientalist caricatures, but as discussed in the following sections we can partly see professional wrestling as offering intensified values of ideologies prevalent in broader sporting cultures and society.

Because professional wrestling exists in a universe replete with moral dichotomies, and where 'good' and 'evil' are apparently personified, much critical attention has seen it as an extension of theatrical genres. Two especially prominent suggestions are that wrestling can be positioned as either a 'contemporary' reincarnation of a (medieval) morality play or, somewhat more convincingly, theatrical melodrama. Descriptions of wrestling as a morality play, whether in passing or as a cornerstone of study, can be found in analyses across much academic engagement with the sport.[13] Henricks' argument provides a summary of how such arguments are normally presented, claiming that the sport is an 'exaggerated morality play fervently manipulating the prejudices of its audiences as quickly as it could perceive them'.[14] Rooted in medieval cultures, morality plays offered religious and moral lessons to their audiences.

Beyond the simplistic description of how audiences engage with wresting, the problem with Henrick's reading, and others like this, is that they fail to address the form, function and, most critically, context in which both medieval morality plays and professional wrestling exist. Such accounts are mostly based on a thin description of the events almost entirely predicated on the fact that both contain condensed and performative tales around 'morality'. So, too, do Hollywood films, soap operas, pop songs, novels and a swathe of contemporary cultural items, but comparisons to the reasonably obscure performance tradition are less forthcoming, and would raise further critiques and questions about the context in which they are performed. Important questions, furthermore, are left unaddressed: do wrestling promoters deliberately seek inspiration from morality plays, or can we track a development from one to the other in the same manner we can track inspirations from the music hall or circus stage?

Comparisons to melodrama are easier understood and much more convincing. At the forefront of such arguments, and certainly the most comprehensive and most influential, is Henry Jenkins' essay, 'Never Trust a Snake'. Writing about the World Wrestling Federation in the early 1990s, he describes how:

> Wrestling, like conventional melodrama, externalises emotion, mapping it onto the combatant's body and transforming their physical competition into a search for moral order. Restraint or subtlety has little place in such a world. Everything that matters must be displayed, publicly, unambiguously, and unmercilessly.[15]

For Jenkins, (WWF) wrestling combines the codes and conventions of sport and fuses them to the 'personal, social, and moral conflicts that characterized nineteenth-century theatrical melodrama'.[16] Professional wrestling, therefore, moves from a domestic setting to the public setting, often stressing conflicts around work, and because of this wrestling can be considered a masculine melodrama. Chapter 5 will also examine the ways in which 'masculine melodrama' has been utilised in other studies of sports.

There is much merit to Jenkins' work, especially when we consider the sheer theatricality of his case study, early 1990s American wrestling. More readily understandable than discussions of medieval morality plays, however, there still arises similar problems with straight comparisons. Is it possible to trace a history of this genre to the squared circle of the WWF, and to what extent does the sport take influence from melodramatic novels or plays? Such challenges are invariably left undiscussed, and beyond a few prize-fighters performing in melodramatic theatrical productions, there is little evidence to suggest that wrestling promoters or wrestlers themselves were taking inspiration from such texts. Such questioning could be considered unfair, and I do not want to detract from an otherwise important and engaging essay that has been a cornerstone for much analysis of professional wrestling. Yet such interrogation does point towards some of the difficulties in seeking to place cultural forms squarely in aesthetic or generic traditions, particularly when we consider the importance of fields in structuring meanings, historical development and reception of cultural texts.

The main issue here, of course, is the malleability of the word melodrama. In both everyday parlance and broader critical thinking 'melodrama' serves a dual purpose. On the one hand, it refers to a very specific set of codes and conventions located in the late eighteenth- and nineteenth-century literary genres, with some clear continuities in contemporary film and television, often encompassing:

> [S]trong emotion, both pathetic and potentially tragic, low comedy, romantic colouring, remarkable events in an exciting and suspenseful plot, physical sensations, sharply delineated stock characters, domestic sentiment, domestic

settings and domestic life, love, joy, suffering, morality, the reward of virtue and the punishment of vice.[17]

On the other hand, melodrama serves as a broad description for many things loosely structured around these same ideas, chiefly notions of strong emotion, morality, and remarkable events. One way of uniting these two positions is to think about what Peter Brooks describes as the melodramatic mode, where melodrama is conceived both as a genre but also as 'as a mode of conception and expression'.[18] Drawing on Brooks, a swathe of cultural historians and theorists have identified this 'mode' in many cultural forms and articulations. Seeking to categorize such thinking, Rohan McWilliam has gone so far as to suggest that postmodern, cultural history has undergone a 'melodramatic turn'.[19] Elaine Hadley, at the forefront of this turn, suggests that melodrama plays 'a significant role, along with other appearances of the melodramatic mode (in politics, journalism, and the novel) in the formation of modern culture'.[20] The emphasis on forms of literary or journalistic representation, and then the relationship between the two cultural forms, is key to understanding the melodramatic mode. During the eighteenth and nineteenth centuries, the period in which the melodramatic mode emerged, newspapers represented public figures from a range of fields, indicative of what Nick Couldry describes as media's 'meta capital'.[21] In these representations, as we will see in further detail shortly, individuals were turned into fictionalized and invented characters, stripping them of intersecting coordinates, contexts and nuances and turning them into melodramatic characters. These are also the same processes in which systems of stardom and fame emerged. Central to the ubiquity of the melodramatic mode, then, was the emergence of what we might broadly call 'celebrity culture' in the eighteenth and nineteenth centuries, and the role of the press is key in melodrama's ubiquity. Understanding how celebrity operates in professional wrestling, and then understanding celebrity culture more broadly as the exemplar expression of the melodramatic mode, are key to making sense of the sport.

Certainly, a variety of authors have argued that versions of melodrama operate across fame. Stars and celebrities of contemporary culture 'embody ethical forces',[22] stimulate 'debates about fundamental moral and social issues'[23] and operate via a 'repertoire of melodrama'.[24] After talking to fans of contemporary gossip magazines, Joke Hermes concludes that readers take pleasure from reading about celebrity's marriages, affairs, divorces, and all the other turns of fortune, because 'there is also a deep sense that the world is unjust', when celebrities are experiencing misfortune audiences can speculate about 'cosmic (rather than political) justice taking its toll'.[25] Because sport often places competitions between local groups or nations (or individuals representing nations), or because sport offers a space in which competitions between races and ethnicities are foregrounded, the moral discussions that circulate around sportspeople are especially fruitful for thinking about melodrama.

Garry Whannel, in the most serious examination of sport stars and moralities, has described the ways in which sporting celebrities have often been infused with 'discourses of moral censure'.[26] These are very precisely how celebrities in professional wrestling are constructed, and reveals that professional wrestling offers a type of melodramatic mode that exists across all contemporary culture.

Less analysed is the historical relationship between celebrity and melodrama, an historical relationship in which the melodramatic mode and celebrity culture grew from the same fundamental social, economic and cultural conditions. Peter Brooks suggests that melodrama 'expresses the anxiety brought by a frightening new world in which the traditional patterns of moral order no longer provide the necessary social glue',[27] and celebrities express those same anxieties. A whole swathe of interconnected changes can be identified as underscoring both the expansion of both melodrama and celebrity cultures: the growth of industrialism, the subdivision of labour, and with it the development of private and public dichotomies; the decline in power of traditional institutions like the monarchy and the court and the church; the expansion of a commodity culture; expansions in urban living, and with it the threat of crowds, expressed most explicitly in the French Revolution.[28] In short, the fielding of society, and attempts to deal with new power structures and struggles, identities and expressions of self that emerge from these transformations. The very material and structural changes from which modernity emerges change the way we feel about ourselves and each other, and celebrity and melodrama are fundamentally and foundationally fused.

Rather than seeing professional wrestling as being a continuation of melodrama in simple, theatrical terms, or using melodrama as a broad description of all things emotional and moralistic in their storytelling, then, articulations of melodramatic sensibilities can be found across a wide variety of cultural subfields and their celebrities, and this includes professional wrestling. In other words, while it does not defend or justify the stereotypes perpetuated, if sporting celebrities often serve as lightning rods for tensions and desires around nationality and race, then professional wrestling did the same. Professional wrestlers, however, were stripped of all nuance and complexities of character, usually built in intensive paratextual networks of representation, that often accompany sporting stars. The types of characters in professional wrestling operated as a condensed and intensified type of celebrity culture, but one that could be identified across many cultural forms, and built into a very specific set of historical conditions.

Intensity is difficult to measure, though, and a more complex analysis can be offered. The form of celebrities that emerged in wrestling existed across competing fields, and have often struggled with the competing demands of theatrical, television and sporting celebrity. While all celebrities exist as part of the melodramatic mode, the form of the melodramatic sensibility expressed in, say, contemporary politics is clearly different to that expressed in sport. Just as economic changes are experienced differently in different fields, so too are the expressions of the melodramatic mode. Sensibilities are not expressed uniformly, but are instead expressed in the specific structures and representational logics of fields. A field's logics are rooted in historical conditions that mask those structures. Analysing professional wrestling historically, and its intersection, conflicts and compromises, reveals the competing logics and codes and conventions of intersecting fields.

A national concern

The eighteenth century was ripe for the birth of celebrity culture, and to understand the characters of contemporary professional wrestling we need to return to the boxing booths of that century. Celebrity cultures are rooted in changes to commercial cultures, and the prize-fighting venues of the early eighteenth century demonstrate some of the earliest examples of these shifts. Many of the codes and conventions of professional wrestling today can be traced to these shifts, particularly in the way identities and morals were perpetuated in these newly formed commercial sporting arenas. In the following section, we will see how these conditions produced a form of melodramatic celebrity. First, though, it is important to see how embryonic celebrity, roughly between 1700 and 1780, grew. Commercialised boxing venues expanded from the existing London bear gardens – informal animal baiting meets supplemented by other human blood sports – that had been a semi-institutionalised quasi-carnival entertainment throughout much of the early modern period. Figg's Amphitheatre opened in 1724, and appears to have been the first venue dedicated solely to prize-fighting. The opening was closely followed by Stokes' Amphitheatre in 1726.

A key way of assessing the commercial differences between the bear gardens and amphitheatres is to look at the changes in promotion. For the bear gardens, the primary form of communication was performance day processions through the surrounding area. Although this was much to the annoyance of some residents, their irritation has left us with a vivid description. In 1701, a presentment of the grand jury in Middlesex described what preceded these performances:

> We having observed the late boldness of a sort of men that stile themselves masters of the noble science of defence, passing through this city with beat of drums, colours displayed, swords drawn, with a numerous company of people following them, dispersing their printed bills, thereby inviting persons to be spectators of those inhuman sights which are directly contrary to the practice and profession of the Christian religion ... we think ourselves obliged to represent this matter, that some method may be speedily taken to prevent their passage through the city in such a tumultuous manner, on so unwarrantable a design.[29]

Processions retained the colour and noise of festival culture. They were clearly designed to garner attention and attract audiences, but their reach was limited.

Processions, after all, could only attract those within the immediate vicinity. The blossoming newspaper business, however, had influence across the whole city, and in some cases, the country. As the press grew, small notes promoting the forthcoming fights at the bear gardens became prominent in the classified advertisement pages, replacing the procession through the city as the primary form of promotion. One early advertisement, with the text likely a word-for-word copy of the handbills handed out on the processions, declared:

> This present Tuesday, being the 26th of September, will be perform'd (at His majesty's Bear Garden in Hockley in the Hole) a trial of skill, between John Anderson the Famous highlander, and John Terrewest of Oundle in North-Hamptonshire, at all the usual weapons.[30]

Compared to what advertisements were to become, the tone is subdued. The names are listed, as is one hometown, but otherwise there is little information to be taken. There is certainly no sense of personal resentment between the two men. The colour of the event itself – the blood, costume, characters and drama – is absent. The mushrooming of the popular press is one of the eighteenth century's defining characteristics, and the venues took advantage. In the early 1720s one newspaper advertisement for a prize-fight at the Bear Garden read:

> Whereas I Edward Sutton, pipe-maker, from Gravesend in the county of Kent, Master of the noble Science of Defence, thinking myself to be the most Celebrated master of the noble Science of Defence, thinking myself to be the most Celebrated Master of that kind in Europe, hearing the famous James Figg, who is call'd the Oxfordshire Champion, has the character to be the onliest Master in the World, do fairly invite him to meet me, and exercise at the usual Weapons fought on the stage, desiring no favour from the hero's hand, and not question in the least but to give such satisfaction, that has not been given for some years past by that Champion. I, James Figg, from Thame in Oxfordshire, Master of the Said Science, will not fail to meet this celebrated Master, at the place and time appointed; and to his request of no favour, I freely grant it, for I never did, nor will show any to no man living, and doubt not but I shall convince him of his own brave opinion.[31]

The challenge and acceptance that had been used on the stages of the bear gardens and transferred to the press in the early decades of the century, but now utilised a greater range of promotional hyperbole and ballyhoo. Viewers of contemporary wrestling will recognise, moreover, the repetition and dramatization of these 'promos'.[32] In the above, Sutton is convinced of his superiority where Figg implies his challenger is arrogant and egotistical: the contests operated 'within the framework of challenges issued and accepted, with manliness, strength and courage held to be as much at issue as fighting skill'.[33] Honour was used as a device to generate interest in the reading and listening public, and if 'the build-up could give an impression of rancour between the fighters it was likely to whet more appetites and increase the takings'.[34] The added spice of rivalry that the promoters constructed in the press successfully maximised the profits of the promoters and pugilists, who benefited financially from larger attendances.

An easy way of generating promotional frisson was in the performance of local and national identities, though sports performers representing wider identities was not necessarily new. Organised combat sports throughout the medieval and early-modern period drew on the wider identities of the competitors. During the carnivals in which wrestling contests took place, fights between men were pregnant with intense symbolism and meaning. Indeed, long before wrestling became a theatrical attraction on the sawdust stages of the London halls, the theatrical quality of pugilism had been noted by observers. In the records of wrestling meetings in the pre-industrial villages of England during festival periods of celebration, the matches often deliberately incorporated images of the theatrical, at least to outsiders. Richard Carew noted the proceedings of a typical fight:

> For performing this play, the beholders cast themselves in a ring, which they call making a place; into the empty middle space whereof the two champion wrestlers step forth, stripped into their doublets and hosen, and untrussed, that they may so the better command the use of their limbs, and first shaking hands in token of friend ship, they fall presently to the effects of anger; for each striveth how to take hold of the other, with his best advantage, and to bear his adverse party down.[35]

In the performance of wrestling, the participants played characters that transcended their individual self. Like the carnival more broadly, gendered, working or local identities were embellished or exaggerated. Wrestling matches, for instance, provided an outlet for local rivalries, and competitions were often fought between villages. In other instances, prize-fights were fought between men of different trades.[36]

The earliest promoters in the newly formed commercial sporting cultures recognised that such performance of identities and rivalries were a core attraction for spectators in such events, and, using the press, they sought to amplify these identities further. In 1725, Figg's advertised a fight between an Italian, the 'Venetian Gondolier', and an Englishman, Whitacre. The prospect of the international fight created huge interest in the press and presumably the reading public. Figg and those involved in the fight further encouraged this speculation in inventive ways. There even appears to have been an early form of 'press conference' conducted at a local coffee-house with the sole intention of stoking further gossip in the papers, encouraging higher ticket prices, and generally promoting Figg and his enterprise:

The combatants have had an interview, when the English Champion took the Italian by the hand, and invited him to one bout for love (as he termed it) before-hand; but he declined it. In a word, the publick daily enter into this affair with so much passion for the event, and gentlemen are so warm on both sides, that it looks like a national concern.[37]

The notion of a 'national concern' is important, and would remain so throughout pugilism promotion in the coming centuries. Newspapers reported the happenings of an individual sporting star to a much large audience than the small numbers in attendance at an event. Increasingly, an 'imagined community' of nation,[38] and some London papers clearly had a national readership in mind, could keep up-to-date with the activities of individuals who they had likely never met. In Francesco Alberoni's influential account, celebrity exists when 'each individual member of the public knows the star, but the star does not know any individuals'.[39] This is perhaps a simplification, because it is not a requirement for the entire public to recognise a performer, but for a field or social circle to be sufficiently large that an individual can be recognised by most within it, beyond the village or local context. Some of the prize-fighters of the period appear to have partly met this definition. Newspaper reports and advertisements would have reached some households across England. Their fame, moreover, had surpassed simply those who had witnessed fights first hand. A poem by John Byrom claimed of Figg, 'To the towns, far and near, did his valour extend, And swam down the river from *Thame* to *Gravesend*.'[40] We might be critical of Byrom's reasons for extolling Figg, but his poem may have been attempting to capture a particular historical moment where fame was being distributed across the country with help from the press.

Just as newspapers were indicative of the commercial culture that was growing around them, many theories of celebrity posit that 'celebrity culture is irrevocably bound up with commodity culture'.[41] A subject's marketability is the moment that marks modern celebrity: 'the point at which a public person becomes a celebrity is the point at which a sufficiently large audience is interested in their actions, image and personality to create a viable market for commodities carrying their likeness'.[42] Celebrities, then, are products in themselves as well as being used as a selling point in order to attract paying audiences to a particular entertainment. One of the reasons the amphitheatres developed when they did may have been because of the increasing attraction to named individuals rather than the broader appeal of animal baiting. Celebrities were also devices to sell newspapers, periodicals and pamphlets. Finally, celebrities' images were used to create and sell merchandise for other products destined for the market. In the eighteenth-century prints commemorating various sporting occasions and sporting celebrities were being produced by various entrepreneurs,[43] not least by the sportsmen themselves. On 19 January 1731, newspapers were advertising the publication of:

The Stage Gladiators: A Clear Stage and No Favour, with the effigies of the Champions curiously engraven on copper. Printed for Messieurs Figg and Sutton, and sold by the Pamphlet-mongers of London and Westminster. Price 6d.[44]

These goods are important precisely because they indicate the complexities that society and the economy were undergoing at this period, and the centrality of celebrity culture in such changes. Such items had been produced utilising new industrial and labour techniques, and a market was created partly because both the working and middle classes had an increase in money to spend on such items. These new working conditions, moreover, created a growing demand for regular forms of commercialised and professionalised entertainment, adapting from being a predominantly local carnival culture to a professionalised, commercialised and national popular culture. In general terms, the prize-fighting amphitheatres served as a pivot from the carnival cultures of the early modern period, described in Chapter 1, to the professionalised entertainments of the industrial revolutions, including the growth of circus, theatres and commercial sports. These broader social and economic changes, however, also created tensions, and celebrities came to be central in articulating those anxieties.

Slang-whang reporters

By the final quarter of the eighteenth century, fame had become a dominant promotional technique in Britain's commercial popular cultures (see Chapter 1). Building on the forms of promotion in the early commercialised boxing venues, the importance of established names in these venues was critical. From 1800, theatrical star salaries demonstrated, 'a dramatic upward movement quite out of proportion to other theatrical earnings'.[45] In towns and cities, popular boxers were met by fans eager to see the performer they had read about. Daniel Mendoza, whose trilogy of fights with Richard Humphreys between 1788 and 1790 marked him as an especially popular fighter, recorded how fame operated:

> [A]n occurrence happened, which will serve to shew the popularity I at that time possessed. The inhabitants, having, by some means, gained information of my being in the chaise, surrounded us, on our entrance in the town, in such numbers, that we were actually prevented from proceeding on our journey, till after Sir Thomas had addressed them, and proposed that in order to gratify their curiosity, we should stand for some time on one of the benches in the market place.[46]

The expansion of star systems can be partly explained by changes in the media field. While the early newspapers outlined in the above section were important for establishing celebrity in the boxing amphitheatres, they did not have the form or content to be described as a full sporting press. Newspapers were restricted to advertisements or occasional treatises or political opinion pieces. Aware of this, resourceful prize-fighters used advertisements as shop windows, celebrating individuals and in their own way conjuring stories about heroic individuals. Advertisements referred to previous matches and on-going rivalries, with the presumption that audiences would be familiar with such accounts. In nearly all the advertisements for the various amphitheatres there is an acknowledgement – sometimes implicit, sometimes explicit – that readers had already heard about those taking part. In so doing, this early form of the press turned fighters into celebrities, and as celebrities they could stand in for wider identities, but regular and dedicated descriptions detailing the match as it took place were wholly absent, and bibliographical anecdotes were practically non-existent.

Between 1790 and 1840, a spate of dedicated sporting periodicals, or at the very least periodicals with a heavily skewed interest in sport, were published, including *The Sporting Magazine* (1792) and *Bell's Life in London and Sporting Chronicle* (1822). Magazines and newspapers helped to disseminate the commercial sporting culture to growing national audiences: rules were written down and distributed, and histories, results and forthcoming events were recorded. Betting hints were given, and events, products and tickets advertised and promoted.[47] In these reports, albeit building on the types of promotion found earlier in the century, sporting celebrities were cemented. From the 1780s, magazines and newspapers featured 'vivid accounts of boxing matches ... particularly with the development of a star system round boxers such as Mendoza'.[48]

The establishment of fields also helps explain the emergence of celebrity. Before the industrial revolutions, social roles and tasks had more fluidity, with individuals moving between forms of production and leisure, with boundaries between work and leisure less clearly demarcated. Wrestlers participating in earlier folk forms of the sport would have retained other social roles, particularly as labourers. Winners of wrestling matches would often win a prize, perhaps an animal or some gold or silver.[49] Social standing in the local community, furthermore, was an important attraction for those taking part. Malcolmson claims that 'sports provided channels for gaining personal recognition. In fact, they were among the few kinds of opportunities which labouring men had to perform publicly for the esteem of their peers.'[50] In Cumberland, an archive note suggests, 'villages had their local champions and it was custom for the new champion after winning at one of these brideswains to parade to Church next Sunday decked in the long decorated leather belt'.[51] Critically, however, wrestlers were still ensconced within their local community and, while enjoying some of the benefits of renown, the performers were not separate from the rest of the village or town. Even the most talented wrestler had to work the same jobs, and had access to the same opportunities, as those around him.

Where prize-fighters in Figg's often retained their everyday employment, from the eighteenth century onwards many prize-fighters performed full-time, fighting, training and entertaining, touring the nation's newly created theatres, circuses and fairgrounds. As social and economic fields emerged, then, individual's roles and positions became defined by the jobs they were expected to undertake, and thus positioned more firmly in that specific field. For a select few, those positions were in the sporting and cultural fields. For many others, their positions were as workers drawn into the industrialising cities and subjected to more explicit time-work discipline with sharper boundaries drawn between work and leisure. In these conditions, interests or skills not relevant to their primary tasks became secondary. In terms of sport and other forms of entertainment, fighters could take up full employment in the commercialising popular cultures, but by default that left other audience members excluded, drawing sharper distinctions between performer and audience who is 'present at, shares in, but does not act'.[52]

The industrial labour conditions that commercial popular cultures developed alongside also produced key changes to how contemporary life was experienced. Where work increasingly lay beyond the boundaries of the home, living in cities widened the number of social circles and fields that people existed in. Individuals developed discrete 'masks' that were performed across different fields and social contexts, creating tensions between public and private lives.[53] Amidst the expansion of anonymous, urban living, melodrama in all its forms explicitly dramatised this new social life, hinting at the conflicts between public and private lives. Operating across multiple fields and social circles explains the 'raw material of [domestic] melodrama' seen on the stage, because working in industrial sectors meant that the home had to be a site of redemption, but could never relieve the alienation of working life.[54] The melodramatic mode, moreover, echoed the conflicts (and to a lesser extent the compromises) of fielding society, played out in everyday life via the imagined subject positions seen in Chapter 3. If everyday life is characterised by ongoing conflicts and compromises, seeking to establish or sustain one's own social position, such conflicts were captured in the melodrama of celebrity. Finally, the tension of performativity is also central to the melodramatic mode. The types of heightened performances seen in melodramatic novels and plays expressed the pressures of individuals developing performances for public life. All of these anxieties were expressed particularly in the celebrity cultures that were emerging at this time, and continue to be reflected in today's systems of fame.

Performativity was central to newspaper reporting, and celebrities, with their own intense performances of public and private life, both eased and exacerbated these tensions. In some regards, representations of celebrities in the press helped to manage the public/private dichotomy by bridging the gap between public and private in their reporting of celebrities. A key feature of sporting magazines, for example, was to supplement information about fights with 'personal' information about the competitors. Newspaper biographies were supplemented by the appearance and subsequent growth of sporting (auto) biographies. In 1816, the *Memoirs of the Life of Daniel Mendoza* offered a tone and narrative that would be recognisable in many modern sports autobiographies, cataloguing childhood difficulties and later triumphs.[55] These forms of autobiography attempted to create a coherent narrative that aligned the public and private identities that existed across multiple fields and social circles.

Attempts to 'humanise' celebrities, however, were often dwarfed by articles that fictionalised those they were reporting about. Newspapers frequently embellished the 'public' character to the point where 'private' persona was masked or even erased. In so doing, readers engaged with public figures as a type of mythologised, fictional text. A classic example of this reporting was 'the Queen Caroline affair'. At the Prince Regent's coronation, prize-fighters, including Mendoza, were hired as pages with the explicit order to keep out Queen Caroline. The Queen Caroline affair freely borrowed conventions of theatrical melodrama, writing about the Queen 'as if she were a fictional character'.[56] In so doing, individuals were turned into flattened-out 'characters' in keeping with the sorts of characters from the stage or novel. With the press turning individuals into 'characters', then, those characters were imbued with the melodramatic mode.

Sports reports from the period are a particularly good example of this. A typical report set the scene, described in detail the location and the crowd; explained fighters' colourful entrances, detailed their costumes, their interactions with the audience; and recorded clearly invented inner monologues and insights, generously littered stylistic subcultural language that folded readers into that world.[57] Just as 'theatrical entertainment focused on variety and spectacle', then the press imitated this style and 'in *Boxiana*-style reports'.[58] Pierce Egan, at the forefront of such writing, often exaggerated and embellished pugilists, describing the boxers 'in dramatic, fictionalized terms, elevating them to immortal status'.[59] Newspaper descriptions emphasised any hint 'of nobility of character in the pugilist' which was then 'lauded to the skies'.[60] Grandstanding was reflected in the names that the press christened fighters: 'The Gasman, the Wheeler Black Diamond, Master of the Rolls, Colonel, Blackee, Massa and African'.[61] Jon Bee's wonderfully titled dictionary of slang explained that such grandiloquent names were often 'put upon them by the slang-whang reporters, who, when a new man appears, inquire "what name he will go by?"'[62] John Ford, reflecting on this in 1971, accurately commented that these traditions had been passed on to professional wrestling in the twentieth century.[63]

In an intensified melodramatic mode of reporting, prize-fighters almost always embodied ethical characteristics or stood in for wider political tensions. As with all celebrities, they served in 'facilitating identifications, channelling desires, defining relations within a community, proscribing behaviours and legitimating values'.[64] Writing on celebrity and stardom posits that a celebrity can refract 'instabilities, ambiguities and contradictions'.[65] Fights and fighters served as lightning rods for wider social tensions around gender, nation, race and class. They often stood in for the national or racial identities they represented, channelling desires or anxieties,[66] or reassured audiences that strong and dominant masculinity existed in a world of industrialism and commercialism.[67] When prize-fighters performed their theatrical and circus sparring tours (see Chapter 1), they were performing these already exaggerated melodramatic characters which were then further embellished by the conventions of the stage. A newspaper report from 1836 described a wrestling performance of Cornish, Devonshire, and Cumbrian wrestling at the Pantheon theatre. It captures the way representations of race and local identity, so regularly performed in the pages of the press, were then re-performed and caricatured on the stage for paying audiences.

> Jack Adams danced a Highland fandango, in regular costume, during the evening; and that Sambo Sutton did a little pankey punkey business, by dancing on his head, and beating time with his feet. A female in the pit was so delighted with the extraordinary agility of the Black, that she rose from her set, and exclaimed, 'Here's sixpence, my lad!'[68]

By the mid-nineteenth century, prize-fighting had developed into a commercial sport with a complex promotional system. Out of the carnival cultures in which fighters represented their villages, pugilists now represented complex intersections of identities around nation and race, and these were shot through with melodramatic reporting and embellished, sometimes fictionalised, accounts of public life. Fighters then performed versions of these characters to the paying publics in the commercial entertainments around the industrial urban centres. Professional wrestling on the music hall stage continued these traditions, but then added further theatrical embellishments to these characteristics.

A splendid showman

Professional wrestling's emergence on the music hall stage can be attributed to showpeople's continuation of older models of performance. Entrepreneurs like P.T. Barnum displayed an acute understanding of how to create local, national and international publicity to further their own or their performers' celebrity, whipping national and regional newspapers into a frenzy, spreading gossip and intrigue. By the turn of the twentieth century, further improvements in printing techniques and distribution allowed for the growth of daily commercial tabloids in the 1880s, the 1890s and the 1900s. Newspapers continued the gossip of earlier papers, but further established codes and conventions of reporting politics, crime, entertainment and sport, and their associated celebrity. Other advances in communication technologies, particularly photography and cinema,[69] changed the intimacy and recognition of celebrities the public had with performers.

Promoters implicitly understood the role of the press in distributing fame. When the impresario C.B. Cochran began managing Georg Hackenschmidt, a moment important to wrestling's development to performed entertainment (see

Chapter 2), one of his earliest acts was secure an article in the *Daily Mail* entitled 'Is Great Strength Genius?'[70] The gushing piece, noting Hackenschmidt's body and good grace, served as a feature-length advertisement. 'Take such a man as Georges Hackenschmidt now appearing at the Tivoli Music Hall,' the article chimed, 'He shows you natural born strength in all its wonderful supremacy.'[71] Other examples of professional wrestlers utilising new communication technologies could be found. Some of the earliest films featured performed boxing exhibitions, and films of wrestling throughout the period were distributed around the world.

On the music hall stage, different skills were emphasised. Wrestlers developed a range of entertaining skills (like strongman or early strongman routines, witty patter, or sideshow performances) that could be drawn upon. It was also in this period that the blue-eye/villain model of promotion was developed, with touring wrestling troupes usually having a wrestler who could antagonise the audience (by abusing the referee or insulting the crowd) before ultimately being defeated in an exhibition match. These promotional techniques extended into legitimate sporting contests. A wrestler's success was as much about their ability to garner support or antagonise the public than merely athleticism. Reflecting on Zbysco's talents, for example, Cochran suggests:

> The British hated [Zbysco] as cordially as they liked Hackenschmidt. Nevertheless he was a great drawing card. Whereas they came with the hope of seeing Hackenschmidt win, they came hoping to see Zbysco beaten. He was a splendid showman, and gave the public exactly what they wanted.[72]

In some regards, the most successful professional wrestlers of the period were not necessarily the most athletically gifted or those with the ability to garner the most wins. Values more in keeping with the stage, like embodying and expressing characterisations, entertaining audiences, and gaining press reaction, became more valued than the amateur ideal prevalent in the sporting and athletic field. Wrestling promoters adopted many of the promotional techniques more familiar in the theatrical fields.

Building on the ways that celebrities had become quasi-fictionalised melodramatic characters in the sporting press, showpeople embellished and then crystallised these melodramatic characteristics, both on the stage but also in the private lives of performers. Here, there was an understanding that 'private lives' structured an audience's relationship with the performer on the stage, but they also recognised that private lives could be fictionalised and embellished to create further public interest.[73] Actresses like Adah Isaacs Menken utilised, for instance, the newly forming public relations industry to spread rumours about marriages, divorces, and relationships that blurred the boundary of fiction and reality, creating a public figure that was an 'invented character'.[74] Likewise, P.T. Barnum recognised that celebrity was defined by an interest in performers' private lives, but he also recognised that private lives could be fictionalised and embellished in order to create further public interest. Audiences took great pleasure in debates about where private and public persona met. In so doing, celebrities displayed the marks of melodrama, and dramatised and eased many of the anxieties of the day.

Thinking about 'invented characters', and the role of theatrical entrepreneurs in these inventions, is a useful way of analysing the changes that happened to professional wrestling cultures between 1890 and the 1920s, and it is perhaps no great surprise that Barnum and other showpeople were influential in these developments. Where reporters earlier in the century had been eager to fictionalise and embellish melodramatic characters in prize-fighting, and then prize-fighters had toured these identities in the theatres, promoters took the lead in developing those characters for the press to distribute. William Brady, for example, a theatrical showman and wrestling promoter in America, explained how he used costume and characters to construct theatrical meanings:

> To replace his ragged clothes I took him to a theatrical costumer's and laid in the fanciest Turkish costume money could buy – red turban, baggy green, gold-laced jacket, fez and all the rest of it ... The reporters had been duly tipped off to be on hand and the next morning the Terrible Turk – my new nickname for him – was on every front page in the country.[75]

Other examples from this period abound: Madrali wore a 'long heavy fur coat and a Turkish fez'[76] and Ali Hassan wore a turban, dark eye make-up and a cape. Thereafter, photographs of various performer in their 'national dress' were circulated in newspapers and magazines. Likewise, photographs of The Great Gama displayed him standing on the hide of a leopard carrying a gada (an Indian ceremonial mace).[77] With the help of costume, characterisation, promotional photos, press conferences, staged events, and a variety of other puffery techniques from the fairground, promoters and fighters established celebrity personas for wrestlers that would be carried into both legitimate competitions and music hall shows alike. By the 1930s, these 'invented characters' had become the dominant model of promotion, with wrestlers adopting outlandish personas removed from the notion of the 'real' person.

As these costumes demonstrate, and like prize-fights earlier in the century, professional wrestling characters on the music hall stage often served as a conduit for broader anxieties and pleasures around race and ethnicity. Professional wrestling promoters, and we should remember that Charles Cochran also managed Harry Houdini, who frequently used such imagery,[78] clearly took influence from these fashionable Orientalist images popular elsewhere on the stage. Orientalised imagery had a long history on Western stages, and in these performances, 'the stereotypical, orientalist British perspective upon the East or Orient was not particularly discerning and rarely respected national, cultural, or geographical boundaries'.[79] The press, too, were clear in the pleasures these might offer their audiences. When the Gama, 'the champion wrestler of the punjab', visited England in 1910 he fought the American Dr. B.F. Roller, an ex-American footballer. *The Times* hoped the match 'would throw some light on the question much discussed of late years, of the relative merits of the Oriental physique and that of the Occidental strong man'. Building on the performance of local, and then national, identities that wrestling and prize-fighting presented, wrestling offered a further consolidation of pleasures that sport channelled. Promoters and wrestlers worked in tandem to create invented characters that provided a form of celebrity that stripped away the nuances and complexities of individuals, leaving a vivid character. Race and ethnicity offered a simple way of delineating fighters whom the public were encouraged to support or reject, and in some ways offered a theatricalised version of the types of pleasures seen in all sports, which allowed for the performance of 'emotional intensity and … acute feelings of community and identity'.[80]

While it would be too simplistic to suggest that there was a clear dividing line where foreigners were simply awarded the villainous role (after all, Hackenschmidt was billed as the Russian Lion), many wrestling narratives continued to position 'foreign' as villainous. The sheer number of Terrible Turks and Terrible Greeks in Britain, France and America is telling, and often the two forms of villainy – Otherness and cheating – intersected and interacted. In a match between Zbysco and Suliman in 1908, newspapers were duly informed about the tendency of Turkish wrestlers to spread themselves in grease before the match. Cochran later stated, most likely writing with a smile, '[I] insisted that the contestants should have a warm bath in the theatre before taking to the mat.'[81] The contestants were given that bath the day of the match, much to the delight of the press. A few days after the fight, however, *The Sporting Life* ran an exposé on the match, claiming the fight was fixed, bathing was only a publicity stunt, and the wrestlers were corrupt. The reaction is worth quoting at length:

> Here are two foreign wrestlers hoaxing the British public as it has not been hoaxed for many a long day. There were challenges and counter challenges, affected quarrels, threatened breaking off of negotiations, meetings at the *Sportsman* office, the deposit of money on behalf of Mr. 'Constantin Papiani,' who does not exist, charges of skin-greasing, and to crown it all, hot water baths for the two friends who were soon to be in each other's deadly embrace … While we admit to the humour of the situation, we cannot shut our eyes to the seriousness of the matter, and we ask, how long is the generous-hearted supporter of wrestling to be imposed upon by these gentlemen from the continent? If a state of matters exist such as we have shown existed between Zbyszko and Suliman, what confidence can we have that when the men, after due palaver, do meet, we are to have real honest wrestling? … Is this wrestling farce never to end?[82]

Borrowing forms of promotion that had been developed in sideshows and theatrical venues, showmen and their wrestlers drew upon traditions more familiar in the theatrical field. As we have seen in earlier chapters, *The Sporting Life's* pleas for the wrestling farce to end reflected a general unease with professional wrestling's distance from the forms of promotion and dissemination of celebrity associated with the wider sporting field. The enduring possibility of professional wrestling extended into its form of celebrity. Ballyhoo was broadly tolerated in the circus, fairground, and sideshow, but it ran against the underlying and negotiated values of the sporting field. When sporting teams or celebrities rooted in the dominant values of amateurism attempted such promotional techniques, as when the Sheffield Zulu teams played charity matches between 1879 and 1882 'dressed as members of the Southern African Zulu tribe', stressing uses of costume that would be more suited to the commercial stage, sporting bodies were quick to stamp this out.[83] In the absence of a strong national or international governing body, then, showpeople borrowed promotional tactics from the theatrical field – a field that had influenced earlier sporting cultures – that positioned wrestling on the fringes of the sporting field. The types of promotion found in wrestling were tolerated, and even encouraged, on the stage, but for a serious sport this contravened the established promotional and forms of fame found in that cultural space. Professional wrestlers, then, were developing characters more akin to the stage, and often offering versions of celebrity in conflicts with the types more generally distributed in the sporting press.

Sporting celebrity refracted wider tensions in society, but it also reproduced the specific values and hegemonies of the field's terrain. W. G. Grace, the exemplar sporting celebrity of Victorian England, was celebrated precisely because he seemed to exemplify the amateur nonchalance of the public school boy, even of stories surrounding him were very often mythologised. Narratives of 'local lads done good', insouciant amateurs, or dedicated purists, the most common stories surrounding sporting celebrities in this period, reproduced the very specific power structures of the sporting field. Though professional wrestling celebrity clearly echoed sporting celebrity, and was imbued with the melodrama that existed across all forms of celebrity culture, without the framing structures, supporting logics, or support of the sporting field, its stars often lacked coherency, and this only accelerated as the century continued. The invented characters of the squared circle, complete with theatrical flourishes of the stage, displayed a type discursive instability, an instability that would become increasingly apparent.

Keeping his identity intact was an obsession

When professional wrestling became an entirely pre-arranged performance in the 1920s and the 1930s, promotors took the notion of 'invented characters' and stretched them further. Not unlike the Victorian and Edwardian showpeople, colourful characters were created which helped tell both in-ring and ongoing narratives. Promoters and wrestlers created characters that were instantly and immediately recognisable to audiences, whether in their demeanour or looks or attitude to rule breaking. The types of Nazis, Arabs, glam rockers, ballet dancers, and a range of other stereotypes described at the beginning of this chapter, became a dominant model of characterisation. Though clearly building on melodramatic mode reporting and the theatricality of Victorian and Edwardian showpeople, it was also during this period that the villain and blue-eye dichotomy solidified. Where the Mountevans Committee sought to restrict these characters, stressing wrestling as a 'real' sport, colourful characters still predominated the type of wrestling that could be seen on ITV on Saturday afternoon.

One wrestler encapsulates the complex ways in which fame operated in professional wrestling: Kendo Nagasaki. Debuting in 1964, Nagasaki's 'true' identity was a hotly debated topic among wrestling fans and journalists alike. Drawing on a tradition of masked wrestlers that had been popular in British professional wrestling since at least the 1930s, Nagasaki had been the subject of much gossip, with a *TV Times* feature describing the wrestler as 'a riddle wrapped in a mystery inside an enigma'.[84] Not only did he wear a mask,

> [he] liked to portray a broody darkness, as if he had endured a terrible life and was now taking vengeance on all humanity. He liked to hit his opponents with savage force, and refused to take a dive in any of his matches … He had strange Samurai rituals, including a salt-throwing routine, and he had half a finger missing from his left hand, which hinted at some cultish and bloody initiation ceremony at the behest of the Yakuza.[85]

It was amid great anticipation, then, when Nagasaki, from the Wolverhampton Civic Hall on New Year's Eve 1977, willingly revealed his face to the world for the first time. Matching the character's own theatrically, the flamboyant unmasking ceremony involved cult-like acolytes, salt throwing, and the burning of the mask. The Wolverhampton crowd's reaction was suitably bemused, albeit a bemusement mixed with intrigue, anticipation and occasional shouted insults. As well as supporting arguments about representations of race and orientalism in the sport, the strange ceremony, and professional wrestling more broadly, can tell us a lot about the complexities and contradictions of 'celebrity' in contemporary society and culture.

Masks have a long history in several wrestling traditions, perhaps most notably Mexico. Masks allowed some wrestlers to perform twice in an evening, but beyond such practicalities wrestlers with masks offer a fruitful way of thinking about some of the contradictions about the forms of celebrity that operate in professional wrestling cultures. If celebrity culture offers public presentation of personas rooted in melodrama, then professional wrestlers generally, and masked wrestlers specifically, were the ultimate model of this system. The mask denies a private persona is playing the part, collapsing all the nuances, complexities and contexts that a 'real' person exhibits. Instead, that person is replaced with a very public and intensified fictionalised and melodramatic performance. In masking the 'private' identity of the performer, the mask becomes a symbol in which highly potent characters can be performed without the messiness of a living human shaping those identities.[86]

Though it is appealing to see the forms of celebrity produced by professional wrestling as an incongruence, a set of fictionalised characters in a fake sport compared to the 'real' celebrities of 'real' sport, this would be a mistake. A range of other media and cultural industries have produced complex promotional systems based around the creation of characters. Just as in professional wrestling, those systems have created colourful, embellished, exaggerated, and sometimes even fictionalised, melodramatic characters, and central to most contemporary analyses of celebrity or stardom is that the mediated personas are not 'real' in any easily understood sense. Producers, managers, personal assistants, stylists and a variety of individuals, stage manage celebrity personas in highly codified and complex paratextual and intertextual networks, and this often involves the careful curation or even invention and then dissemination of biographical details. In other words, professional wrestlers are certainly constructed characters, but professional wrestling's embellished and intensified characters are no more or less 'constructed' than other celebrities.

Though they are no less real or fake, professional wrestlers feel more embellished, less coherent and stable than forms of celebrity operating across other fields, and this can be explained by two interconnecting factors: adherence to kayfabe and the intersecting of both the sporting and theatrical fields. As we saw in Chapter 3, at its most basic kayfabe refers to the presentation of performed professional wrestling as a legitimate sport, with characters extending into the 'real' world. Despite the obviously colourful characters, then, Dale Martin Promotions were always quick to dismiss comments about 'gimmickry' and 'phoney foreigners'.[87] There might be some emphasis and embellishment, was their usual defence, but all their wrestlers, were from the countries of origins and the characters in the ring were merely an extension of those in real life. One article quoted Leslie Martin as stating, 'You can make a personality out of a wrestler but you can't make a wrestler out of a personality.'[88] Expressed simply, wrestlers and promoters often maintained that the types of characters in the ring were continuations of the characters outside of the ring, like sportspeople more broadly, rather than actors playing fictional characters.

Outlandish characters might have made this defence difficult, but such arguments were partly helped by the fact that not all wrestlers had characters that were outlandish: many wrestled in plain trunks, with their own names, and without any obvious gimmicks. As the *Daily Mail* claimed, 'villains … are usually matched against a clean competitor', describing Billy Joyce, wrestling under his real name and town, who 'sticks strictly to scientific wrestling'.[89] Other wrestlers were clearly out-and-out fictions, though. Peter Gotz, an amateur champion of the sport, decried the fact that 'the promoters' chief aim is to secure the services of big, muscular well built young men, regardless of their wrestling knowledge'. Further, he claimed, 'They are often then billed as champions of this or that country, county or continent with such prefixes as;- Butcher, Killer, Phantom or Devil'.[90] Even when wrestlers were played straight, they existed in the diegesis with such characters, and there is little doubt that the colourful wrestlers with 'gimmicks' were often the main attraction. The different and sometimes competing character types that the media and promotional cultures have struggled to untangle in professional wrestling appear in ways that other cultural forms do not. Jackie Pallo was not wrong when he argued, perhaps somewhat playfully, that 'Wrestling has its gimmicks and its personality building procedures, but what entertainment hasn't?'[91] Other entertainments had personality building procedures, sometimes offering entirely fictionalised 'private' characters, but they had complex promotional systems to sustain, stabilise and anchor these characters. Wrestling, on the other hand, did not, at least for much of the twentieth century. The sport never fully developed a stable set of codes and conventions about the production, dissemination and reception of its celebrities in the mainstream press, and they similarly lacked the financial, cultural or social support of the sporting field to implement them.

While there are underlying and structural similarities, fields and subfields, 'genres and media formats'[92] develop specific systems for producing and disseminating celebrity. Indeed, this can partially explain the ongoing debates in film, media and cultural studies about the differences between film stardom, television personalities, and celebrity, and the extensive typologies that have been developed in these fields.[93] At its broadest, film and stage stardom has traditionally relied heavily on a 'duality of image', fuelled by the promotion of a screen actor's public persona and the circulation of information about their 'private' life.[94] This mediated private life, distributed in magazine features, interviews and other mediated texts, then ultimately reinforces the fictionalised stage or screen performance. The 'real' personas could be highly stage-managed, layered, or outright fictions, but they conformed to particular codes and conventions, giving access narratives of backstage or off-screen relationships, gossip, and other paratextual titbits. Though some competing versions of film stardom have developed, emphasising the actor as a performer, these still produce paratexts about training, 'method' preparation and others. Importantly, the notion of 'real' actor performing 'fictional' character is the basic, structuring device.

Sporting celebrity, on the other hand, claims that a person performing on the field or in the ring is an extension of the person off the field. Players could stand in for wider forces, around race, nation or gender, and encapsulate ideological shifts,[95] but they were not supposed to be read as obviously fictional characters. The sports player does not adopt a fictional character when they enter the field of play, and the dressing room is not where the 'real' person prepares for their role. The growth of television (explored in more detail in Chapter 5), furthermore, changed sporting celebrity. Television made players seem more intimate (broadcast into living homes each week) yet more distant. Players relationships with popular cultural forms like music and fashion made sporting stars seem more glamourous. And these expansions combined with the expansion of daily sports coverage, particularly the growth of redtop tabloids, and its institutionalised gossip. Despite these changes, though, sporting players mapped onto an obvious off-pitch persona, and there was supposed to be a coherent link between the two.

Regardless of the field, celebrity reporting almost always focused on the possibility of capturing that 'real' performer in their day-to-day lives, and celebrities can be defined as being 'the point at which media interest in their activities is transferred from reporting on their public role … to investigating the details of their private lives'.[96] Professional wrestling struggled with this: kayfabe insisted that characters in the ring were not fictional, but struggled to provide the 'real' lives of characters behind the performers. Music hall wrestlers could broadly adopt to both sporting and theatrical forms of representation, with an underlying logic of a 'real' person behind those performances. In this logic, they were sportspeople and when they appeared on the stage, they sometimes adopted more fictionalised characteristics, not unlike other actors and performers on the stage. From the 1930s, however, this became impossible. Admitting that characters were fictional meant admitting it was not a real sport, and in their place other types of representation would need to be developed.

On insisting that wrestlers were sportsmen, promoters often struggled to gain regular coverage in newspapers, sporting magazines and other types of press. The problem was mostly readily materialised by newspapers' reluctance to report on wrestling in the manner that other sports had developed. For the first three years of the 1930s, *The Times* had reported on all-in wrestling, but as it became apparent that the sport was 'fixed', newspapers became wary. They claimed:

> Let us admit then that these champions (and there are a vast number of them) have properly heroic names – Atholl Oakeley and the Black Devil, for instance, might have walked straight out of the pages of romantic fiction – but their wrestling is too lacking in the graces and too redolent of what looks like, but probably in reality is not, crude brutality to be included in the catalogue of heroic sports.[97]

Other newspapers also stopped reporting on professional wrestling in the manner that other sports were reported on. Articles, match reports, biographies and other features that were a fixture of sporting coverage remained absent for professional wrestling in the UK press throughout the twentieth century. In its place, dedicated wrestling magazines covered professional wrestling performers as if there was no separation between performer and character. Though there was a broad acceptance that showmanship and embellishment might exist, such magazines accepted that the sport was legitimate and that those characters existed 'in real life'. In so doing, professional wrestling's celebrities operated in a representational field outside and beyond the boundaries reserved for the rest of the sporting field.

The popularity heralded by television, though, began a limited interaction between newspapers and wrestling which had not happened in any meaningful way since the early 1930s. Modes of reporting established throughout the twentieth century to cover sports and sporting celebrities seemed inadequate in the face of professional wrestling.[98] Roy Blackman, in the lead-up to the big FA Cup day match between McManus and Pallo in 1963, produced a report which attempted to apply the codes and conventions of sports reporting to professional wrestling: he visited the wrestlers at their homes and at the gym and explored the men 'behind' the characters. To bypass the (fairly) obvious conclusion that the match was a performance, the report speculated that, despite understanding that the match was not competitive, there really existed a rivalry between the two:

> They won't be shaking hands. They won't even be civil. In fact you can bet your last half-crown they'll be downright nasty … [and I am] prepared to believe it. Kidding aside, I thought they really don't like each other.[99]

With his tongue firmly in his cheek, the report was keen to stress that Pallo and McManus genuinely held a grudge against one another. Indeed, this seemed to fuel the eagerness with which the public awaited the match. Conversely, when the *T.V. Times* interviewed Nagasaki in 1976, the author struggled in the types of classical reporting needed to bring private and public persona together. For Nagasaki, retaining the mythology of his character was of great importance – Peter Thornley from Stoke-on-Trent was kept as an intense secret that few people knew. Nagasaki's determination to keep himself masked, however, extended beyond magazine features. Max Crabtree, in an interview to Simon Garfield, explained, 'from the moment [Nagasaki] arrived at the hall he'd have the mask on … Keeping his identity intact was an obsession.'[100] This broadly extended into reports that sought to find the 'real' performer behind the character: 'He does not wish to discuss his background, reluctantly admits that it was rural, concedes that his voice indicates it was Northern. He says that he has "detached" himself from that, preferred to bury it.'[101]

Taken together, both accounts hinted at the contradictions and complexities of professional wrestling and how it had developed. Neither sports nor theatrical or film models seemed particularly useful, and writers sought various coping mechanisms to represent the characters as they were presented to them, seeking authenticity and playing along with the game as it appeared to them, yet overall struggling to place them into a specific field's logics.

Where newspapers and magazines struggled, audiences were better attuned to deconstructing these celebrity texts. Just as kayfabe is a pleasurable and productive, audiences seeking to peek behind the mask were a regular feature of wrestling. One writer to the MO explained that what they enjoyed most about the wrestling was 'trying to determine what or who is beneath the costumes and masks, which several wrestlers appear in'.[102] The playful response to personas has some overlap with wider celebrity culture. According to Joshua Gamson, one of the central attractions of celebrity culture is the way that audiences play with the celebrity image, including trying to decipher what public presentation is 'true' and what is 'performance'.[103] Gamson refers to this playfulness as a game, but the rules of the games are very much rooted in the field or fields in which the celebrity exists. Professional wrestling therefore offered a condensed pleasure of celebrity culture, and kayfabe explained the relationship to these games, but kayfabe also referred to the absence of otherwise structuring rules of the field.

Writing about Chris Benoit, the Canadian professional wrestler, who in 2007 committed the murders of his wife and young child, before eventually killing himself, and the nature of professional wrestling stardom, Tom Phillips suggests that '[The] constant interplay between reality and fakery means that constructing a celebrity image for a professional wrestler with separate professional, official private, and "real"personas is decidedly complex.'[104] Phillips is right, but this complexity extends across any number of celebrity cultures. The complexity he is hinting at describes the discursive and field-specific stability many celebrities exhibit, born from the representational logics of fields developed over hundreds of years, a stability that professional wrestling has often struggled with. Both 'fakery' and 'melodrama' sit at the heart of celebrity culture, but the rules for how those celebrities are produced, disseminated and received by audiences are more readily understood and grounded in the specific logics and histories of the fields.

Conclusion

Professional wrestling's form of celebrity points towards the complexities and contradictions of celebrity more broadly. The villain and blue-eyes dichotomies, its masculine melodrama, its invented characters, and the games audiences play in untangling characters offer condensed versions of the pleasures of celebrity cultures more broadly. These pleasures, the chapter has argued, are rooted in the historical conditions of a fielding society, and tracing professional wrestling's development reveals some of these tensions. Celebrity culture and the melodramatic mode are fused together: the expansion of industrialism, combined with the media's metacapital in the eighteenth and nineteenth centuries, created celebrities that operated in the melodramatic mode. This turned sportsmen and women into celebrities-cum-quasi-fictional-characters. Thereafter, in the circuses, fairgrounds and music halls, and in keeping with other performers of the day, these characters were displayed to audiences with an embellished and exaggerated manner. Until the early 1930s, wrestlers-as-celebrities continued this arrangement, with the public persona loosely matching and mapping onto a private persona, but by the mid-twentieth century it was extremely difficult to get a sense of where characters begun or ended. Individuals adopted out-and-out fictionalised personas that had been condensed to a degree that they merely signalled a flattened-out caricature which resisted acknowledgement of a private self. Professional wrestling promoters took this form of sporting celebrity, and then further intensified those performances, leaving a highly concentrated set of characters. These very often took the form of caricatures about race, ethnicity and nationality, but removed many of the nuances and complexities that sporting celebrities otherwise exhibited.

In existing between intersecting fields, however, professional wrestling also reveals how important fields are in structuring the representational logics of celebrity cultures. Stage (and then film) and sport have developed highly codified forms of celebrity, with their own codes and conventions, and individuals have trained themselves for specific skills and talents. Ultimately, moreover, celebrities reveal the wider social field's ideologies and tensions, but also tensions, ideologies and conflicts in the specific field. Because wrestling has existed as an enduring possibility, at odds with the wider sporting field, and often drawing on theatrical characterisations and embellishments, celebrities in professional wrestling have often felt unnatural. Promoters in the 1970s, the 1980s and the 1990s, particularly Vince McMahon, did a good job of realigning the wrestling subfield, but for much of the twentieth century the celebrity of professional wrestling was unstable, working against pre-existing values and ideologies.

Notes

1. Joe Nguyen, 'How Pro Wrestling Helped Shape Muhammad Ali's Charismatic Persona', *The Denver Post*, 4 June2016. Available at: www.denverpost.com/2016/06/04/how-pro-wrestling-shaped-muhammad-alis-charismatic-persona.
2. Lawrence A. Wenner (ed.), *Fallen Sports Heroes, Media and Celebrity Culture* (Oxford, 2014).
3. 'Like It or Not, Wrestling is Here to Stay', *Daily Mail*, 8 Oct. 1964, p. 15.
4. Roland Barthes, *Mythologies*, trans. Annette Lavers (Reading, 1993), p. 18.
5. Jeffery J. Mondak, 'The Politics of Professional Wrestling', *The Journal of Popular Culture*, 23(2) (1989), pp. 139–149.
6. John W. Campbell, 'Professional Wrestling: Why the Bad Guys Win', *Journal of American Culture*, 19(2) (1996), pp. 127–132;
7. Mondak, 'Politics of Professional Wrestling', p. 146.
8. Correspondence, MO, box SxMOA1/5/E/8.
9. Nicholas Porter, 'Grappling with the New Racism: Race, Ethnicity, and Post-Colonialism in British Wrestling During the 1970s and 80s', in Broderick Chow, Claire Warden and Eero Laine (eds), *Performance and Professional Wrestling* (London, 2017), pp. 177–186.
10. Bob Findlay, 'Wrestling is Not All-In', in *Grandstand Sport* (London, 1962), p. 119.
11. Kent Walton, *This Grappling Game* (London, 1967), p. 43.
12. Ibid., p. 43.
13. Campbell, 'Why the Bad Guys Win'; Thomas Henricks, 'Professional Wrestling as Moral Order', *Sociological Inquiry*, 44(3) (1974), pp. 177–188; Gerald W. Morton

and George M. O'Brien, *Wrestling to Rasslin: Ancient Sport to American Spectacle* (Bowling Green, OH, 1986).
14 Henricks, 'Wrestling as Moral Order'.
15 Henry Jenkins, '"Never Trust a Snake": WWF Wrestling as Masculine Melodrama', in Nicholas Sammond (ed.), *Steel Chair to the Head: The Pleasure and Pain of Professional Wrestling* (Durham, NC, 2005), p. 34.
16 Ibid., p. 39.
17 Michael R. Booth, *Theatre in the Victorian Age* (Cambridge, 1991), pp. 150–151.
18 Peter Brooks, *The Melodramatic Imagination: Balzac, Henry James, Melodrama and the Mode of Excess* (New Haven, CT, 1976), p. xiii.
19 Rohan McWilliam, 'Melodrama and the Historians', *Radical History Review*, 78 (2000), pp. 57–84.
20 Elaine Hadley, *Melodramatic Tactics: Theatricalized Dissent in the English Marketplace, 1800–1885* (Stanford, CA, 1995), p. 8.
21 Nick Couldry, 'Why Celebrity Studies Needs Social Theory (and Vice Versa)', *Celebrity Studies*, 6(3) (2015), pp. 385–388.
22 Christine Gledhill, 'Signs of Melodrama', in Christine Gledhill (ed.), *Stardom: Industry of Desire* (London, 1991), p. 120.
23 Sofia Johansson, '"Sometimes You Wanna Hate Celebrities": Tabloid Readers and Celebrity Coverage', in Su Holmes and Sean Redmond (eds), *New Directions in Celebrity Studies* (London, 2006), p. 349.
24 Joke Hermes, 'Media Figures in Identity Construction', in Pertti Alasuutari (ed.), *Rethinking the Media Audience: The New Agenda* (London, 1999), p. 80.
25 Ibid.
26 Garry Whannel, *Media Sport Stars: Masculinities and Moralities* (London, 2002), p. 36.
27 Brooks, *Melodramatic Imagination*, p. 20.
28 P. David Marshall, *Celebrity and Power: Fame in Contemporary Culture* (Minnesota, 1997); Chris Rojek, *Celebrity* (London, 2001).
29 Quoted in William A. Boulton, *The Amusements of Old London* (London, 1901), p. 4.
30 Classified advertisement, *Post Boy*, 23 Sept 1699.
31 Classified advertisement, *Daily Post*, 10 Apr. 1723.
32 Claire Warden, 'Pops and Promos: Speech and Silence in Professional Wrestling', in Broderick Chow, Claire Warden and Eero Laine (eds), *Performance and Professional Wrestling* (London, 2017), pp. 17–25.
33 Dennis Brailsford, *Bareknuckles: A Social History of Prize-Fighting* (Cambridge, 1988), p. 129.
34 Ibid., p. 130.
35 Richard Carew, *Carew's Survey of Cornwall* (London, 1811), p. 199.
36 Douglas A. Reid, 'Beasts and Brutes: Popular Blood Sports c. 1780–1860', in Richard Holt (ed.) *Sport and the Working Class in Modern Britain* (Manchester, 1990), p. 20.
37 Anon., *The London Journal*, 16 Jan. 1725.
38 Benedict Anderson, *Imagined Communities: Reflections on the Origin and Spread of Nationalism* (London, 1991). For a wider discussion of the relationship between nation and celebrity in the eighteenth century see Jason Goldsmith, 'Celebrity and the Spectacle of Nation', in Tom Mole (ed.), *Romanticism and Celebrity Culture, 1750–1850* (Cambridge, 2009), pp. 21–40.
39 Francesco Alberoni, 'The Powerless "Elite": Theory and Sociological Research on the Phenomenon of the Stars', in Dennis McQuail (ed. and trans.), *Sociology of Mass Communications: Selected Readings* (Harmondsworth, 1972), p. 77.

40 John Byrom, *Miscellaneous Poems* vol. 1 (Manchester, 1773), p. 43.
41 Rojek, *Celebrity*, p. 14.
42 Simon Morgan, 'Celebrity: Academic "Pseudo-Event" or a Useful Concept for Historians?', *Cultural and Social History*, 8(1) (2011), p. 97.
43 Michael Harris, 'Sport in the Newspapers Before 1750: Representations of Cricket, Class and Commerce in the London Press', *Media History*, 4(1), (1998), p. 27.
44 Classified advertisement, *London Evening Post*, 19 Jan. 1731.
45 Michael Baker, *The Rise of the Victorian Actor* (London, 1978), p. 117.
46 Daniel Mendoza, *Memoirs of the Life of Daniel Mendoza Containing a Faithful Narrative of the Various Vicissitudes of his Life and an Account of the Numerous Contests in Which he has Been Engaged, With Observations on Each* (London, 1816), p. 165.
47 Adrian Harvey, *The Beginnings of a Commercial Sporting Culture in Britain, 1793–1850* (Aldershot, 2004), pp. 33–34.
48 Jeremy Black, *The English Press, 1621–1861* (Stroud, 2001), p. 60.
49 Isaac T. Gate, *Great Book of Wrestling References, Giving the Last Two, Three and Four Standers of about 200 Different Fights in all the Principal Rings in England from 1838 to the Present Day* (Carlisle, 1874), p. iv.
50 Robert W. Malcolmson, *Popular Recreations in English Society 1700–1850* (Cambridge, 2007), p. 85.
51 Clicker wrestling notes, 16 Feb. 1973, Cumbria archive centre, DSO 48/25.
52 Alberoni, 'The Powerless "Elite"', p. 79.
53 McWilliam, 'Melodrama and the Historians'.
54 Chuck Kleinhans, 'Notes on Melodrama and the Family under Capitalism', in Marcia Landy (ed.), *Imitations of Life: A Reader on Film and Television Melodrama* (Detroit, 1991), p. 200.
55 Matthew Taylor, 'From Source to Subject: Sport, History and Autobiography', *Journal of Sport History*, 35(3) (2008), p. 477.
56 Thomas W. Lacquer 'The Queen Caroline Affair: Politics as Art in the Reign of George IV', *The Journal of Modern History* 54(3) (1982), p. 458.
57 David Snowdon, 'Drama Boxiana: Spectacle and Theatricality in Pierce Egan's Pugilistic Writing', *Romanticism on the Net*, 46 (2007).
58 Ibid., para 25.
59 Harvey, *Commercial Sporting Culture*, p. 38.
60 Brailsford, *Bareknuckles*, p. 32.
61 Jon Bee, *Slang: A Dictionary of the Turf, the Ring, the Chase, the Pit, of Bon-Ton and the Varieties of Life, Forming the Most Completest and Most Authentic Lexicon Balatronium Hitherto Offered to the Notice of the Sporting World... Interspersed with Anecdotes and Whimsies, With Tart Quotations and Rum Ones...* (London, 1823), p. 203.
62 Ibid.
63 John Ford *Prizefighting: The Age of Regency Boximania* (Devon, 1971), p. 55.
64 Goldsmith, 'Celebrity and the Spectacle of Nation', p. 22.
65 Richard Dyer, *Stars* (London, 1998), p. 31.
66 Quoted in Paul Magriel, 'Tom Molineaux', *Phylon*, 12(4), (1951), p. 331.
67 Karen Downing, 'The Gentleman Boxer: Boxing, Manners, and Masculinity in Eighteenth-Century England', *Men and Masculinities*, 12(2), (2010).
68 Anon., 'Wrestling and Other Athletic Amusements', *Bell's Life in London and Sporting Chronicle*, 3 Jan. 1836, p. 3. See also Harvey, *Commercial Sporting Culture*, p. 174.
69 Dan Streible, *Fight Pictures: A History of Boxing and Early Cinema* (Berkeley, CA, 2008).

70 Cochran wrongly claims the article was featured on the front page. It was actually featured on page 4. Mary Nugent, 'Is Great Strength Genius?', *Daily Mail*, 2 Apr. 1902, p. 4.
71 Ibid., p. 4.
72 Charles B. Cochran, *The Secrets of a Showman* (London, 1925), p. 117.
73 Joshua Gamson, 'The Assembly Line of Greatness: Celebrity in Twentieth Century America', *Critical Studies in Mass Communication*, 9(1), (1992).
74 Renée M. Sentilles, *Performing Menken: Adah Isaacs Menken and the Birth of American Celebrity*. (Cambridge, 2003), p. 4.
75 William A. Brady, *Showman* (New York, 1937), pp. 215–216.
76 Charles B. Cochran, *Showman Looks On* (London, 1945), p. 275.
77 Joseph S. Alter, 'Subaltern Bodies and Nationalist Physiques: Gama the Great and the Heroics of Indian Wrestling', *Body & Society*, 6(2), (2000), pp. 45–72.
78 One of Houdini's first short films (1906) was entitled *Houdini Defeats Hackenschmidt*, See Mathew Solomon, *Silent Film, Houdini and the New Magic of the Twentieth Century* (Chicago, 2010), pp. 152–153.
79 Sarah Dadswell, 'Jugglers, Fakirs, and Jaduwallahs: Indian Magicians and the British Stage', *New Theatre Quarterly*, 23(1), (2007), p. 9.
80 Tony Collins, 'Early Football and the Emergence of Modern Soccer, c. 1840–1880', *The International Journal of the History of Sport*, 9 (2015), p. 12.
81 Cochran, *Secrets of a Showman*, p. 119.
82 Quoted in Graham Noble, '"The Lion of the Punjab" – Gama in England, 1910', *InYo: The Journal of Alternative Perspectives on the Martial Arts and Sciences*. Available at: http://ejmas.com/jalt/jaltart_noble_0502.htm (accessed 13 March 2013).
83 Graham Curry, 'Football Spectatorship in Mid-to-Late Victorian Sheffield', *Soccer & Society*, 8(2–3), (2007), pp. 189–190.
84 David Nathan, 'The Peaceful Faith Behind the Violent Mask...Kendo Nagasaki', *TV Times*, 12 Dec. 1976, p. 3.
85 Simon Garfield, 'Who is that Masked Man?', *The Guardian*, 7 Oct. 2001. Available at: www.theguardian.com/observer/osm/story/0,6903,562562,00.html
86 Heather Levi, *The World of Lucha Libre: Secrets, Revelations, and Mexican National Identity* (Durham, NC, 2008).
87 Letter from Dale Martin Promotions to Howard Thomas, 6 Apr., Sporting Events "Wrestling", vol. 1, IBA, box 01097.
88 Bob Findlay, 'Wrestling Is Not All-In'.
89 'Like It or Not, Wrestling is Here to Stay', *Daily Mail*, 8 Oct. 1964, p. 15.
90 Letter from Peter Gotz to Clyde Wilson, 20 March, 1933, LCC, box CL/PC/01/026.
91 Findlay, 'Wrestling Is Not All-In'.
92 Su Holmes and Sean Redmond, 'Understanding Celebrity Culture', in Su Holmes and Sean Redmond (eds), *New Directions in Celebrity Studies* (London, 2006), p. 13.
93 See Rojek, *Celebrity*.
94 Christine Geraghty, 'Re-examining Stardom: Questions of Texts, Bodies and Performance', in Christine Gledhill and Linda Williams (eds), *Re-Inventing film Studies* (London, 2000), p. 187.
95 David L. Andrews and Steven J. Jackson (eds), *Sport Stars: The Cultural Politics of Sporting Celebrity* (London, 2002).
96 Graeme Turner, *Understanding Celebrity* (London, 2004), p. 8.
97 Quoted in Robert Snape, 'All-in Wrestling in Inter-War Britain: Science and Spectacle in Mass Observation's "Worktown"', *The International Journal of the History of Sport*, 30(12), (2013), p. 1423.
98 Whannel, *Media Sport Stars*.
99 Roy Blackman, 'The Duel at 1.20pm: It's the Fight They Wouldn't Put on for Prince Philip This Week', *Daily Mirror*, 25 May 1963, p. 9.

100 Simon Garfield, *The Wrestling* (London, 2007), p. 128.
101 David Nathan, 'The Peaceful Faith Behind the Violent Mask ... Kendo Nagasaki', *TV Times*, 12 Dec. 1976, p. 3.
102 Correspondence, MO, box SxMOA1/5/E/8.
103 Gamson, *Claims to Fame*, p. 173.
104 Tom Phillips, 'Wrestling with Grief: Fan Negotiation of Professional/Private Personas in Responses to the Chris Benoit Double Murder–Suicide', *Celebrity Studies*, 6(1) (2015), p. 74.

Bibliography

Alberoni, Francesco, 'The Powerless "Elite": Theory and Sociological Research on the Phenomenon of the Stars', in ed. and trans. Dennis McQuail, *Sociology of Mass Communications: Selected Readings*, Harmondsworth, Penguin, 1972, pp. 75–98.
Alter, Joseph S., 'Subaltern Bodies and Nationalist Physiques: Gama the Great and the Heroics of Indian Wrestling', *Body & Society*, 6(2), (2000), pp. 45–72.
Anderson, Benedict, *Imagined Communities: Reflections on the Origin and Spread of Nationalism*, London, Verso, 1991.
Andrews, David L. and Jackson, Steven J. (eds), *Sport Stars: The Cultural Politics of Sporting Celebrity*, London, Routledge, 2002.
Baker, Michael, *The Rise of the Victorian Actor*, Lanham, MD, Rowman and Littlefield, 1978.
Barthes, Roland, *Mythologies*, trans. Annette Lavers, Reading, Vintage Press, 1993.
Bee, Jon, *Slang: A Dictionary of the Turf, the Ring, the Chase, the Pit, of Bon-Ton and the Varieties of Life, Forming the Most Completest and Most Authentic Lexicon Balatronium Hitherto Offered to the Notice of the Sporting World...Interspersed with Anecdotes and Whimsies, With Tart Quotations and Rum Ones...*, London, T. Hughes, 1823.
Black, Jeremy, *The English Press, 1621–1861*, Stroud, Sutton, 2001.
Booth, Michael R., *Theatre in the Victorian Age*, Cambridge, Cambridge University Press, 1991.
Boulton, William A., *The Amusements of Old London*, London, John C. Nimmo, 1901.
Brady, William A., *Showman*, New York, Curtis Publishing, 1937.
Brooks, Peter, *The Melodramatic Imagination: Balzac, Henry James, Melodrama and the Mode of Excess*, New Haven, CT, Yale University Press, 1976.
Byrom, John, *Miscellaneous Poems*, vol. 1, Manchester, J. Harrop, 1773.
Campbell, John W., 'Professional Wrestling: Why the Bad Guys Win', *Journal of American Culture*, 19(2), (1996), pp. 127–132.
Carew, Richard, *Carew's Survey of Cornwall*, London, T. Bensley, 1811. Cochran, Charles B., *The Secrets of a Showman*, London, William Heinemann Ltd, 1925.
Cochran, Charles B., *Showman Looks On*, London, J.M. Dent & Sons Ltd, 1945.
Collins, Tony, 'Early Football and the Emergence of Modern Soccer, c. 1840–1880', *The International Journal of the History of Sport*, 9, (2015), pp. 1127–1142.
Couldry, Nick, 'Why Celebrity Studies Needs Social Theory (and Vice Versa)', *Celebrity Studies*, 6(3) (2015), pp. 385–388.
Curry, Graham, 'Football Spectatorship in Mid-to-Late Victorian Sheffield', *Soccer & Society*, 8(2–3), (2007), pp. 189–190.
Dadswell, Sarah, 'Jugglers, Fakirs, and Jaduwallahs: Indian Magicians and the British Stage', *New Theatre Quarterly*, 23(1), (2007), pp. 3–24.

Dyer, Richard, *Stars*, London, BFI Publishing, 1998.
Ford, John, *Prizefighting: The Age of Regency Boximania*, Devon, David and Charles, 1971.
Gamson, Joshua, *Claims to Fame: Celebrity in Contemporary America*, Berkeley, CA, University of California Press, 1994.
Gamson, Joshua, 'The Assembly Line of Greatness: Celebrity in Twentieth Century America', *Critical Studies in Mass Communication*, 9(1), (1992), pp. 1–24.
Garfield, Simon, *The Wrestling*, London, Faber & Faber, 2007.
Gate, Isaac T., *Great Book of Wrestling References, Giving the Last Two, Three and Four Standers of about 200 Different Fights in all the Principal Rings in England from 1838 to the Present Day*, Carlisle, Steel Brothers, 1874.
Geraghty, Christine, 'Re-examining Stardom: Questions of Texts, Bodies and Performance', in Christine Gledhill and Linda Williams (eds), *Re-Inventing film Studies*, London, Bloomsbury, 2000, pp. 183–202.
Gledhill, Christine, 'Signs of Melodrama', in Christine Gledhill (ed.), *Stardom: Industry of Desire*, London, Routledge, 1991, pp. 207–232.
Goldsmith, Jason, 'Celebrity and the Spectacle of Nation', in Tom Mole (ed.), *Romanticism and Celebrity Culture 1750–1850*, Cambridge, Cambridge University Press, 2009, pp. 21–40.
Hadley, Elaine, *Melodramatic Tactics: Theatricalized Dissent in the English Marketplace, 1800–1885*, Stanford, CA, Stanford University Press, 1995.
Harris, Michael, 'Sport in the Newspapers before 1750: Representations of Cricket, Class and Commerce in the London Press', *Media History*, 4(1), (1998), pp. 19–28.
Harvey, Adrian, *The Beginnings of a Commercial Sporting Culture in Britain, 1793–1850*, Aldershot, Ashgate, 2004.
Henricks, Thomas, 'Professional Wrestling as Moral Order', *Sociological Inquiry*, 44(3), (1974), pp. 177–188.
Hermes, Joke, 'Media Figures in Identity Construction', in Pertti Alasuutari (ed.), *Rethinking the Media Audience: The New Agenda*, London, Sage, 1999, pp. 69–86.
Holmes, Su, and Redmond, Sean, 'Understanding Celebrity Culture', in Su Holmes and Sean Redmond (eds), *New Directions in Celebrity Studies*, London, Routledge, 2006, pp. 1–16.
Jenkins, Henry, '"Never Trust a Snake": WWF Wrestling as Masculine Melodrama', in Nicholas Sammond (ed.), *Steel Chair to the Head: The Pleasure and Pain of Professional Wrestling*, Durham, NC, Duke University Press, 2005, pp. 33–66.
Johansson, Sofia, '"Sometimes You Wanna Hate Celebrities": Tabloid Readers and Celebrity Coverage', in Su Holmes and Sean Redmond (eds), *New Directions in Celebrity Studies*, London, Routledge, 2006, pp. 343–358.
Kleinhans, Chuck, 'Notes on Melodrama and the Family under Capitalism', in Marcia Landy (ed.), *Imitations of Life: A Reader on Film and Television Melodrama*, Detroit, Wayne State University Press, 1991, pp. 197–204.
Lacquer, Thomas W., 'The Queen Caroline Affair: Politics as Art in the Reign of George IV', *The Journal of Modern History*, 54(3), (1982), pp. 417–466.
Levi, Heather, *The World of Lucha Libre: Secrets, Revelations, and Mexican National Identity*, Durham, NC, Duke University Press, 2008.
Magriel, Paul, 'Tom Molineaux', *Phylon*, 12(4), (1951), pp. 329–336.
Malcolmson, Robert W., *Popular Recreations in English Society, 1700–1850*, Cambridge, Cambridge University Press, 2007.
Marshall, P. David, *Celebrity and Power: Fame in Contemporary Culture*, Minnesota, University of Minnesota Press, 1997.

McWilliam, Rohan, 'Melodrama and the Historians', *Radical History Review*, 78, (2000), pp. 57–84.

Mendoza, Daniel, *Memoirs of the Life of Daniel Mendoza Containing a Faithful Narrative of the Various Vicissitudes of his Life and an Account of the Numerous Contests in Which he has Been Engaged, With Observations on Each*, London, Hayden, 1816.

Mondak, Jeffery J., 'The Politics of Professional Wrestling', *The Journal of Popular Culture*, 23(2), (1989), pp. 139–149.

Morgan, Simon, 'Celebrity: Academic "Pseudo-Event" or a Useful Concept for Historians?' *Cultural and Social History*, 8(1), (2011), pp. 95–114.

Morton, Gerald W. and O'Brien, George M., *Wrestling to Rasslin': Ancient Sport to American Spectacle*, Bowling Green, OH, Bowling Green State University Press, 1986.

Noble, Graham, '"The Lion of the Punjab" – Gama in England, 1910', *InYo: The Journal of Alternative Perspectives on the Martial Arts and Sciences*. Available at: http://ejmas.com/jalt/jaltart_noble_0502.htm (accessed 13 March 2013).

Phillips, Tom, 'Wrestling with Grief: Fan Negotiation of Professional/Private Personas in Responses to the Chris Benoit Double Murder–Suicide', *Celebrity Studies*, 6(1), (2015), pp. 69–84.

Porter, Nicholas, 'Grappling with the New Racism: Race, Ethnicity, and Post-Colonialism in British Wrestling During the 1970s and 80s', in Broderick Chow, Claire Warden and Eero Laine (eds), *Performance and Professional Wrestling*, London, Routledge, 2017, pp. 177–186.

Reid, Douglas A., 'Beasts and Brutes: Popular Blood Sports c. 1780–1860', in Richard Holt (ed.), *Sport and the Working Class in Modern Britain*, Manchester, Manchester University Press, 1990, pp. 12–28.

Rojek, Chris, *Celebrity*, London, Reaktion Books, 2001.

Sentilles, Renée M., *Performing Menken: Adah Isaacs Menken and the Birth of American Celebrity*, Cambridge, Cambridge University Press, 2003.

Snape, Robert, 'All-in Wrestling in Inter-War Britain: Science and Spectacle in Mass Observation's "Worktown"', *The International Journal of the History of Sport*, 30(12), (2013), pp. 1418–1435.

Snowdon, David, 'Drama Boxiana: Spectacle and Theatricality in Pierce Egan's Pugilistic Writing', *Romanticism on the Net*, 46, (2007).

Solomon, Matthew, *Silent Film, Houdini and the New Magic of the Twentieth Century*, Chicago, University of Illinois Press, 2010.

Streible, Dan, *Fight Pictures: A History of Boxing and Early Cinema*, Berkeley, CA, University of California Press, 2008.

Taylor, Matthew, 'From Source to Subject: Sport, History and Autobiography', *Journal of Sport History*, 35(3), (2008), pp. 460–471.

Turner, Graeme, *Understanding Celebrity*, London, Sage, 2004.

Walton, Kent, *This Grappling Game*, London, Compton Printing Ltd, 1967.

Warden, Claire, 'Pops and Promos Speech and Silence in Professional Wrestling', in Broderick Chow, Claire Warden and Eero Laine (eds), *Performance and Professional Wrestling*, London, Routledge, 2017, pp. 17–25.

Wenner, Lawrence A. (ed.), *Fallen Sports Heroes, Media and Celebrity Culture*, Oxford, Peter Lang, 2014.

Whannel, Garry, *Media Sport Stars: Masculinities and Moralities*, London, Routledge, 2002.

Chapter 5

'Everything is eventually going to find its way on the goggle-box'

Television and spectacle

Between 1880 and 1950, the core values, ideologies and capitals of the sporting and exercise field had been established, often through conflict and compromise. By the turn of the twentieth century, the terrain of the field had been set with various groups and sports taking their positions. Limited commercialism was permitted if 'amateur' sporting groups and institutions had ultimate control, restricting the types of payments made and making sure values, ideologies and forms of capital were foregrounded. In the post-war period, the terrain of the sporting field was radically altered by changes in the media field and the increasing overlaps between the two. The introduction of television producers and controllers into the field of sport, especially after 1955, was the most dramatic restructuring since the genesis of the field in the late nineteenth century. In turn, this dramatically changed professional wrestling. and studying those consequences offers a useful way of thinking through the relationship between sport and television.

The chapter begins by examining the establishment of the BBC and ITV, and sport's relationship to these institutions. Because of the public service broadcaster's existing connection with sporting organisations, ITV at first struggled with broadcasting sports. Upon establishing *World of Sport*, their competitor to the BBC's *Grandstand*, they soon found a common partner in Joint Promotions, and professional wrestling became the channel's most popular sporting programme in the 1960s and the 1970s. Television, furthermore, adopted and adapted existing cultural forms while simultaneously and fundamentally changing the audience's view and understandings of these texts. Applying camera angles, editing, commentary and establishing 'flow' turned sport into a televisual text. Audiences' primary experience of professional wrestling was a mediated reconstruction.

Commercial television was critical for professional wrestling, and their seemingly symbiotic relationship has been described in popular and academic texts. Less commented upon is professional wrestling's relationship with Pay-TV in the 1960s, a topic the chapter then discusses. In the wake of the Pilkington Report, a limited pay television licence was granted to media entrepreneurs. In preparation for the channel, Joint Promotions were bought by the company

Viewsport to offer pay-per-view content. Pay-TV ultimately proved to be a discarded possibility, but the experiment drove up the cost of television sports rights contracts and left professional wrestling with a succession of owners who were eager to create a more colourful and entertaining project, much to the chagrin of some commentators. If coin-in-the-box Pay-TV served as a discarded possibility, the underlying notion of commercial, subscription and pay-per-view television became a reality in the 1970s and the 1980s. Like ITV and Pay-TV, the launch of Sky television in Britain has fundamentally altered the terrain of the sporting field and professional wrestling. Specifically, the World Wrestling Federation (WWF) found a regular broadcaster, and ITV cancelled *World of Sport* in response to challenges posed by Sky's broadcasting of sports.

The chapter concludes by analysing the ways in which sport became an entertaining spectacle in the 1980s, and how it has moved closer to a position historically occupied by wrestling. The influence of television controllers and sponsors means that sport is now concerned with entertainment, establishing editing, framing and narrative techniques, and the growth of celebrity cultures associated with sport. While not all sports have taken the route that professional wrestling took (fixing contests to guarantee heightened dramatic and emotional release, giving championships to trusted performers, and the other advantages that pre-arranged contests heralded), most sports have gone to great lengths to offer as much entertainment as they can muster, embracing rule and presentational changes to simplify contests, expand audiences, and secure sponsorship and television deals. As an enduring possibility, then, wrestling's primary purpose is to make other sports look real where we might otherwise consider them entertaining spectacles.

Something better than a ringside seat

In the decades following the Second World War, television became the most ubiquitous and well-practised leisure pursuit in English society. The way most people were entertained the clear majority of the time moved from the cinema screens, stages of variety theatres, pitches of football stadiums, and rings of the circus to living rooms in the home. This was not, of course, an instantaneous transformation. Radio had laid the groundwork earlier in the century. For the study at hand, however, radio and wrestling were never particularly well-matched. Professional wrestling performed complicated moves, often in quick succession, with a specialised terminology.[1] It was predominantly a visual sport which a detailed spoken explanation would struggle to keep up with. Rugby union, football, rowing, cricket, and Wimbledon tennis were better suited to radio's demands, and these sports were providing the blueprints for the style and form of presenting and commentating on sport via mass media.[2]

Experiments in television were conducted before the Second World War, and in 1938 the BBC screened short exhibitions of matches in the catch style. These matches, judging by the *Radio Times* descriptions, were very much in the style of exhibition and presentation rather than out-and-out professional matches.[3] Throughout 1938 and 1939, forms of exhibition wrestling were presented on the still prototypal television channel, and they were often presented alongside other forms of fighting, notably boxing and fencing. As the *Radio Times* argued, 'television can provide something better than a ringside seat'.[4] Just as wrestling had been suited to the music hall because it was contained, compact and easy to light, wrestling was well suited to television's early experiments with sport. Its difficulties in broadcasting on radio made it ideal for television. Experiments with television before the outbreak of the Second World War were limited to small geographical areas and by minimal television ownership, however. The new medium had little impact within the field of media and even less impact on the sporting field.

After its re-launch, television's popularity and ubiquity rocketed: between 1946 and the launch of commercial television in the 1950s numbers of licences grew from 15,000 to 4.5 million.[5] In media historiography the Queen's Coronation and the Stanley Matthews Cup Final in 1953 play a near-mythical role in securing television as *the* medium of the late twentieth century.[6] The introduction of a British commercial television channel was a crystallisation of television as a powerful sub-field and, consequently, a vigorous restructuring of power within the media field. Discussed in the 1950s, the possibility of adding a second channel funded by private companies was finally introduced in 1955. As was discussed in Chapter 3, the arrival of commercial television focused debates about the role of mass media, commercialisation, popular culture and fears of Americanisation.[7] The Television Act was passed in 1954 on the understanding that the Independent Television Authority (ITA) would govern regional companies that composed Independent Television (ITV).[8]

ITV was an intriguing case study of the ways in which competing fields and parties negotiated and compromised. ITV was to be funded by commercials and could be profitable, thus pleasing those entrepreneurs who wanted to profit from the potential of new media. The state, however, exerted a control over rules and regulations for programming – including a limit on American imports – as well as occasionally producing reports outlining how the channel should proceed in the future (the most famous of which, the Pilkington Report, could demand changes to programming and content).[9] The introduction of a second commercial channel almost immediately altered the institutional and political set-up of broadcasting.[10] For the first time there existed a competition for audience share, doubly so because ITV's operating budgets and profits relied on audiences watching advertisements between programmes. The BBC had its own charter and responsibilities to fill. So, too, did ITV. The situation created institutions with differing attitudes to what made, and what should be deemed, successful television.

Sport did not register highly on the ITV's priorities for the first five years of its existence. The BBC had already built up extensive contracts with sporting organisations, and the old-boy network of the BBC complemented the old-boy network of amateur sporting bodies.[11] The BBC's Head of Outside Broadcasting claimed that the organisation and Wimbledon's cosy relationship existed as a 'deliberate policy of an amateur sport towards a public service'.[12] In other words, intersecting fields and proximity in social space structured the relationship between BBC controllers and amateur sporting bodies. The regional structuring of ITV, as opposed to the London-focused BBC, further complicated relationships between the channel and sporting bodies often situated in the city. Bernard Sendall later noted that in the early years, 'ITV handled sport rather gingerly; coverage, compared with the BBC's, seemed sparse, random, and sometimes amateurish.'[13] Early attempts to create a sporting programme on the channel resulted in the London-based AR's *Cavalcade of Sport*'s one-hour programme that ran on Wednesday nights. For the most part, *Cavalcade* was disappointing, haphazardly thrown together at the last minute,[14] and 'promising rather more than it gave'.[15] Its legacy, it would turn out, was its televising of professional wrestling which began on the 9th of November 1955 with the match between Bert Royal v. Cliff Beaumont and provided by Dale Martin Promotions for the wider Joint Promotions.

By the mid-1960s, however, sport was a crucial form of programming in which the BBC and ITV competed for viewers. *World of Sport* was conceived as a direct competitor to *Grandstand*, the BBC's own Saturday afternoon sports magazine show. The problems that had initially repelled ITV from sport persisted, though: the BBC still had a majority of sporting contracts, they continued to have expertise in filming and presenting live sport, and they were not burdened by advertisement breaks.[16] Professional wrestling, aside from the small problem that it was not a sport in any commonly understood way, ticked nearly every box of John Bromley's conditions for televised sport:

> [T]he sport must have simple rules and be easily understood; it must be visual; it must be possible to televise without involving too much extra work and expense, i.e. it must be practical to televise it; and the event must be capable of drawing a reasonable crowd at the venue.[17]

Wrestling was indoors, it was easily lit, and, as we have already seen, sporting connoisseurship was neither required nor particularly desired. It could also attract an audience, on television and at arenas. Added to these considerations, British professional wrestling had an organisation which had a near monopoly over the sport. With the arrival of television in the 1950s, Joint Promotions were perfectly poised to use their monopoly to become the premiere and sole provider of televised wrestling. With a regular and recurring time slot, professional wrestling became a 'signature' of the channel,[18] airing on Saturday afternoons between 3.45 and 4 p.m.–5 p.m. during *World of Sport*,[19] wrestling remained by far the most watched sport on ITV on a Saturday afternoon.

Given the rivalry between the two stations and professional wrestling's popularity, there were occasional suggestions that the BBC might attempt to screen professional wrestling themselves. The Head of BBC's Outside Broadcast had other ideas. 'We don't look on wrestling as a sport,' he told one newspaper, 'wrestlers are entertainers.'[20] Away from the glare of the press, in private, the BBC *were* worried about wrestling's successes on the rival channel denting *Grandstand*'s ratings. Some went so far as to internally petition for the channel to produce their own version of professional wrestling. Lew Grade stated that:

> The BBC who are quite keen to do wrestling could of course have gone to some of the other independent promoters, but they must apparently be of the opinion that they could not put on wrestling programmes of calibre otherwise I am sure they would have approached them.[21]

Joint Promotions' closed-shop approach certainly caused the BBC problems, but more realistically the 'governors remained adamant that professional wrestling was not a suitable sport for the BBC'.[22] Aside from a single BBC broadcast in May 1965, professional wrestling chimed with the commercialisation associated with ITV (see Chapter 3 for further details). Professional wrestling, however, was something of a mixed blessing for the commercial broadcaster. Though popular, athletic associations were reluctant to have their sports transmitted alongside the spectacle of professional wrestling, which was viewed by some with amusement or derision.[23] For many, and most importantly to those who provided contracts to television, ITV's continued association with professional wrestling 'betray[ed] a lack of seriousness in ITV's approach to sport'.[24] Thus, *World of Sport* relied on a mix of unusual, niche and/or imported content to fill the four hours of programming on Saturday afternoons. Despite this, professional wrestling's status as television institution, and the culmination of Joint Promotion's rehabilitation of the sport post-Mountevans, arrived in 1961: professional wrestling matches featured before the FA Cup Final and wrestling on cup final day became a tradition for the next two decades. Put simply, professional wrestling remained immensely popular throughout the 1960s and the 1970s, and was regularly the channel's most watched sport.

It is difficult to ascertain how many viewers watching wrestling on a television screen had seen a variant of wrestling live. Given its ubiquity at fairgrounds, summer camps and seaside resorts, presumably many had *some* experience of watching the performance in person. From the 1960s onwards, however, television provided audiences with their primary experience of the sport. In their audience study for ITV, Ian Dobie and Mallory Wober, recorded 'one in twenty of the adult sample claims to have attended a live wrestling performance in the last twelve months. Among those who are interested in wrestling, this rises to one in eleven.'[25] In their report, the authors drew parallels between the live and broadcasted form:

> All observers agree that participation by comment, applause, jeering, with the possibility of having a wrestler land upon or close to one's person, or of

throwing things at the ring is an important facet of being a wrestling spectator ... it may be that the viewer obtains, in lesser measure, similar experiences as does the 'live' spectator.[26]

There was a primary difference between electronic mass media and older forms of popular culture: first, via photography, then cinema, and perfected by television, audiences were positioned as 'witnesses' to a broad range of events which they did not have access to before.[27] Television sports reporting added commentators, producers, presenters, and editing techniques. Professional wrestling, and indeed all sporting contests, used televisual conventions to add another layer of mediation to the live performance. Those watching at home had an engagement with storytelling and narrative construction that those in the stadium did not have access to.

One of the clear ways in which narratives were constructed in sport was through camera angles and editing. While professional wrestling started life on television as a fairly static affair with one hard camera relaying the performance, by the mid-1960s, improvements in technology were helping to construct the narrative in particular ways.[28] Kent Walton described,

Today we have platform mountings where the 'zoom' lenses really come into their own providing us with exiting close-ups from above the ring. True, we still get shots at canvas level but the new, modern techniques mean these are selected by, instead of forced upon, the Director.[29]

In line with developments across television production, the use of three cameras and zoom technologies allowed the performance to be seen in ways that were impossible with the human eye. Audiences at a live sporting event had a fixed viewpoint from the stands, audiences at home could be directed towards moments considered by the director to be of interest. Television, thus, could direct the home audience's attention to narratives as they developed (a close-up of the face of wrestler in a submission, perhaps). Thus, the director became an important purveyor of meaning for the wrestling spectacle. Further technological improvements in the 1970s – such as slow-motion replays – further allowed sporting contests to construct narratives and focuses on stories and sporting celebrities. Not all viewers were necessarily thrilled about this. One viewer wrote to the ITA complaining that editing techniques meant audiences 'lost trends of fights when all we get is sweating faces and behinds – all very dramatic but can't follow sport that way'.[30] It is a criticism one could make of television sports editing more generally.[31] But, as the writer attests to, editing did complement narratives and highlight individuals in the match.

Another purveyor of meaning were the commentators who provided yet another layer of dramatisation and interpretation. A commentator addressed audiences personally and warmly, balancing reporting with entertainment and blending texture with explanation.[32] Commentary was a vital component of televised professional wrestling's success. The sound of Kent Walton's voice as he introduced another week of action became as identifiable for audiences as the wrestlers themselves. In some ways, Walton's job was like that of sports commentary more generally. He needed to provide a knowledgeable understanding of holds, wrestlers and continuing narratives. Garry Whannel has contended that commentary 'brought analysis to the foreground' and often privileged former professionals with experience and expertise in the sport.[33] In other regards, professional wrestling did not follow this trajectory: if a commentator explained technique and helped the audience understand how movement or body shape were used to create the performance, they would be giving away the secrets of the wrestling ring. The commentator's job in professional wrestling, then, was to draw attention to the distractions and sleights of hand used to help camouflage the cooperative movements used by wrestlers. One ITA member wrote to another to explain the commentator's function: 'by means, of a variety of unsubtle devices, [the commentators] would have us [believe it is real]. It is curious how successful these methods can be.'[34] On the one hand, professional wrestling commentary was developing alongside other practices of television reporting, on the other, there was still an element of fairground barkers who exaggerated and embellished and were part of the performance as much as commenting on it. The point remained, though, that commentators had an important role in adding drama and entertainment where there might not be otherwise to the televised sporting action.

The presenter's job, furthermore, was to help manage the 'flow' of television.[35] As we have seen, television drew on many different cultural forms that existed alongside each other. Rob Turnock explains that television 'was a unified cultural form that placed discrete and separate cultural activities in a direct relationship with each other. News programmes could now coexist alongside sitcoms, opera alongside variety, [and] drama alongside music.'[36] Part of television's appeal was its ability to move audiences from location to location, drawing together disparate entertainments and popular cultural forms. The magazine television format, and television in general, served a similar purpose to the dedicated sporting press of the Georgian period (see Chapter 4). The magazine format was ideally suited to television because broadcasting 'depends on attracting and securing a mass audience ... hence the imperative to develop programme forms ... without alienating too much of the potential audience for too long'.[37] Like the sporting newspapers and magazines in the nineteenth century, these programmes helped to delineate the field:[38] *World of Sport* literally gave a 'unity [to] the world of sport'.[39]

Sports broadcasting followed the magazine format for much of the twentieth century.[40] Eamonn Andrews or Dickie Davies, *World of Sport*'s presenters, linked disparate sports from various locations. They serve as a useful illustration of how television presenters were used to manage the flow of television. Television presenters, being recognisable celebrities, also operated across programming, further helped to manage the flow of the medium. Eamonn Andrews, in particular, is a good example of this. Andrews made his name presenting the BBC panel show that had popularised Gilbert Harding, *What's My Line*? Later he became a presenter on *World of Sport* and was also given his own show, *The Eamonn Andrews Show*, a programme that borrowed heavily from America's established celebrity interview late-night shows.[41] If the magazine programme spoke of a unified world of sport, then particular television celebrity-cum-presenters offered a unified world of television. On a particularly famous episode in January 1967, Mick McManus and Jackie Pallo rekindled their long-running feud with a dramatic argument, linking the Sunday night show to the Saturday afternoon sports programme in more ways than one (as well as giving the two wrestlers, Joint Promotions and *World of Sport* publicity).

The establishment of television and then a commercial television channel was crucial in the history of British professional wrestling. Joint Promotions secured its near-monopoly status, and audience's interactions with the sport became dominated by television. Television controllers, directors, and producers, furthermore, created their own style and form of representation for sport generally. In the minds of the public and academic writing, the two were closely entwined. Another television channel would have an important influence on professional wrestling's development, but unlike ITV this channel has not received much coverage in either popular or academic writing: the Pay-TV experiments in the 1960s and the 1970s.

Black masks, stomachs the size of saucepans and glittering gowns

Max Crabtree, manager of Joint Promotions in the 1970s, was not exaggerating when he told Simon Garfield that 'there were lots of deals over the years'.[42] From the early 1960s to the mid-1970s, professional wrestling experienced fundamental changes in ownership as individuals tactically positioned themselves for perceived economic and technical transformations in the media field stemming from the announcement, test and then ultimate cancellation of pay television between 1964 and 1968. Though Pay-TV now represents an intriguing discarded possibility, an experiment that ultimately does not have much consequence in wider television or sporting history, that is not how it was experienced. Pay television was a test for the political, social and cultural role of television as technology. Before and during the experiment, the threat and/or possibility of pay television was considered worthy of intense discussion and debate. These debates involved journalists, politicians, sporting bodies, theatrical groups and unions, technology companies, and audiences. Moreover, investments were made by a broad range of broadcasting companies, including but not limited to ATV, Granada, Rediffusion, Rank, Horizon Pictures, Paramount Picture Corp. For the investors at least, pay television was not only a possibility but a likely development. Pay-TV, then, demonstrates the far-reaching influences that changes in one field can have in another, the way individuals, agents and institutions prepare for conflicts and seek to structure the field, and the power dynamics between sub-fields and fields. In other words, Pay-TV fundamentally altered professional wrestling in Britain.

Using cable technologies and a coin box connected to the television that unscrambled channels, the potential of pay television served as a clear departure from the public service broadcasting and commercial television duopoly that dominated British broadcasting in the 1950s, the 1960s and the 1970s. As the BBC claimed:

> [Pay television] is a radical idea, with far-reaching implications. The existing services of television would be greatly affected by the successful introduction of pay television. So would also many of the various industries and interests that are concerned with television. The introduction of any system of pay television would be likely, therefore, to affect the public in a very material way.[43]

Arguments about the possibilities of pay television gained traction in the 1950s, reaching a crescendo in 1960 with the formation of the Pilkington Committee. Pilkington set up an investigation into the quality of national television cultures, and awarded a third television channel, in which pay television was a possibility. Upon the announcement of the committee, numerous wire relay companies merged with content providers, and those companies were eager to position pay television as offering a genuine alternative to either public service broadcasting or commercial television.[44] Given the political context in which the committee was sitting and the desire to differentiate pay television against existing broadcasters, the companies stressed to Pilkington the potential to provide programming that covered 'minority tastes and interests'.[45] These included programming like 'opera, ballet and educational purposes'[46] and 'large sporting events which otherwise would not be seen by the majority of people'.[47] In spite of widespread objections about the pressures on public service broadcasting, and cynicism about the type of programming offered, the Conservative government supported an experiment in pay television.[48] While several companies were developed to offer regional experimental services, refusal by the Post Office to guarantee expansion beyond the experiment, difficulties in securing Hollywood films and apparent failures of similar pay television services in America left only one company willing to take up the experimental deal. British Home Entertainment, who had been petitioning for the experiment since 1960, announced their participation with British Relay Wireless, and the group later named the company Pay-TV.

Pay-TV started broadcasting on 7 January 1966 in a small area of London and in Sheffield with a combined 9000 subscribers. Despite promises made to deliver culture and education, Hollywood movies and sport became key attractions. In a sample period recorded by the channel, there were shown seven live football matches (three European cup games and four League Cup games), ten boxing matches, 21 horse races and 60 recorded wrestling broadcasts from Chicago, America. Crucially, Pay-TV's sister company, Viewsport, had an agreement with Harry Levene Ltd. to the live rights of Muhammad Ali fights.[49] On 21 May 1966, Henry Cooper met Muhammad Ali at Arsenal's Highbury Stadium, and the fight was the first heavyweight contest for the world championship to have been staged on British soil for a long time and had attracted significant interest from the press.

Given the overall costs of sporting coverage, and the limited chances of regaining that money via pay television subscribers, the group had other ways of making money. During the summer of 1964, the Hurst Park Syndicate, a group of businessmen and promoters building a business portfolio following the sale of the Hurst Park racecourse, formed Viewsport Ltd. Shortly after the pay television experiment announcement, a spokesperson for the group claimed that the company's intention, referring directly to pay television, was to 'look to make use of these new opportunities'.[50] By the time Pay-TV started broadcasting, Viewsport had an agreement with the channel to provide all their sporting programming.[51] More importantly for the Hurst Park Syndicate, Viewsport also screened live sporting contests via closed-circuit television in cinemas. Thus, the disparity in the number of subscribers in the Sheffield/London experiment to the channel and the costs of acquiring heavyweight boxing contracts could be bypassed by also charging audiences across the country to attend cinema screenings. This dual approach proved to be a successful formula. Pay-TV were given top sporting events, and Viewsport were given two modes of screening, as well as placing themselves in prime position if the experiment was extended.

The Viewsport/Pay-TV combination radically altered the terrain of the media field and the sporting field. Around sports rights, the BBC and ITV were forced into competitive bidding wars, either losing out to pay television or having to increase their costs and investment. According to one sympathetic report, 'the broadcasting authorities now have a real competitor for the most interesting sporting events'.[52] As well as repeated conflicts about rights to air boxing, football was something over which the different broadcasters battled. After experiments in the 1965/66 season, for the 1967–68 season the BBC, ITV and Viewsport all competed with one another for live Football League broadcasting rights. Despite the large amounts of money involved, many clubs were unhappy with this arrangement. Burnley's chairman, Bob Lord, likened live televised football as a 'possible cancer … because it has the effect of keeping people away from the matches themselves'.[53] Commentators in the press agreed. In his *Daily Mirror* column, Peter Wilson argued that:

> Once the idea catches on that EVERYTHING is eventually going to find its way on the goggle-box, the sense of 'occasion' will rapidly drain away from sport … What I fear is that sport – and soccer is the obvious target – will sell out wholesale, dazzled by the admittedly vast sums at the disposal of the TV authorities.[54]

Ultimately, the Football League agreed and rejected both the BBC's and Viewsport's offers, but the amounts of money and influence that media entrepreneurs could wield ultimately radically altered the structures of the sporting field. Over one million pounds had been spent by Pay-TV in the hope that the channel would be rolled out nationally upon the experiment's completion.[55]

It was in this context that Viewsport invested heavily in professional wrestling. In 1964, Jarvis Astaire, operating under Hurst Park Syndicate, bought first Dale Martin Promotion[56] and then shortly after Best Wryton Promotions and Morrell and Beresford.[57] In so doing, he essentially bought the monopoly of Joint Promotions, and *The Observer* would later write that 'under the ample Astaire wing lies most of what you can see in the halls and all of what you see on the box'.[58] Professional wrestling was a popular sport, and had a similar structure to boxing insofar as big matches had serious pay-per-view appeal. Unlike football and other sports with complicated ownership structures rooted in the field's development in the late nineteenth and early twentieth centuries, wrestling was most importantly easily traded. For wrestling at least, these changes were of huge importance, but in the context of the wider sporting and media fields, wrestling was a minor attraction.

Despite promises to the contrary, the Pay-TV experiment was never expanded past its first three years, with the Labour government anxious that Pay-TV would expand commercial television and undercut broadcasting as a public service,[59] and Astaire was left with a set of wrestling promotions he has little use for. Though Astaire was said to be a wrestling fan, and often defended wrestling to journalists, professional wrestling was only one of 22 companies held under Hurst Park. The promotions had clearly been bought with the expectation that the field of television would be changed dramatically by the introduction of subscription-model television.[60] In the wake of Pay-TV's failures, the Hurst Park Syndicate were obtained by William Hill in 1971 to maximise their presence on the high street. The same year, William Hill were acquired by Sears Holdings Limited.[61] According to Crabtree, wrestling was never a major concern for William Hill,[62] and more generally Sears had broad interests (including shoe making and high street fashion). Initially, Joint Promotions kept their original management and organisation structures, but as they eventually retired or were bought out, they were apparently replaced by 'secretaries', at least according to one wrestler at the time.[63] By the mid-1970s, Max Crabtree, who had spent much of the 1960s working outside of the Joint Promotions monopoly, became managing director of the group.

Conflicts between the ITA and Joint Promotions (see Chapter 2), the reasonably frequent changes in ownership, and the developments in television technology all produced noticeable alterations to the televised professional wrestling product. As the older generation of sporting promoters who had agreed to the Mountevans Committee rulings were replaced, elements of all-in that the Mountevans had been so desperate to restrict were creeping back in the televised spectacle. Not everyone was a fan of the new style. In an interview with the 1979 *World of Sport* annual, Kent Walton warned of the dangers of moving too far away from the sporting pleasures of wrestling.

> [F]licked wrists, dropped shoulders and Boston crabs [had once] ruled, black masks, stomachs the size of saucepans and glittering gowns have barged in. And wrestling's great worry now is that all the razzamatazz and showmanship that has appeared will take over from the proper stuff.[64]

It was not difficult to see who these criticisms were directed at. For some, Big Daddy, Max Crabtree's brother, was an embodiment of everything that was wrong with wrestling. In 1979, one irate viewer pleaded to the IBA, 'Please let us have good class wrestling as it used to be. None of your "Big Daddys". That's not wrestling.'[65] Another viewer suggested that Big Daddy's 'performance was … awful, having got on the canvas he had great difficulty in getting up'.[66] They further argued that Max Crabtree's nepotism and relationship with his brother had created a situation in which Big Daddy 'was kept … on his feet' with matches only lasting 'about 2 mins'.[67] Adrian Street's suggestion that Max Crabtree did this in order to run down the business and buy it off from Astaire seems a little harsh.[68] On the one hand, Big Daddy was one of the era's most popular performers, but the criticisms of his matches were fair: they were exceptionally short, and he often had to be placed in tag matches to help mask his shortcomings.

Such assessments point to a wider problem with televised wrestling in the latter half of the 1970s. It was an old problem: should professional wrestling be presented as a legitimate sporting competition? Should skill and talent in the ring be emphasised over entertainment? Promoters who had always been at great pains to protect professional wrestling's secrets and promote the performance as genuine sporting competition also came to be critical of the sport's less believable showmanship. Norman Morrell, who had played such a pivotal role in the creation of the Lord Mountevans style and Joint Promotions, found himself increasingly disillusioned with professional wrestling on television. In a long series of letters to the IBA from 1975 to 1980, Morrell, who was always quick to point out his previous involvement with the sport, decried the current situation. Aside from a few letters in reply, his calls for the ITV bosses to take a more active regulation over televised wrestling fell on deaf ears. In 1980, his frustration was such that he accused Joint Promotions of being, 'no longer a body of independent promoters [having ceased] to have authority and [are] just another subsidiary in the great conglomerate'.[69] In the same letter, the IBA were branded a puppet for, 'the mammoth commercial empire that owns Joint Promotions [and their] … destruction of wrestling as any form of sport'.[70]

Critics like Morrell contended that the problems faced by wrestling in the 1970s and the 1980s were born out of an embrace of theatricality: wrestling had abandoned all pretence of being a legitimate sport, and in so doing had abandoned its audiences. Others attached to wrestling blamed the influence of American wrestling. Ken Walton, for example, declared:

'Sell the seats and forget your cares' is the normal American slogan – and maybe there is some worth in the argument. But in the case of wrestling, there is rather more to it as long as you're assessing the merits of the sport in Britain. The American version is, as they say, a whole new ball game with such delights as eye gouging presented for the mob's delight. Happily, *World of Sport* viewers can see wrestling of a rather higher calibre each Saturday afternoon … [but] wrestling's great worry now is that all the razzamatazz and showmanship that has appeared will take over from the proper stuff.[71]

Such critiques did reflect changes in how professional wrestling was represented, but they both romanticise the past. Showmanship and razzmatazz had been central to wrestling since the early twentieth century. The emergence of American professional wrestling, however, would radically alter the British sport, and in response to the changing terrain of the sporting field the World Wrestling Federation would embrace showmanship and entertainment.

Stuck in about 1955, and the world had changed

Though ultimately Pay-TV served as a discarded possibility, Pay-TV's experiment hinted at key intersecting tensions around sports broadcasting in the post-war era: influxes of money into some, though not all, sports; serious challenges to amateurism; and increasing globalisation. Likewise, sport in the post-war period offers a useful study for thinking about how fields operate and interact at local, national and global contexts. For Bourdieu, fields often exist at a national level. This is unsurprising, given that the fielding of society was often intensely tied up with the formation of national laws and economies. Evidently, though, cultural forms exist at a transnational level. Whether in the expansion of sports and games linked to colonialism or in international sporting megaevents like the Olympics, sport has been intensely linked to international flows of culture, ideology and capital. Applying Larissa Buchholz's notion of multi-scalar global fields can be useful here. Writing about international art, for Buchholz, multi-scalar global fields can be described as a 'globally extended sphere of specialized practice that displays a relatively autonomous logic of competition vis-à-vis other types of fields as well as other field levels within the same realm of practice'.[72] The global field of sport is an independent field to national fields, but drawing on Simmel we can also posit that many individuals or institutions belong to both national fields and the global field, and their relationships and capitals are structured in these intersections.

Put another way, studying sport in the twentieth century is a matter of studying local, national and international power dynamics, and how that power is articulated across numerous overlapping fields. Though a global sporting field had existed since at least the nineteenth century, developments in broadcasting, and political attitudes to the role of the mass media, meant significant changes for specific sports, and both national and global sporting fields. Tracking those changes in wrestling reveals the complex ways in which such developments take place. If global and national sporting fields can be described as operating vertically, and other fields are placed horizontally, then we get a sense of the complex topographies of contemporary social fields in a global society. Changes in fields are refracted but also reverberated, altering the terrain in sometimes distant fields in unpredictable, multidirectional ways. Professional wrestling is interesting precisely because it has rarely been central to the sporting field, and it has intersected with various other fields. Transformations in both the political fields and media fields, however, have dramatically altered the history of professional wrestling in unintended ways. It is evidence of the reverberating nature of fields.

After the failures of Pay-TV, a fourth channel was added to British terrestrial television in 1982. When it came to sports, Channel Four, as the new channel was named, was reluctant to engage with a market that was already covered by the BBC and ITV.[73] Hence, the channel sought sports that covered minority interests, and which were not already covered by the two main channels. One sport that took advantage of this new development in the UK was American Football. For the National Football League (NFL), it was not simply a matter of selling the television rights to a station in need of cheap and effective sports programming. Rather, television opened a new market who, the league hoped, would indulge in the myriad merchandise which became available in Britain.[74] The influence of NFL on Channel Four would ultimately have consequences for a range of sports on British television, demonstrating the types of multi-scalar refractions across the media and sporting fields.

One of the key changes that NFL offered was in its presentation. Channel Four decided 'that the traditional form of British sports coverage was no longer appropriate'.[75] Both *Grandstand* and *World of Sport* could generally be characterised by an emphasis on seriousness, a reliance on long shots on hard cameras and an inclination to display the action as the spectator would see the game from the stadium. Televised American sports, in comparison, employed multi-camera shooting, an array of editing techniques and slow-motion replays to offer a stylised (re)construction of the game.[76] Channel Four took existing American Football game highlights, kept intact with original American commentary, and repackaged the games for British audiences using 'popularist presenters, rock 'n roll title music, and colourful graphics'.[77] Derek Brandon, in charge of producing the show, commentated on the difference between the two national styles:

> The televising of sport in America is simply stunning. They make it fun, they make it stylish, and they make it a family occasion. These are the things that we've lost from British sport. If LWT [London Weekend Television – *World of Sport* producers] had done American Football … they'd have been back to the presenter in the blazer with the glass of water.[78]

World of Sport was caught between the BBC's monopoly on traditional and respected sporting events and the seemingly fresher and more exciting, at least to some viewers, American or American-influenced sports on Channel Four, not to mention the marketing forces that accompanied these brands. Furthermore, compared to the style and tone of Channel Four's new ventures, *World of Sport* looked positively dated. Since its conception, *World of Sport* had struggled to compete with first the BBC, and then Viewsport, and now Channel Four was offering a fast-paced alternative. In 1981, an internal party was created to investigate whether both *World of Sport* and professional wrestling should be kept on the air. Though their recommendation was that they should remain so, a mere two years later in 1983, another internal party was set up to review the station's sport outlook and output.[79] The Sports Experts Group (SEG), made up of ITV's regional heads of sport, came to a more pessimistic, though perhaps more realistic and pragmatic, verdict than their earlier colleagues. The report summarised:

> ITV Sport needs reviewing and reviving, of that there can be no doubt. Disenchantment among some controllers, disputes over scheduling and disappointing ratings in some areas are outweighing the undoubted success stories in others. ITV has never broken free of its 'Racing and Wrestling' image.[80]

The channel's sports broadcasting had become old-fashioned, 'diffused, uneconomic and inevitably political'.[81] To counteract the problems outlined, the SEG recommended, 'the dismantling of *World of Sport* in its present form, substituting major event coverage, live wherever possible, from 15.00–16.40. This would allow alternative programming from 13.00–15.00.'[82] The group also suggested the dropping of professional wrestling, but was granted a reprieve.

Despite the sweeping changes that came into effect in the early autumn of 1985, professional wrestling remained in the schedules, but its programming was affected. The separate and contained professional wrestling programme brought with it contract renewals, and lacking the backing and support of the SEG, Joint Promotions found they had neither manoeuvrability nor bargaining power when it came to negotiations. Consequently, to save costs and revitalise the programme, Joint Promotions were forced to share the new broadcasting rights with its rival, All Star Promotions, and, crucially, with America's World Wrestling Federation (WWF). Without *World of Sport* to anchor professional wrestling in a regular time slot, the programme jumped around the schedule, shown at 12.30 one week and 13.55 the next with little or no pre-warning. Thus, all but the most ardent and attentive audience members were left with no real understanding of when to expect the show. When viewers could find professional wrestling, the shared television rights, with three separate companies, and three sets of rosters and styles, all competing for time and attention, meant there was little uniformity or cohesion from one week to the next. WWF's presence on British screens indicated the increasing intersections between the national and global media and sporting fields. Critically, changes in American broadcasting were refracted in Britain.

Taking advantage of the expansion of cable television in America, thanks to Reagan's deregulation of pricing, ownership and content, Vince McMahon seized opportunities to build a national following for his WWF shows, producing a variety of weekly cable television programmes. These included *Tuesday Night Titans* (USA, 1984–1986), *WWF All American Wrestling* (USA, 1983–1994), and *WWF Prime Time Wrestling* (USA, 1985–1993); syndicated shows, *Superstars of Wrestling* (1986–1996), *Wrestling Challenge* (1986–1995); and network specials, most famously *Saturday Night's Main Event* (NBC, 1985–1992). He also created closed circuit and pay-per-view events, most notably the transmedia event *Wrestlemania*. This approach was in stark contrast to how American professional wrestling had been promoted for much of the twentieth century. Prior to the 1980s, a collective of wrestling promotions grouped under the National Wrestling Alliance (NWA) had broadcast to regional areas, and this cartel relationship suited the localised manner of promoting professional wrestling. Much to the chagrin of the NWA, McMahon broke with this model and pursued an expansionist strategy.

As part of this expansion, McMahon also looked across the Atlantic to bolster the company's profit margins.[83] In the UK, he was to find another neo-conservative government with a similarly Reaganite attitude to media regulation in the process of expanding its television market via cable and Direct Broadcasting by Satellite (DBS). Driven by Margaret Thatcher's free market principles, the Conservative government embraced the concept of the market in broadcasting, and multi-channel television was the cornerstone of those changes.[84] Two companies emerged as the frontrunners in the British media field, British Satellite Broadcasting (BSB), the company awarded the official government endorsement, and Sky, the European-based company that would directly challenge BSB. The two companies battled over exclusive content, and by the late 1980s both Sky and BSB were haemorrhaging money that neither could particularly afford. The imminent arrival of two DBS services, moreover, also proved to be harmful to both the BBC and the ITV. Given their own commercial pressures, it was ITV who looked like they would potentially struggle in this new environment.

The channel, however, seemed set for the fight, particularly about sport. In 1988, 'ITV reached the peak of its sporting ambitions':[85] Greg Dyke and David Elstein, LWT programme controllers, outbid both the BBC and BSB in a competitive series of negotiations to win a four-year contract for Football League matches at an unprecedented £11 million per season. BSB's colossal overspending in Hollywood and their commitment to investing money in their own programming had served ITV well during the bartering for privileged league rights. If *World of Sport*'s cancellation had been detrimental to Joint Promotions, then the Football League contract was to prove fatal. As Dyke explained;

Even though £11 million doesn't sound like much when you consider ITV's annual programme budget is £400 million, we will still have to trim costs elsewhere. Cutting wrestling, darts, gymnastics and bowls would save about one and a half million pounds.[86]

In another interview, Dyke was also willing to admit that wrestling's cancellation was part of a wider positioning of the channel in a new multichannel media environment, seeking programming that attracted more lucrative advertising. Joint Promotions had failed to attract a younger audience, with only 2 per cent of 18–34s claiming to be 'extremely interested' and 7 per cent 'very interested' in professional wrestling.[87] As Dyke explained:

When I took over the sports in 1988, ITV was losing badly in the ratings to BBC. We were stuck in about 1955, and the world had changed, and we were too downmarket. Wrestling was clearly never a proper sport – that was part of the problem. It was unfortunate really. Wrestling was unlucky, but it was so tarnished with the old-style look of ITV that it had to go. We got rid of a lot of game shows for the same reason. (Dyke, cited in Garfield, 2007, pp. 145–146)

Any hope that British wrestling might have had in securing a deal with Sky's rival were dealt a final blow when BSB and Sky merged to form BSkyB in November 1990, illustrating again how fields are structured by compromise as much as conflict. Rupert Murdoch had once described sport as 'the battering ram' of his pay TV services,[88] and BSkyB turned their attention to acquiring that weapon. While ITV's Football League contract had been something of a coup in 1988, they had inadvertently fed the league's commitment to commercial expansion. By 1992, when ITV's contract expired, The Football League Division One had formed the FA Premier League Ltd and sold their television rights to BSkyB for an annual £60 million over a five-year contract.[89] ITV were left with few sporting contracts, and their 'live and exclusive' banner was short-lived. If *World of Sport* had become old-fashioned and stuffy in comparison to Channel Four's American sport coverage, BSkyB opted for the latter broadcasting model. Premier League coverage featured multi-camera perspectives, fast editing, instant replays and stylish presentation, accompanied by longer introductions and post-match analysis.

Vince McMahon was well placed to provide BSkyB with their wrestling content. The WWF fitted well on a network that frequently exploited News Corporation's extensive entertainment links, airing American drama, comedy and movie content. McMahon, furthermore, was already making wrestling programming for American syndication, and could sell the same to BSkyB for the cost of a videotape, making his money back on live tours and merchandising. As Crabtree explained:

> After Sky started broadcasting the American wrestling, I went to see the head of programmes there ... [We] talked about doing some British wrestling shows, and he said to go and do thirty tapes for him. I asked him how much we'd get. He said same as Americans. He put his hand up showing five fingers. I thought he meant £5,000, but he meant £500 – £500 an hour. I worked it out. To make a tape of three forty-minute shows ... would cost £20,000. So there was clearly no way back.[90]

As had been demonstrated at ITV repeatedly, it was difficult for the quasi-sport to be the cornerstone of a channel's sporting output. As the Premier League deal proved, BSkyB were happy to pay a premium for programming which was attractive to new customers – professional wrestling was considered a convenient but non-lucrative filler. This philosophy to programming echoed through much of their content: pay big money for the most popular British sports and Hollywood movies, and fill the remainder of the schedules with cheaper American imports. Sky television, however, represented just part of radical changes that were taking place in sport, in some ways merely a continuation of conflicts and compromises that had been undergoing in television since commercial television in the 1950s, and the experimentation with Pay-TV in the 1960s. Money was flooding in, and those involved with the television field were taking ever more prominent positions on the sporting field's terrain.

Entertain the public who will not otherwise pay to watch it

Since its establishment in the 1950s, the media field's terrain has been radically altered by television, and shifts in one field can be refracted and ultimately consequential in another, particularly the sporting field. As this book has stressed, a field's terrain is partly produced by intersections, individuals and organisations that operate across multiple fields. The deregulation and expansion of globalised markets combined with a continued flux of money into competitive sport continues to alter ownership of sporting teams while simultaneously calling into question the legacy of control that sporting bodies wield. Writing about sport shortly before his death in the shadow of France's hosting of the soccer World Cup, Bourdieu illustrated the many actors and agents that had become increasingly-active in the sporting field.

> Sport as spectacle, in the form that we know it as televised sporting spectacle, presupposes a system of competition in which, alongside sporting actors transformed into objects of spectacle, there are other actors. These are sports industry managers who control television and sponsoring rights, the managers of television channels competing for national broadcasting rights (or rights covering linguistic areas), the bosses of major industrial companies such as Adidas or Coca-Cola competing with each other for

exclusive rights to link their products with the sports event, and finally television producers.[91]

The large sums of money heralded by television moved control away from the amateur ideal more closely to commercial interests. While the amateur ethos retained some of its discursive power, sport become first and foremost a commodity which was produced for national and global television audiences. By the 1980s and the 1990s, even the staunchest advocates of amateurism, like the International Olympic Committee, had come to allow certain factors that encourage this. In these intersections, the power and values of the sporting field have been challenged, and notions of entertainment and spectatorship have been established as the key values of the field.

Sport's unadulterated moments of joy can offer moments of escapism from the drudgery of everyday life: a last-minute winning goal can trigger adrenaline, excitement and a feeling of getting lost in a crowd. Yet while most spectators will be able to recognise some of these feelings, even the most passionate sports fan will be able to recall turgid 0–0 draws, lifeless test days being deadened by defensive batsmen, and one-horse races delivering predictable results. Asking audiences to part with their money to watch an event in which quality and entertainment are left to chance seems an improbable business model in a century which saw ever-increasing Fordism (and then post-Fordism) and standardisation across cultural and economic commodities. Where some sporting organisations experimented with entertainment in the interwar years, many amateur sporting bodies insisted that entertainment was a by-product rather than central attraction. As Garry Whannel has argued, however,

> The increased penetration of sport by capital and the resultant infusion of spectacular, internationalised and glamorised forms of entertainment can be viewed an attempt to reduce the uncertainty of the sporting commodity, at least as far as its entertainment value is concerned.[92]

In the post-war period, entertainment became one of sport's defining features.

Adapting rules and catering for audiences have been an ongoing project since the debates about professionalism in the nineteenth century (see Chapter 2), and this has escalated since the arrival of television as a mass medium in the 1950s and the 1960s. Sporting bodies were eager to adapt rules to attract television producers to screen their sport, for reasons that we will look at in more detail shortly. Badminton, for example, experimented with different point scoring systems to better provide natural lulls in play for close-ups and slow motions which 'increased the drama and excitement without falsifying the sport'; water polo shortened the playing area and added balls to create the feeling of speed and excitement; and table tennis organisations proposed changes that included wrestling-style fanfares, master of ceremonies and entrances and exits.[93] Elsewhere, less niche sports adopted wholesale rule or presentational changes in order to better fit the demands of television broadcasting. For example, the advent of one-day and then Twenty-20 cricket marked an attempt to provide faster-paced, more easily televised entertainment suited to the sped-up temporality of an increasingly urbanised world.

Where rules have not been changed, or sports created in the manner of the Twenty-20, televisual technologies and codes and conventions have helped to heighten, and sometimes artificially create, entertainment. Television offers a singular viewpoint, and constructs a representation quite different from that experienced in the stadium, one made up of 'varying shots, angles, positions and the fragmentation of time through replays and slow motions'.[94] Over this, commentators frame narratives, embellish events, and generally exhibit excitement.[95] Where sports contest still have the potential to disappoint, filming, editing and other layers of mediation, characterised by their 'excitement, speed ... and sensory bombardment',[96] seek to limit the potential for disappointment. In other words, sport has become first and foremost a televised spectacle. Writing about football, Baudrillard, one of postmodernism's most prominent thinkers, suggested that a European football game, which he dubs 'the phantom football match', between Real Madrid and Napoli held in the empty *Estadio Santiago Bernabéu* stadium encapsulates the spirit of postmodernism: a game which no one witnessed directly, 'but everyone will have received an image of;' where 'every real referent must disappear so that the event may become acceptable on television's mental screen;' in which the 'pure event ... [is] devoid of any referent in nature, and readily susceptible to replacement by synthetic images'.[97]

As part of these shifts to sporting entertainments, since the 1960s, the role of sports players has changed as well. With television, and its close-ups, bringing players existing in exciting narratives into the homes of the national and globe, many sports players have increasingly become celebrities. Sports players have also more frequently been folded into celebrity cultures. Responding to the tabloidization in the 1960s and the 1970s, gossip about sports stars, their relationships, and their 'moral' digressions, have become a regular feature of modern society. Alongside this, athletes have sought better wages, sponsorship deals, and other financial gains, eroding the notion of amateurism almost entirely by the 1990s.

In this context, sport on television has been read as increasingly melodramatic.[98] For Ava Rose and James Friedman, for example, 'sports programs are ... open-ended, cyclical, and melodramatic',[99] because narratives emphasising 'personal struggle, social tension, and moral conflict' with 'extremes of emotion ... exaggerated, and opposing forces are pitted against each other in absolute dualisms'.[100] In the UK, Sky Sports developed sleek modes of presentation, building narratives before, during and after the game or match via edited montage packages, complete with dramatic music. In the twenty-first century, television viewers of association football matches have become less concerned with unpredictable outcomes or competition and more interested in narratives starring their favourite sporting stars. The 'classic notion of a pure sporting contest', Babatunde Buraimo and Rob Simmons suggest, 'has been replaced with one in which the preference is for sporting entertainment delivered by superstars'.[101]

In the glare of 24-hour news cycles; million-pound contracts for players and billion-pound contracts for clubs, leagues and organising committees; and red-button, multi-camera, multi-angle television, professional sports are closer to the position historically occupied by professional wrestling than they have ever been before. Sport has not gone to the radical lengths that wrestling promoters settled on in the 1920s, but many have taken great lengths to offer as much entertainment as they can muster, embracing rule and presentational changes to simplify contests, expand audiences, and secure sponsorship and television deals. In some ways, today's stress on entertainment, audience pleasure and spectacle can be understood as a re-emergence of the imperatives of sporting cultures before the rise to prominence of the amateur ethos in the nineteenth century, albeit adapting to the needs of global capital and the digital media. If this is the case, we may very well view 'amateurism' – or the 'classic notion of pure sporting contest' – to be a historical blip of the mid-nineteenth to mid-twentieth century.[102] If professional wrestling has been an enduring possibility for an older model of sporting display, then those possibilities have partly been realised since the 1970s.

Individuals involved with professional wrestling have responded to these changes in the field's terrain in different ways. Early in the 1960s, when television's influence was first beginning to be felt, the problems facing other sports adapting to the new broadcasting environment, and the concessions 'purer' sporting bodies were having to make, were not lost on professional wrestling promotors. With the sporting field becoming increasingly orientated towards entertainment, promoters pointed to changes in the sporting field as evidence of professional wrestling's legitimacy, and used these examples and others to defend themselves from criticism from television producers. As early as 1966, a letter from Dale Martin Promotions not unfairly reasoned:

> Most professional sport is presented with the major object of attracting large crowds, and to do this, it has to entertain the public who will not otherwise pay to watch it. In this respect, one merely has to bear in mind the campaign which has been mounted for brighter cricket in the face of decreasing attendances, or the cry for less defensive football in the interests of halting the decline in its support.[103]

H.W. Abby rationalised that wrestling was merely part of a wider movement to play sports more interesting and engaging for those watching and for those seeking commercial contracts: it just so happened that professional wrestling had been more successful and had been doing it for longer.

While both former wrestlers and fans have sometimes decried wrestling's disregard of sport entirely, the cultural context for professional wrestling's shifts in the 1980s might well be explained by wider changes in the sporting world. Where once wrestling's focus on entertainment had marked it as a fringe position, by the 1980s and the 1990s, it was generally the dominant value in the field. Given that part of professional wrestling's attraction has been in caricaturing, parodying and critiquing the wider sporting field, the new terrain of multi-channel, global sports has seen wrestling promoters embrace increasingly outlandish characters. This could partly be seen in the complaints about the 'black masks, stomachs the size of saucepans and glittering gowns' described above. Professional wrestling's success has been driven by its excesses, and its clearly embellished characters, and Vince McMahon's decision to acknowledge the existence of kayfabe, going public about its pre-arranged status in 1989 (see Chapter 3 and Chapter 4), may have been a tactical realignment on a terrain in which sports were increasingly resembling professional wrestling.

As part of this realignment, McMahon decidedly pursued intersections with the field of entertainment and popular culture, seeking co-promotional events with channels like MTV, encouraging wrestlers to appear in music videos, popular television shows, and films.[104] McMahon's style of wrestling, furthermore, looked different. Coming out of Mountevans, British wrestling retained its own style: it was methodical, slower-paced but technically more accomplished, using complex submission holds, and the 2 out of 3 falls match structure. Vince McMahon's version of professional wrestling was different to the type that Joint Promotions had encouraged. Any pretence that professional wrestling was a legitimate sport was removed entirely. WWF matches were considerably shorter, sometimes lasting no longer than two or three minutes, and often used any number of 'gimmicks'. Though more character-based wrestlers and larger-than-life figures had emerged in the 1970s, it was still based on the notion that it was a legitimate sport. WWF television shows featured an array of brightly coloured characters that could almost pass for cartoon characters. Any pretence that these were professional sportsmen was difficult to maintain in a television show that presented wrestlers as hillbillies and evil drill sergeants.

Sitting on the fringes of the sporting field, professional wrestling has historically questioned and critiqued the possibilities that were actualised in other sports, haunting the amateur purists, and serving as a reminder of sport's theatrical past. Occupying this position on the sporting field's terrain, professional wrestling has been used by concerned commentators as an example of all that is wrong with professionalism, commercialism and spectators. One of the first writers to critique the expansion of commercialism in sport, Gregory P. Stone, for example, used the example of professional wrestling as a warning for the direction other sports might take. He suggested:

> The game, inherently moral and ennobling of its players, seems to be giving way to the spectacle, inherently immoral and debasing. With the massification of sport, spectators begin to outnumber participants, and the

spectator as the name implies, encourages the spectacular – the dis-play. In this regard the spectator may be viewed as an agent of destruction as far as the dignity of sport is concerned.[105]

Spectator sports, as discussed in Chapter 3, devalued the capitals associated with the establishment of the field, undercutting the ideologies and hegemonies closely associated with its structures. Since the arrival of television, and particularly commercial television, the terrain of the sporting field has been radically altered, and the possibility of professional wrestling has been actualised, albeit with sports embracing entertainment and profit in different ways. Because of this, professional wrestling has adapted to that terrain, itself becoming ever-knowingly dramatised, and acknowledging its performativity (see Chapter 3), and these changes have served the wider sporting field well.

Just as journalists had used wrestling as a warning to boxing in the late 1910s and early 1920s, professional wrestling continues to be the comparator, particularly regarding the World Wrestling Federation, when contemporary journalists want to register their disgust at contemporary sporting culture. In February 2012 at a Dereck Chisora vs Vitali Klitschko post boxing match press conference in Munich, Chisora and David Haye exchanged insults and wound up in a brawl in front of the world's press. A fight between the two was announced despite the BBBC not licensing the match. In the press conference leading up to the event, a steel fence was placed between the two competitors. Sports columnists were, overall, appalled by the proceedings. Professional wrestling, albeit American, was again used as a comparison.

> Many WWE [World Wrestling Entertainment] elements were there – key action taking place outside the ring, for instance, and Chisora's nice line in unconvincing mawkishness ... If not quite WWE, then it was boxing's version of structured reality, the term used to describe cultural offerings such as *The Only Way is Essex* and *Made in Chelsea*.[106]

Such comments have not been restricted to boxing, a sport that has always been reasonably close to wrestling in the field. In football, Martin Kelner has designated reporting and coverage of the final few games of the season as the 'time of the year when football adopts the language of WWE wrestling, when every day is Judgment Day'.[107] Despite sport's almost wholesale embrace of many of the values of sporting entertainment, wrestling still serves as a useful marker on the sporting field's terrain, continuing to operate as an enduring possibility. As other sporting events became increasingly postmodern and commoditised, the presentation of professional wrestling as pseudo-sport served to conceal the fact that all sports had become hyperreal. Thinking in these terms, Baudrillard's famous conception of Disneyland is useful. For him, the theme park was 'presented as imaginary in order to make us believe that the rest is real, when in fact all of Los Angeles and the America surrounding it are no longer real'.[108] In an age where the vast majority of sport is consumed on television, with an expectation that entertainment is heightened, professional wrestling's cultural role has changed. Rather than serving as a warning, it now convinces audiences that the rest of the sporting field is 'real'.

Conclusion

The introduction and intersection of television producers and controllers into the field of sport, especially after 1955, were the most dramatic shift in terrain since the genesis of the field in the late nineteenth century. For the first time in sport's existence, spectator sports were not played for the enjoyment of those taking part, nor performed for the crowds in stadiums. First and foremost, professional sports were now predominantly about securing and sustaining television audiences. By the 1980s, the amateur ideal, so central to muscular Christians in the Victorian and Edwardian periods, was all but a vague value alluded to but never strictly enforced. In 1988, the Olympics, one of the last strongholds of strict amateur sport separation, allowed professionalism.

Professional wrestling, in this regard, was no different. Both television and the development of a global sporting and media field generated substantial changes in the ownership, production, dissemination and consumption of the sport. First, with their contract with ITV, Joint Promotions generated a cartel-like relationship over the sport. The possibility of pay television, however, meant that the sport was bought by eager investors hoping to provide popular content for pay-per-view television content. Upon its failure, Joint Promotions was passed between promoters before ultimately being surpassed by American wrestling on Sky and then cancelled on ITV. Television's, and commercial and pay television's, influence on British sport since the 1970s cannot be understated. Television has changed the structure and feel of sport, and organisations have adapted rules to make sports more entertaining. In other words, sports moved closer to the capital, pleasures and values of professional wrestling. Televised sports needed to be engaging, entertaining and commercially viable. In response, promoters like Vince McMahon have shifted the position in which professional wrestling sits, still serving as an enduring possibility of how sport might have developed, and might develop next.

Notes

1 Scott M. Beekman, *Ringside: A History of Professional Wrestling in America* (Westport, CT, 2006), p.83.
2 Mike Huggins, 'BBC Radio and Sport 1922–39', *Contemporary British History*, 21(4), (2007), pp. 491–515.
3 Anon., 'Television', *Radio Times*, 4 Mar. 1938, p. 29.
4 Anon., 'Cures for Interference', *Radio Times*, 10 Mar. 1939, p. 15.
5 Edward Royle, 'Trends in Post-War British Social History', in James Obelkevich and Peter Catterall (eds), *Understanding Post-War Britain* (London, 1994), p. 13.

6 Martin Johnes and Gavin Mellor, 'The 1953 FA Cup Final: Modernity and Tradition in British Culture', *Contemporary British History*, 20(2), (2006), pp. 263–280.
7 Jonathan Bignell, 'And the Rest is History: Lew Grade, Creation Narratives and Television Historiography', in Catherine Johnson and Rob Turnock (eds), *ITV Cultures: Independent Television Over Fifty Years* (Maidenhead, 2005); Janet Thumim, *Inventing Television: Men, Women and the Box* (Oxford, 2004), p. 17.
8 In 1972, the ITA was restructured and renamed the Independent Broadcasting Authority (IBA).
9 Rob Turnock, *Television and Consumer Culture: Britain and the Transformation of Modernity* (London, 2007), p. 22.
10 For a discussion of field in relation to television history see Pierre Bourdieu, *On Television* (New York, 1996), pp. 41–42.
11 Bernard Sendall, *Independent Television in Britain*, vol. 1: *Origin and Foundation, 1946–62* (London, 1982), p. 324.
12 Richard Holt, *Sport and the British: A Modern History* (Oxford, 1989), p. 321.
13 Sendall, *Independent Television in Britain*, vol. 1, p. 324.
14 Kent Walton, *This Grappling Game* (London, 1967), p. 11.
15 Sendall, *Independent Television in Britain*, vol. 1, p. 323.
16 Garry Whannel, *Fields in Vision: Television Sport and Cultural Transformation* (London, 1992), p. 52.
17 Ibid., p. 78.
18 John Ellis, 'Importance, Significance, Cost and Value: Is an ITV Canon Possible?' in Catherine Johnson and Rob Turnock (eds), *ITV Cultures: Independent Television Over Fifty Years* (Maidenhead, 2005), p. 43.
19 Unless otherwise stated, all information regarding television schedules has been taken from the TV Times Project, Bournemouth University(www.tvtip.bufvc.ac.uk), the TVRoom Plus archive (www.tvlistings.thetvroomplus.com) and The Christopher Griffin-Beale Radio Times Collection, Sussex University.
20 Clifford Davies, 'Ring Stars Join Variety Union: Wrestlers Fight for Bigger TV Purse', *Daily Mirror*, 23 Apr. 1962, p. 11.
21 Letter from Lew Grade to Bernard Sendall, 18 Apr. 1967, Sporting Events "Wrestling", vol. 1, IBA, box 01097.
22 Whannel, *Fields in Vision*, p. 49.
23 Ian Dobie and Mallory Wober, *The Role of Wrestling as a Public Spectacle: Audience Attitudes to Wrestling as Portrayed on Television*, Independent Broadcasting Authority (London, 1978), Paul Bonner and Lesley Aston, *Independent Television in Britain*, vol. 5: *ITV and the IBA 1981–92: The Old Relationship Changes* (Basingstoke, 1998), p. 109.
24 Bonner and Aston, *Independent Television in Britain*, vol. 5, p. 109.
25 Dobie and Wober, *The Role of Wrestling*, p. 3.
26 Ibid., p. 10.
27 John Ellis, *Seeing Things: Television in the Age of Uncertainty* (London, 2000), pp. 6–38.
28 Turnock, *Television and Consumer Culture*, p. 61.
29 Walton, *This Grappling Game*, p. 15.
30 Internal memo about viewer complaint, 11 Jan. 1965, Sporting Events "Wrestling", vol. 1, IBA, box 01097.
31 Holt, *Sport and the British*, p. 317.
32 Whannel, *Fields in Vision*, pp. 27–28.
33 Ibid., p. 31.
34 Letter from F.W. Bath to F.H. Copplestone, 30 Aug., 1967, Sporting Events "Wrestling", vol. 1, IBA, box 01097.

35 Raymond Williams, *Television: Technology and Cultural Form* (London, 2003), pp. 77–120.
36 Turnock, *Television and Consumer Culture*, pp. 67–68.
37 Thumim, *Inventing Television*, p. 4.
38 Jacques deFrance, 'The Making of a Field with a Weak Autonomy', in Philip S. Gorski (ed.), *Bourdieu and Historical Analysis* (Durham, NC, 2013), p. 301.
39 Whannel, *Fields in Vision*, p. 37.
40 Ibid.
41 Francis Bonner, *Personality Presenters: Television's Intermediaries with Viewers* (Farnham, 2011), p. 80.
42 Simon Garfield, *The Wrestling* (London, 2007), p. 148.
43 Paper no. 19, BBC memorandum (no. 4), Cmnd. 1819, *Report of the Committee on Broadcasting, 1960*, vol. I. Appendix E, 1960, p. 158.
44 Paper no. 214, British Home Entertainment Limited Second Submission, Cmnd. 1819, *Report of the Committee on Broadcasting, 1960*, vol. I, Appendix E, 1960, p. 1059.
45 Paper no. 215, British Telemeter Home Viewing Limited, Cmnd. 1819, *Report of the Committee on Broadcasting, 1960*, vol. I, Appendix E, 1960. p. 1059.
46 'Licenses for Five Pay-TV Groups', *The Times*, 12 Dec., 1963, p .4.
47 Paper no. 216, Choiceview Limited, Cmnd. 1819, *Report of the Committee on Broadcasting, 1960*, vol. I, Appendix E, 1960, p. 1065.
48 Postmaster General, *Broadcasting: Further Memorandum on the Report of the Committee on Broadcasting* (London, HMSO, 1962), p. 11.
49 'TV Firms Reject Fight Terms', *The Times*, 20 Apr. 1966, p. 6.
50 'Hurst Park Forms Pay-TV Offshoot', *The Times*, 12 Aug. 1964, p. 12.
51 IBA, box 01039, 'Pay Television, vol. 1', 'Sir Hugh Greene, Pay Television and Closed Circuit Television Developments: Note to Members of the Administrative Council', 26 May 1966.
52 'Box Fighting', *The Economist*, 14 May 1966, p. 716.
53 'BBC's £781,000 Bid for TV Football', *The Times*, 14 Mar., 1967, p. 3.
54 Peter Wilson, 'TV Spells Danger', *Daily Mirror*, 15 Mar. 1967, p. 27.
55 Anon., 'Pay Television Stakes Its Claim', *Illustrated London News*, 15 Jan. 1966, pp. 10–11.
56 Anon., 'Hurst Park Forms Pay-TV Offshoot', *The Times*, 12 Aug. 1964, p. 12.
57 Garfield, *The Wrestling*, p. 148.
58 David Hunn, 'They All Dance to Astaire's Tune', *The Observer*, 8 Apr. 1973, p. 25.
59 Des Freedman, *Television Policies of the Labour Party 1951–2001* (London, 2003), p. 60.
60 Anon., 'Hurst Park Forms Pay-TV Offshoot', *The Times*, 12 Aug. 1964, p. 12.
61 Andrew Davenport, 'Betting on the Bookmakers: Sears Holdings' Bid for William Hill', *The Guardian*, 25 Nov. 1971, p. 24. For a summary of turnovers and takeovers of bookmakers during this period, see Roger Munting, *An Economic and Social History of Gambling in Britain and the USA* (Manchester, 1996), pp. 89–116.
62 Garfield, *The Wrestling*, p. 148.
63 Ibid., p. 153.
64 Peter Bills, 'Beware: Too Much Showmanship Could Ruin Wrestling, says Kent Walton', *World of Sport Annual* (London, 1979).
65 Unsigned correspondence, date unknown, Sporting Events "Wrestling", vol. 5, IBA, box 01097.
66 Unsigned correspondence, date unknown, Sporting Events "Wrestling", vol. 6, IBA, box 01097.

67 Unsigned correspondence, date unknown, Sporting Events "Wrestling", vol. 6, IBA, box 01097.
68 Garfield, *The Wrestling*, p. 153.
69 Letter from Normal Morrell to Michael Gillies and Teresa Newberry, 16 Jul. 1980, Sporting Events "Wrestling", vol. 6, IBA, box 01097.
70 Letter from Norman Morrell to Michael Gillies, 23 Apr. 1980, Sporting Events "Wrestling", vol. 5, IBA, box 01097.
71 Peter Bills, 'Beware: Too Much Showmanship Could Ruin Wrestling, says Kent Walton', *World of Sport Annual* (London, 1979).
72 Larissa Buchholz, 'What is a Global Field? Theorizing Fields beyond the Nation-State', *The Sociological Review Monographs*, 64(2). (2016), p. 42.
73 Stephen Lambert, *Channel Four: Television With a Difference?* (London, 1982), p. 149.
74 Joseph Maguire, 'American Football, British Society, and Global Sport Development', in Eric G. Dunning, Joseph A. Maguire and Robert E. Pearton (eds), *The Sports Process: A Comparative and Developmental Approach* (Champaign, IL, 1993), pp. 207–230.
75 Ibid., p. 210.
76 Margaret Morse, 'Sport on Television: Replay and Display', in E. Ann Kaplan (ed.), *Regarding Television* (Los Angeles, 1983), pp. 50–51.
77 Maguire, 'American Football', p. 210.
78 Brandon in Maguire, 'American Football', p. 210.
79 Bonner and Aston, *Independent Television in Britain*, vol. 5, p. 109.
80 Sports Experts Group in ibid., p. 110.
81 Ibid.
82 Ibid.
83 I have explored these issues in further detail in Benjamin Litherland, 'Selling Punches: Free Markets and Professional Wrestling in the UK, 1986–1993', *Journal of Historical Research in Marketing*, 4(4), (2012), pp. 578–598.
84 Peter Goodwin, *Television Under the Tories: Broadcasting Policy 1979–1997* (London, 1998).
85 Bonner and Aston, *Independent Television in Britain*, vol. 5, p. 112.
86 Greg Dyke, in 'Snatch of the Day', *TV Times*, 29 Oct.–4 Nov. 1988. Available at: www.johnlisterwriting.com/itvwrestling/article882.html (accessed 5 July 2010).
87 Dobie and Wober, *The Role of Wrestling*, p. 17.
88 Campbell Cowie and Mark Williams, 'The Economics of Sports Rights', *Telecommunications Policy*, 21(7), (1997), p. 620.
89 Ibid.
90 Crabtree, in Garfield, *The Wrestling*, p. 146.
91 Pierre Bourdieu, 'The State, Economics and Sport', *Culture, Sport, Society*, 1(2), (1998), pp. 17–18. See also Pierre Bourdieu, *On Television* (New York, 1996), pp. 79–81.
92 Whannel, *Fields in Vision*, p. 79.
93 Ibid., pp. 77–78.
94 Cornel Sandvoss, *A Game of Two Halves: Football, Television, and Globalisation* (London, 2003), p. 146.
95 Jennings Bryant, Paul Comisky and Dolf Zillmann, 'Drama in Sports Commentary', *Journal of Communication*, 27(3), (1977), pp. 140–149.
96 Bob Stewart and Aaron Smith, 'Australian Sport in a Postmodern Age', *International Journal of the History of Sport*, 17(2), (2000), p. 278.
97 Jean Baudrillard, *The Transparency of Evil: Essays in Extreme Phenomena* (London, 1993), p.79.
98 Jim McKay and David Rowe, 'Field of Soaps: Rupert v. Kerry as Masculine Melodrama', *Social Text*, 50, (1997), pp. 69–86.

99   Ava Rose and James Friedman, 'Television Sports as Mas(c)uline Cult of Distraction', in Aaron Baker and Todd Boyd (eds), *Sports, Media and the Politics of Identity* (Bloomington, IN, 1997), p. 2.
100 Ibid., p. 8.
101 Babatunde Buraimo and Rob Simmons, 'Uncertainty of Outcome or Star Quality? Television Audience Demand for English Premier League Football', *International Journal of the Economics of Business*, 22(3), (2015), p. 466.
102 Tony Collins, *Sport in Capitalist Society: A Short History* (London, 2013), pp. 121–122.
103 Letter from H.W. Abby, Dale Martin Promotions, to Lew Grade and Howard Thomas, 21 Jan. 1966, Sporting Events "Wrestling", vol. 1, IBA, box 01097.
104 See Holly Chard and Benjamin Litherland, '"Hollywood" Hulk Hogan: Stardom, Synergy and Field Migration', *The Cinema Journal* (forthcoming).
105 Gregory P. Stone, 'American Sports: Pay and Display', in Eric Dunning (ed.), *Sport: Readings From a Sociological Perspective* (London, 1971).
106 Marina Hyde, 'Why Frank Warren's Chisora-Haye Plot Line Saw Boxing Hit Rock Bottom', *The Guardian*, 9 May 2012. Available at: www.theguardian.com/sport/blog/2012/may/09/frank-warren-haye-chisora (accessed 3 Oct. 2013).
107 Martin Kelner, 'Relegation Hyperbole Reaches a New Level of Massiveness', *The Guardian*, 11 May 2009. Available at: www.theguardian.com/sport/blog/2009/may/11/premier-league-relegation-battle (accessed 3 Oct. 2013).
108 Jean Baudrillard, *Simulcra and Simulation* (Michigan, 1994), pp. 166–184.

Bibliography

Baudrillard, Jean, *The Transparency of Evil: Essays in Extreme Phenomena*, London, Verso, 1993.
Baudrillard, Jean, *Simulacra and Simulation*, Michigan, University of Michigan Press, 1994. Beekman, Scott M., *Ringside: A History of Professional Wrestling in America*, Westport, CT, Praeger, 2006.
Bignell, Jonathan, 'And the Rest is History: Lew Grade, Creation Narratives and Television Historiography' in Catherine Johnson, and Rob Turnock (eds), *ITV Cultures: Independent Television Over Fifty Years*, Maidenhead, Open University Press, 2005.
Bonner, Francis, *Personality Presenters: Television's Intermediaries with Viewers*, Farnham, Ashgate, 2011, p. 80.
Bonner, Paul and Aston, Lesley, *Independent Television in Britain: vol. 5: ITV and the IBA 1981–92: The Old Relationship Changes*, Basingstoke, Macmillan, 1998.
Bourdieu, Pierre, *On Television*, New York, The New Press, 1996.
Bourdieu, Pierre, 'The State, Economics and Sport', *Culture, Sport, Society*, 1(2), (1998), pp. 15–21.
Bryant, Jennings, Comisky, Paul, and Zillmann, Dolf, 'Drama in Sports Commentary', *Journal of Communication*, 27(3), (1977), pp. 140–149.
Buchholz, Larissa, 'What Is a Global Field? Theorizing Fields beyond the Nation-State', *The Sociological Review Monographs*, 64(2), (2016), pp. 31–60.
Buraimo, Babatunde and Simmons, Rob, 'Uncertainty of Outcome or Star Quality? Television Audience Demand for English Premier League Football', *International Journal of the Economics of Business*, 22(3), (2015), pp. 449–469.
Chard, Holly, and Litherland, Benjamin, '"Hollywood" Hulk Hogan: Stardom, Synergy and Field Migration', *The Cinema Journal*, (forthcoming).

Collins, Tony, *Sport in Capitalist Society: A Short History*, London, Routledge, 2013.
Cowie, Campbell and Williams, Mark, 'The Economics of Sports Rights', *Telecommunications Policy*, 21(7), (1997), pp. 619–634.
DeFrance, Jacques, 'The Making of a Field with a Weak Autonomy', in Philip S. Gorski (ed.), *Bourdieu and Historical Analysis*, Durham, NC, Duke University Press, 2013, pp. 303–326.
Dobie, Ian, and Wober, Mallory, *The Role of Wrestling as a Public Spectacle: Audience Attitudes to Wrestling as Portrayed on Television*, London, Independent Broadcasting Authority, 1978.
Ellis, John, *Seeing Things: Television in the Age of Uncertainty*, London, I.B. Tauris, 2000.
Ellis, John, 'Importance, Significance, Cost and Value: Is an ITV Canon Possible?', in Catherine Johnson and Rob Turnock (eds), *ITV Cultures: Independent Television Over Fifty Years*, Maidenhead, Open University Press, 2005, pp. 36–56.
Freedman, Des, *Television Policies of the Labour Party, 1951–2001*, London, Frank Cass, 2003.
Garfield, Simon, *The Wrestling*, London, Faber & Faber, 2007.
Goodwin, Peter, *Television Under the Tories: Broadcasting Policy 1979–1997*, London, BFI Publishing, 1998.
Holt, Richard, *Sport and the British: A Modern History*, Oxford, Clarendon Press, 1989.
Huggins, Mike, 'BBC Radio and Sport 1922–39', *Contemporary British History*, 21(4), (2007), pp. 491–515.
Johnes, Martin, and Mellor, Gavin, 'The 1953 FA Cup Final: Modernity and Tradition in British Culture', *Contemporary British History*, 20(2), (2006), pp. 263–280.
Lambert, Stephen, *Channel Four: Television with a Difference?* London, BFI Publishing, 1982.
Litherland, Benjamin, 'Selling Punches: Free Markets and Professional Wrestling in the UK, 1986–1993', *Journal of Historical Research in Marketing*, 4(4), (2012), pp. 578–598.
Maguire, Joseph, 'American Football, British Society, and Global Sport Development', in Eric G. Dunning, Joseph A. Maguire and Robert E. Pearton (eds), *The Sports Process: A Comparative and Developmental Approach*, Champaign, IL: Human Kinetics Publishers, 1993, pp. 207–230.
McKay, Jim and Rowe, David, '"Field of Soaps": Rupert v. Kerry as Masculine Melodrama', *Social Text*, 50, (1997), pp. 69–86.
Morse, Margaret, 'Sport on Television: Replay and Display', in E. Ann Kaplan (ed.), *Regarding Television*, Los Angeles, American Film Institute, 1983, pp. 44–66.
Munting, Roger, *An Economic and Social History of Gambling in Britain and the USA*, Manchester, Manchester University Press, 1996.
Rose, Ava and Friedman, James, 'Television Sports as Mas(c)uline Cult of Distraction', in Aaron Baker and Todd Boyd (eds), *Sports, Media and the Politics of Identity*, Bloomington, IN, Indiana University Press, pp. 1–15.
Royle, Edward, 'Trends in Post-War British Social History', in James Obelkevich and Peter Catterall (eds), *Understanding Post-War Britain*, London, Routledge, 1994.
Sandvoss, Cornel, *A Game of Two Halves: Football, Television, and Globalisation*, London, Routledge, 2003.
Sendall, Bernard, *Independent Television in Britain*, vol. 1: *Origin and Foundation, 1946–62*, London, Macmillan, 1982.

Stewart, Bob and Smith, Aaron, 'Australian Sport in a Postmodern Age', *International Journal of the History of Sport*, 17(2), (2000), pp. 278–304.

Stone, Gregory P., 'American Sports: Pay and Display', in Eric Dunning (ed.), *Sport: Readings from a Sociological Perspective*, Toronto, University of Toronto Press, 1971.

Thumim, Janet, *Inventing Television: Men, Women and the Box*, Oxford, Oxford University Press, 2004.

Turnock, Rob, *Television and Consumer Culture: Britain and the Transformation of Modernity*, London, I.B. Tauris, 2007.

Whannel, Garry, *Fields in Vision: Television Sport and Cultural Transformation*, London, Routledge, 1992.

Williams, Raymond, *Television: Technology and Cultural Form*, London, Routledge, 2003.

Epilogue

Though the detailed history outlined in this book has been concluded, it is worth sketching some of the transformations that have occurred in professional wrestling since 1988. The history of British wrestling can be traced through a narrative of decline and then resurgence. Though this is something of a simplistic telling of a more complicated history, throughout the 1990s and 2000s, British wrestling has been overshadowed by its American counterpart, particularly World Wrestling Entertainment. In the summer of 1992, the WWF (as they were still called) reached the zenith of its popularity. Taking advantage of BSkyB's market dominance, especially after its capture of Premier League football, and as a response to dwindling markets in the USA, Vince McMahon's company held its second biggest event of the year, *SummerSlam*, at Wembley stadium. The capacity audience of 80,355, waving their foam fingers, decked out in merchandise, were treated to a spectacle. Wrestlers rode the ring on motorbikes, fireworks exploded above the ring, and The British Bulldog – a Lancashire lad who had sought fame and fortune in America – headlined in the main event. The event cemented the WWF's popularity in Britain, and they have not loosened their grip on the market since. Joint Promotions, in comparison, was left to tour town halls. Without a television contract, their dwindling audiences meant that by the mid-1990s the company had gone out of business.

Since the 1990s, Vince McMahon has worked incredibly hard for professional wrestling to be synonymous with the World Wrestling Entertainment (WWE, the name for the now rebranded WWF), at least in America, Europe and Australasia, with an ever-growing number of countries also having access to the company's television product. After a short rivalry with World Championship Wrestling (WCW) in the 1990s, when in America the two companies aired on different channels at the same time on Monday nights, the WWE has been the dominant market leader of professional wrestling. According to its corporate website, WWE is available in over 20 languages to 180 countries. In the global field of entertainment, the company are now important players. Building on the expansion of synergistic media making, and the sporting field's ever closer relationship to entertainment, Vince McMahon has developed WWE into a transmedia phenomenon, incorporating, at one time or another, home video distribution, film production studios, and record labels, and producing a swathe of multimedia texts and merchandise, including animated cartoons, movies, toys, t-shirts, records, foods, and multivitamins.

At points in this historical narrative, it has seemed that Vince McMahon's control over professional wrestling was fixed, with British wrestling serving as an historical legacy – a discarded possibility – supporting the narrative of the WWE as the cutting edge global leader. Fields, though, are never fixed, and neither are their histories. As we have seen throughout this book, fields change, and their changes refract and reverberate at both a micro and macro level. Since the 2000s, a wave of British promotions and training schools have grown, peaking in the mid-2010s, and their influence on the global stage is now fully cemented. As I write this in 2017, British professional wrestling is in a position of strength not seen since the 1980s. Promotions like Insane Championship Wrestling (ICW) (based in Glasgow, founded in 2006), Progress Wrestling (London, 2011), Revolution Pro Wrestling (London, 2012), Fight Club Pro (Wolverhampton, 2009), Attack! Pro Wrestling (Cardiff, 2011) all feature impressive global talents. There are dozens of other promotions, usually centred around a city or town, operating across Britain (and indeed Ireland and the rest of Europe), all working from a core of between 50–100 regular talents, in addition to training schools developing other wrestlers. In 2016, ICW held at an event at Glasgow's 13,000 seat SSE Hydro arena, and Progress have announced they will be holding an event at London's Wembley arena in 2018.

British wrestling's recent popularity can be attributed to several, interconnected factors. First, changes in production, distribution and reception technologies. Whether on America's first national television channels, the Pay-TV experiments, or multi-channel satellite and cable broadcasting, professional wrestling has always been something of a test case for popular entertainments and new technologies. Most British promotions have taken advantage of broader changes in the media environment. Whether with the availability of DVDs, the short-lived The Wrestling Channel broadcast on Sky Digital (2004–2008), and most importantly internet streaming, contemporary British wrestling promotions have developed audiences and brands through emerging technologies. Revolution Pro, Progress, and ICW, for example, have all developed streaming services on demand on Pivotshare. What Culture Professional Wrestling, a YouTube channel that has had some success with wrestling commentary and opinion videos, have likewise created their own wrestling promotion based on YouTube's advertising model, though changes in advertising regulation during the spring and summer of 2017 appear to be causing some problems for the promotion and company.

Second, British wrestling promotions have built dynamic brands. Learning lessons from the post-modern, global sporting super-brands of the 1980s and the 1990s, many contemporary British wrestling companies have created localised micro-brands that attract a good deal of excitement and dedication from their audiences. These brands extend to social and digital media, and operating on post-Fordist logics of production, a stream of merchandise (particularly t-shirts) are created and sold on quick turnovers. Where local indy wrestling groups are apparently often firmly rooted in local towns and cities, they mingle with specific forms of consumer and fan identities that are then performed on global, digital streaming sites. Just as crowds co-produce meanings in wrestling contests (as explored in Chapter 3), British wrestling crowds have developed their own cultures, incorporating terrace-style football songs with the chanting of American sports and wrestling. There is a good deal of pride, and intense senses of ownership, that audiences have for both favourite wrestlers and favourite promotions. Some of these practices (the shouting of 'one fall' in the pre-match announcements, for example) have now been adopted by WWE audiences in America, suggesting the movement of participatory practices between local and international fields.

The notion of a national wrestling style is important to some of these narratives and movements. What is now called the *World of Sport* style is a genre of performing professional wrestling that is recognised as a dominant international style. In contrast to lucha libre's gymnastics, or Japan's hard-hitting style, British professional wrestling has been submission-based and more 'technical', partly rooted in the Mountevans Committee in the 1940s. This description of the British style has been discussed in wrestling fandoms, but also on WWE broadcasts, perhaps because of the prominent role William Regal, a former British wrestler who appeared on *World of Sport*, has as a trainer for the NXT sub-brand attached to WWE. In the past 30 years, a type of global wrestling style has emerged. This style is fast-paced, incorporating lucha elements, hard-hitting, incorporating Japan's 'strong style' ethos, and Britain's technical aspects. In other words, contemporary British wrestlers have updated the *World of Sport* Style, making it faster-paced than it was in the 1960s and the 1970s, and borrowing aspects of other national styles. Yet, even in this global context, localised variations still flourish. A social network analysis of wrestlers' movements across the world, from the 1980s to today, may very well reveal in more concrete terms the structures for how local, national and international wrestlers have helped to create and disseminate these transnational genres.

Indeed, alongside the core of working British wrestling talent described above, British wrestling promotions have supplemented their cards with 'imports', international wrestlers visiting from other countries, often with their own independent circuits. For example, Revolution Pro Wrestling have fostered international links with New Japan Pro Wrestling, Fight Club Pro have working relationships with America's Chikara, and Progress Wrestling have co-promoted shows with Canada's Smash Pro Wrestling and Germany's WXW. Performing this localised version of global styles, British wrestlers have also toured America and Japan, having significant successes in the major wrestling promotions and cultures. For example, Will Ospreay is the first British person to hold the coveted junior heavyweight title, and the second Brit to win New Japan's Best of the Super Juniors. Both Marty Scurll and Zack Sabre Junior have also had significant successes in Japan, and the three have also made popular appearances in American companies. Likewise, British women regularly appear in Japan's *joshi* divisions, including Viper. The WWE, finally, features an array of British and European talent, many of whom have emerged from these divisions, including Jack Gallagher, Drew McIntyre, Finn Balor, Paige, Noam Dar, Killian Dain, Aleister Black, Neville, and Nicki Cross.

In attempts to capture this buzz, in the autumn of 2016, Independent Television announced that they would be reviving wrestling on the channel – billed as *World of Sport: Wrestling* – for a one-off special that aired on New Year's Eve that year. Seemingly in response to the possibility of a rival wrestling company gaining national coverage on free-to-air television, the WWE announced that it too would be launching its own British wrestling promotion, airing on their network, and beginning with a 4-hour-long tournament broadcast over a weekend in January 2017 live from Blackpool to crown the first ever WWE UK Championship. Since then, ITV announced that they were going to revive *World of Sport: Wrestling* as a weekly show, but a series of production problems seems to have stalled those developments, and without the imminent threat the WWE has retreated from its own weekly series. Despite this, WWE have developed 'working relationships' with several British wrestling promotions, most notably ICW and Progress, and many British wrestlers have been retained on short, independent contracts by WWE. As discussed in the book, this jockeying for position, operating as both outright conflict and more nuanced compromise, demonstrates the ever-shifting nature of professional wrestling's history.

The narrative presented in this epilogue represents early reflections on a scene that requires intensive further study. Further research will be aided by empirical studies of these scenes, and historical research will reveal further implications we do not yet see. Indy wrestling – both in Britain and internationally, and the relationship between the two – poses and complicates many existing questions about the nature of fandom and identity in a post-Fordist culture, about how sport is watched and understood, and about how celebrity can operate in those cultures. Certainly, though, the changes underpin many of the arguments outlined in this book, about the nature of historical change, and how those changes are enacted in specific terrains, and how those terrains are partly created by the overlap and intersection of fields. Whether in changes in the technology or media fields, a model of fields, terrains and coordinates offers useful theoretical formulations.

A new generation of studies about professional wrestling, moreover, will do well to consistently stress not professional wrestling's uniqueness, but its continuities and influences on broader culture. Key theoretical approaches developed around kayfabe and performativity, in particular, seem vital in understanding the metamodern politics of contemporary celebrity cultures and politics. This is all the more vital in an era where Donald Trump, a former character in professional wrestling, having appeared in Wrestlemania 23, is the President of the United States. Likewise, the former WWE wrestler The Rock is the biggest grossing actor on the planet, and Hulk Hogan has been a key character in debates around freedom of expression in his Gawker trials. Many of the concepts developed in this book, especially around melodrama and celebrity, and the ways in which taste battles play out on terrains of fields that intersect with other fields, are vital in understanding the culture wars and conflicts of contemporary culture. In very simple terms, professional wrestling is not niche, and its pleasures, complexities, and contradictions serve as a flashpoint for many debates about media, sport, films, politics, and the associated conflicts therein.

Index

advertising, 85–86, 121–125, 163, 178
alcohol, 30, 95
Ali, Muhammad, 114, 156
All Star Promotions, 161
amateurism, 3, 8, 11, 22, 23, 33, 36–43, 54, 61–66, 68–71, 93–94, 96, 99, 133, 135, 150, 159, 166–167
American football, 132, 160
Astaire, Jarvis, 157–58

babyface (see blue-eyes)
Barnum, P.T., 31, 56, 100, 104, 129, 130
Baudrillard, Jean, 166, 169
bear gardens, 121–123
Bell's Life in London, 31, 33
Belle Vue, 13, 67, 104
Bennett, Louis 'Deerfoot', 29
Benoit, Chris, 139
Best, Bill, 72
Big Daddy, 1–2, 99, 105, 158
biographies, 12–13, 54, 102, 127, 128, 137
blood sports, 27, 121
blood, 24–25, 38, 68, 93–95, 97
blue-eyes, 16, 96, 114, 116–117, 139
bodybuilding, 4. See also Sandow the Magnificent.
Bourdieu, Pierre, 6–11, 23, 36, 41, 54, 60, 70, 89–91, 159, 164
Boxiana, 128
Brady, William, 55, 131
branding, 164
British Boxing Board of Control, 39, 66–67, 69–70, 73–74, 169
British Wrestling Board of Control, 71
Butlin's, 73

Cannon, Tom, 56
Carkeek, Jack, 55, 57–58

carnival, 24, 38, 86, 101, 121, 123, 125, 129
Carter, Raich 53
Channel Four, 160–163
Charles, Tom, 73
cinema, 53, 60, 88, 100, 129, 148, 152, 156
circus, 4, 28–33, 38–40, 41, 98–99, 101, 106, 118, 125, 127, 129, 133, 139, 148
class fractions, 7, 27, 90
Cleary, Edwin, 61–62
clowning, 32, 100
Cochran, Charles, 13, 57–60, 62, 95, 129–132
comedy, 16, 32, 84, 92, 100–101, 104–105, 118, 163
commentary (television), 152–153, 160
commercialism in sport, 40–42, 67, 129, 168
Cornwall, 23–24, 26, 39, 43, 64
costume, 4, 29, 44, 56–57, 98, 116, 122, 128–129, 131, 133, 139
Crabtree, Max, 138, 154, 157–158, 163
crowds, 24, 26, 40, 88, 96, 105, 120, 167, 170, 179
Crystal Palace, 65
cultural studies, 5, 9, 89, 136
Cumberland and Westmorland Wrestling Society, 39, 42
Cumbria, 26, 39, 42, 129

Daily Mail, 2, 43, 63, 66, 130, 135
Dale Martin Promotions, 72, 135, 150, 167
Davies, Dickie, 153
Ducrow, Andrew, 98
Dyke, Greg, 162–163

Egan, Pierce, 29, 128
enduring possibilities, 54

F.A. Cup Final, 149, 151
fairs and fairgrounds, 24, 28–29, 31–33, 36, 38, 54–58, 68, 70, 73, 84, 98–101, 106, 116, 127, 131, 133, 151, 153
Fédération Internationale des Luttes Associées (FILA), 65
Figg, James, 121–126
First World War, 86
Football Association (FA), 13, 54, 63–64, 75
Football League, 63, 156–157, 162–163
Fordism, 4, 165
freak shows, 55, 99–100, 104, 130

gambling, 3, 35, 58, 75, 157
Giant Haystacks, 1–4, 99
Gold Dust Trio, 67
Gorgeous George, 101, 114
Gotch, Frank, 59, 65
Grace, W. G., 133
Grade, Lew, 73, 75
Graeco-Roman, 55, 65, 67
Grandstand, 102, 128, 147, 150–151, 160
Great Gama, The, 59, 131–132
Grecian Saloon, 29, 31
Guardian, 1, 72, 74

Hackenschmidt, Georg, 57–59, 65, 95, 98–99, 129–132
Hall, Stuart, 6, 9, 11
heels (see villains)
hegemony, 6, 27, 41, 63, 89

Irslinger, Henry, 67–69

Home Office, 13, 84, 103
Houdini, Harry, 131
Hurst Park Syndicate, 156–157

Independent Television, 1, 4, 13, 16, 74, 84–87, 101–102, 117, 134, 149–154, 156, 158, 160–164, 180
Independent Television Authority/Independent Broadcasting Authority, 13, 74, 84, 102, 103, 149, 152, 153, 157
indoor sports, 61–63, 150
International Olympic Committee (IOC), 165

Japan, 4, 12, 59, 116, 179
Joint Promotions, 12–13, 16, 55, 72–75, 150–151, 154, 157–159, 161, 163, 168, 170

kayfabe, 12, 84, 101–105, 115, 135, 137–139, 168, 180
Kellet, Les, 100

Lancashire, 23–24, 31–32, 42, 55, 64, 72
Lewis, Ed 'Strangler', 56–57, 67
London County Council, 13, 68, 70, 85–86
Lonsdale, 38, 71
lucha libre, 116, 179

Madison Square Garden, 59, 63
Martin, Leslie, 135
Marx(ism), 6, 25, 37
masculinity, 16, 34, 70, 99–100
masks, 116, 121, 127–128, 134, 135, 138–139, 158, 168
mass culture, 87, 102
Mass Observation, 14, 84–85, 93, 96, 98
McMahon, Vince, 101, 103, 140, 162–163, 168, 170, 177–178
McManus, Mick, 1, 83, 97, 115–116, 138, 154
Mendoza, Daniel, 25–26, 30–32, 125–126, 128
Menken, Adah Isaacs, 130
Methodism, 25
Metropolitan Police Act, 25
Miller, David Prince, 31–32
Mondt, Toots, 67
moral panics, 91
morality play, 16, 115, 117
Morrell, Norman, 71, 72, 74, 101
Mountevans Rules, 71–74, 97, 100–102, 134, 151, 157–158, 168, 179
MTV, 168
Muldoon, William, 55–56
muscles, 58, 98–99
muscular Christianity, 34, 36

Nagasaki, Kendo, 116, 134, 138
National Amateur Wrestling Association, 64, 70, 94
National Sporting Club, 38
National Wrestling Alliance, 162
NFL (see American football)

Oakeley, Atholl, 67–69, 71–73, 137
Olympia, 54, 61–63
Olympics, 64–65, 71, 93, 159, 170

Pallo, Jackie, 1, 83, 136, 138, 154
pantomime, 29, 31, 100

Pay-TV, 147, 154–159
pedestrianism, 28–29
Picture Post, 70
Pierri, Antonio, 56, 58
Pilkington Report, 148, 149, 155
police, 6, 14, 25, 57, 83, 93, 103
Premier League, 163–164
Professional Wrestling Board of Control, 65, 71
public schools, 34–37

Queensberry Rules, 38

race, 119–120, 128–129, 131–132, 134, 137, 140
referees, 30, 68, 75, 92, 96, 103, 115–116
Regal, William, 179
Reith, John, 83
Royal Albert Hall, 58, 66
rugby, 4, 24, 39, 41, 43, 148

Saint Monday, 25
Sandow the Magnificent, 58, 99
Sandow, Billy, 67
Second World War, 10, 71, 148–149
Sheffield Zulus, 133
Simmel, Georg, 6, 9, 60, 159

Sky TV, 17, 148, 162–164, 166, 170
Slam Bang Western Style Wrestling, 67
Smith, Davey Boy (The British Bulldog), 177
Starr, Ricki, 100, 116
Street, Adrian, 101, 116, 158

Thatcher, Margaret, 162

villains, 16, 92, 96–97, 116, 135
violence, 6, 16, 24, 54, 68–72, 84, 86, 92–99, 102–105

Walton, Kent, 152–153, 158
weapons, 68, 93, 97, 122
Wimbledon, 4, 148, 150
Wolverhampton Civic Hall, 134
women in wrestling, 69–70
Worktown, 85
World of Sport, 1, 101, 117, 147, 150–154, 160–164, 170, 179
World Wrestling Federation (WWF), 116–118, 148, 161–163, 168–169, 178–181

youth cultures, 24, 42, 85–86

Zbyszko, Stanislaus, 132